MILTON AND FREE WILL: An Essay in Criticism and Philosophy

MILTON AND FREE WILL:
AN ESSAY IN CRITICISM
AND PHILOSOPHY

WILLIAM MYERS

CROOM HELM
London ● New York ● Sydney

© 1987. W.F. Myers
Croom Helm Ltd, Provident House, Burrell Row,
Beckenham, Kent BR3 1AT
Croom Helm, 44-50 Waterloo Road,
North Ryde, 2113 NSW, Australia

British Library Cataloguing in Publication Data

Myers, William
    Milton and free will: an essay in criticism and philosophy.
    1. Free will and determinism
    I. Title
    123   BJ1461
ISBN 0-7099-4620-1

Published in the USA by
Croom Helm
in association with Methuen, Inc.
29 West 35th Street
New York, NY 10001

Library of Congress Cataloging-in-Publication Data

Myers, William, 1939-
    Milton and free will.

    1. Milton, John, 1608-1674   — Philosophy.
2. Free will and determinism. I. Title.
PR3592.P5M94 1987 821'.4   87-423
ISBN 0-7099-4620-1

Filmset by Mayhew Typesetting, Bristol, England
Printed and bound in Great Britain by Mackays of Chatham Ltd, Kent

For my Mother

As to my book it is always most difficult to be exact in one's language, nor is it necessary to be exactissimus in a work which is a conversational essay, not a didactic treatise.

John Henry Newman, 1870

It is scarcely necessary to say that the Author submits all that he has written to the judgment of the Church, whose gift and prerogative it is to determine what is true and what is false in religious teaching.

John Henry Newman, in a note attached to lists of his published works.

Contents

Introduction

Anyone who believes as I do in the strongest possible version of free will, and who hopes to find support for that belief in literature might be expected to dislike the following summary by Terry Eagleton (1983) of the thought of Jacques Derrida. It reads as follows:

> nothing is ever fully present in signs: it is an illusion for me to believe that I can ever be fully present to you in what I say or write, because to use signs at all entails that my meaning is always somehow dispersed . . . Not only my meaning, indeed, but *me*: since language is something I am made out of, rather than a convenient tool I use, the whole idea that I am a stable, unified entity must also be a fiction . . .
>
>   . . . [The] Western philosophical tradition, all the way from Plato to Levi-Strauss, has consistently vilified writing as a mere lifeless, alienated form of expression, and consistently celebrated the living voice. Behind this prejudice lies a particular view of 'man': man is able . . . to be in full possession of himself, and to dominate language as a transparent medium of his inmost being . . .
>
>   Just as Western philosophy has been 'phonocentric' . . . so it has also been . . . 'logocentric', committed to a belief in some ultimate word, presence, essence, truth or reality which will act as the foundation of all our thought, language and experience. It has yearned for . . . the 'transcendental signifier' — and for the anchoring, unquestionable meaning to which all our signs can be seen to point (the 'transcendental signified'). (129–31)

Derrida, it seems, rejects all that I hope to establish in this essay, for I believe in the self as a potentially stable and unified entity in full possession of itself and thereby discovering in the transcendental signifier the transcendental signified. But these ideas do not in fact embarrass me. Instead they remind me of key passages in *An Essay in Aid of a Grammar of Assent* (1870), in which John Henry Newman firmly places himself in the philosophical

1

tradition from which Derrida seeks to withdraw, and so specifies 'deconstructionism' as something which that tradition has already taken into account.

The ethical ideas from which he came to religion, Newman writes, 'are derived not simply from the Gospel, but prior to it from heathen moralists . . .; and as to the intellectual position from which I have contemplated the subject, Aristotle has been my master' (334). From this master, Newman derives convictions about the person which seem very different from Derrida's, affirming in particular that in all 'actions of the intellect, the individual is supreme and responsible to himself' (277). But this is a more complicated position than it seems. It contains three distinct implications: first, that human beings are irreducibly individual: secondly, that they are so by virtue of their intelligence taken as a whole; and thirdly, that though willing requires the action of intelligence, intelligence is itself willed. Hence Newman's assumption that the experience of 'truth' is a necessary condition of conscientious choosing, and yet that the individual has a responsibility to relate conscientiously to the true. His epistemology is thus a moral one. Certitude, he maintains, involves 'an active recognition of propositions as true, such as it is the duty of each individual . . . to exercise at the bidding of reason, and, when reason forbids, to withold' (271). It follows that from one point of view the individual is prior to knowledge yet from another is a consequence of it: persons are constituted by the knowing and willing in which they engage, yet to know they must will, and to will they must know, and to do either they must already be personal beings: 'each of us [Newman asserts] has the prerogative of completing his inchoate and rudimental nature, and of developing his own perfection out of the living elements which his mind began to be' (274).

But this is not, as it may seem, an instance of 'supplementarity'. The concept of supplement, Derrida (1967(a)) writes, 'harbors within itself two significations whose cohabitation is as strange as it is necessary. The supplement adds itself; it is a surplus, a plenitude enriching another plenitude . . . It cumulates and accumulates presence' (144). But for Derrida 'presence' is an illusion, I deceive myself into believing that what a word signifies is fully present to me, and I do so by adding another word to it. I affirm it by saying that it 'is' something else. Thus reasoning in Newman's account — the recognition of propositions as true — is supplemented by willing — such recognitions are also choices.

But willing is similarly supplemented by reasoning: I cannot will without first having engaged in some kind of reasoning. Derrida would say that Newman is here deceiving himself, that each 'of the two significations is effaced or becomes discreetly vague in the presence of the other' (145), and so only effects an illusory presence of 'mind' in Newman's mind. But Newman is not deceived by the supplement. His description of the self as inchoate and rudimental yet capable of rational self-perfection exactly corresponds with Derrida's own description of meaning. 'Meaning', Derrida (1967(b)) writes, 'must await being said or written in order to inhibit itself, and in order to become by differing from itself what it is: meaning' (11). A person, Newman suggests, must wait on thoughts and actions in order to be a self, and so to become what he or she already is — a person. Both writers are aware of the paradoxes concealed in the word 'is'.

Newman on willing, then, and Derrida on meaning do not contradict but illuminate each other. Each rejects notions of the self, the world and other selves as fixable presences to one another. Thus far from leading to the kind of totalitarian closure to which Derrida objects so strongly, Newman's inchoate subject moving, like one of Derrida's sentences, towards itself, issues in the existential isolation of certitude. Real assents, Newman insists,

> are of a personal character . . . They depend on personal experience and the experience of one man is not the experience of another. Real assent, then . . . is proper to the individual, and as such, thwarts rather than promotes the intercourse of man with man. (82–3)

It thus 'deconstructs' the conception of discourse as the potential bearer of some ultimate word, some completely signified and transparent truth, to which all minds must give allegiance. Yet this deconstruction of presence in Newman's thought is not new or radical. On the contrary, as we shall see, it is a problem repeatedly confronted and more or less effectively overcome in the broadly Aristotelian tradition to which he and Milton belonged.

These are necessarily preliminary and compressed remarks, mere gestures towards the argument advanced in this essay. Its hero is John Milton, supported first of all by three very different writers, Newman, Henry James and the present Pope, and by a cloud of other witness including Aristotle, St Thomas Aquinas, Mikhail Bakhtin, Michael Polanyi, Jacques Monod, Anthony

3

Kenny, Donald Davidson, Richard Swinburne, Alvin Plantinga, Daniel Dennett, Derek Parfit and Earl Miner. My argument involves a defence of traditional notions of truth, the self and God, which I believe rationalists, empiricists and deconstructionists have all misread. Many of the latter might agree with this judgement since some of them hold that all readings are misreadings anyway. Be that as it may, the body of (mis)readings I assemble and disassemble in this book constitutes a celebration of the convergence of philosophical, scientific and deconstructionist arguments around the notion of free, intelligent, self-possessing human beings on which alone it is possible to predicate the preservation of humanity and its revolutionary transformation.

For most of this essay, however, deconstructionist arguments remain in brackets while I examine my subject on more traditional lines. This imposition of the phenomenologist's *epoché* is not meant to dispose of fundamental problems, but to keep them open. All I ask is for an opportunity to privilege my own arguments provisionally, that is, to scrutinise the writings of others for their meanings in relative confidence about my own. I hope that my penultimate chapter will justify this procedure.

Another more general concession is sought from the reader. I have held to the conviction at the heart of this book for some twenty years with a growing sense of its relevance to my work as a student and teacher of literature. I have never been a student of philosophy and doubtless many of my arguments and ways of expressing myself will embarrass those who are. I hope anyone so embarrassed will look to my conclusions rather than to the indirect, crook'd ways I get to them. A sound building may be concealed behind ramshackle scaffolding. In any case the ladders I ascend must finally be pushed away, so I ask only to be seen safe up. For my coming down let me shift for myself.

1

Milton and Free Will

1. The priority of free will in Milton's conception of God. 2. The priority of God in Milton's conception of man. 3. The priority of the individual in Milton's conception of the church 4. Difficulties in Milton's account of the generation of the Son 5. Difficulties in Milton's account of the incarnation 6. Milton's personal involvement in the problem 7. The radical disorder in Milton's thought 8. Milner's reading of Milton 9. Milton's perception of ideology 10. Correcting ideological distortion 11. Proto-marxist aspects of Milton's thought 12. Ideology in Milton's hell 13. Ideology and consciousness 14. Ideology and bad faith 15. The case against deliberation 16. The ideology of helplessness \17. The ideology of self-control 18. The legitimacy of pursuing the argument further.

1. The question I address in this essay is whether we can sensibly regard human beings as intelligently free agents. For a number of reasons I find the best answer to this question in the works of Milton. It was a subject about which he wrote extensively and from a position of philosophical literacy. In fact he was obsessed by it and on such a topic obsession matters. The truth or falsity of the proposition that God exists is in no way affected by the quality of my acceptance or rejection of the argument from design, whereas if my enthusiasm for certain arguments about free will shows evidence of being compulsive, the doctrine itself may well be at risk. Ultimately I shall make considerable claims for the quality of Milton's commitment to human freedom in the fullest possible sense. But a poet obsessed is a poet exposed, and I shall first have to consider whether the quality of Milton's interest in freedom is evidence against it. The two possible ways of accounting for this interest which suggest that it is, one psychological, one

5

ideological, are dealt with in this chapter. This leads to a more general consideration of whether the free will problem can usefully be discussed at all.

My first task, then, is to examine the place of free will in Milton's thought. It was apparently the governing idea of his life. He rejects the scholastic teaching that God is *Actus Purus*, for example, because he holds it to be incompatible with what he believes about willing. Without latent powers, he argues in *Christian Doctrine*, God 'could do nothing except what he does do, and he would do that of necessity, although in fact he is omnipotent and utterly free of his actions' (146). A similar motivation explains Milton's anti-trinitarianism. His theory of the generation of the Son is explicitly grounded in convictions concerning the Father's freedom. For, he argues, if freedom necessarily involves the actualisation in time of latent potentialities, then the generation of the Son must have occurred 'within the bounds of time' (209). Consequently the Son is not co-eternal with the Father and is not therefore one in substance with him.

> God [Milton writes] could certainly have refrained from the act of generation and yet remained true to his own essence, for he stands in no need of propagation. So generation has nothing to do with the essence of deity . . . [He] could not have begotten the Son except of his own free will and as a result of his own decree.

This is an argument echoed by Immanuel Kant in a note in *The Prolegomena to any Future Metaphysics* (1783):

> The idea of freedom [he writes] finds a place solely in the relation of the *intellectual* as cause to the *appearance* as effect. Hence we cannot . . . find a concept of freedom appropriate to pure beings of the understanding [purely rational beings], e.g. God, in so far as his activity is immanent. For his activity, although independent of outer determining causes, is yet determined in his eternal reason and in the divine *nature*. Only when something *is to begin* through an act, and the effect is to be encountered in the time sequence, consequently in the world of the senses (e.g. the beginning of the world), does the question arise, whether the causality of the cause must also itself begin or whether the cause can start an effect without its causality itself beginning. (109–110)

6

Committed to the view that the generation of the Son is a free act of the Father's, Milton, in line with the logic of this argument, represents God's trinitarian life as having '*to begin*', and the generation of the Son as 'the beginning of the world'.

Subordinationism has for him the added advantage of clarifying the Son's freedom as well as the Father's, for it is as a created being, he suggests, in *Christian Doctrine*, that the Son is able to act independently of the Father and 'VOLUNTARILY' (416) to perform his office as universal redeemer, imputing 'our sins to himself, and of his own free will [washing] them away' (486). Milton was a subordinationist, therefore, largely because he believed that subordinationism strengthened the free-will thesis, which, before all others, he sought to uphold.

2. The figure of God, finally alone so that he can be free, becomes the premiss of everything else in Milton's thought, and in particular of his conception of human willing. As he points out in *The Art of Logic*, 'Only God does all things with absolute freedom' (227); angels and men, who 'do things through reason and deliberation', act freely only 'on the hypothesis . . . of the divine will, which in the beginning gave them the power to act freely'. But granted this hypothesis, human freedom is incontestable and obvious. In *Christian Doctrine*, therefore, he represents God's first and most fundamental act as the issuing of his General Decree 'by which HE DECREED FROM ETERNITY, WITH ABSOLUTE FREEDOM, WITH ABSOLUTE WISDOM AND WITH ABSOLUTE HOLINESS, ALL THOSE THINGS WHICH HE PROPOSED OR WHICH HE WAS GOING TO PERFORM . . . singly and by himself' (153–4), a distinction between God's proposals and his performances which is only necessary because from eternity God has envisaged creaturely freedom. Hence the line in *Paradise Lost* describing the Father bending

> down his eye,
> His own works and their works at once to view
>
> (III 58–9)

Hence also Milton's insistence that divine foreknowledge does not compromise the moral accountability of created intelligences. Moreover, once granted, freedom is never finally withdrawn: even in the corruption of the fall, Milton asserts in *Christian Doctrine*, free will is not 'entirely extinct' (396), and accordingly he makes large assumptions about the day-to-day autonomy of human beings. 'The end . . . of learning', he writes in *Of Education*

> is to repair the ruins of our first parents by regaining to know God aright, and out of that knowledge to love him, to imitate him, to be like him, as we may the neerest by possessing our souls of true vertue, which being united to the heavenly grace of faith makes up the highest perfection. (366–7)

This distinction between 'true vertue' and 'heavenly grace' implies a capacity for self-realisation on which Milton's entire system of education depends. Not that we are saved by such self-realisation. Salvation is an effect of Grace. But as Michael tells Adam in *Paradise Lost*, even Grace requires our 'free/Acceptance' (XII 304–5), a formula which preserves the autonomy of fallen human beings in the work of salvation itself. This is why Milton can assert in *The Tenure of Kings and Magistrates* that, 'No man . . . can be so stupid as to deny that all men naturally were borne free, being the image and resemblance of God himself' (198).

3. Creaturely freedom, then, has to be willed by God, but what God wills is very strong indeed — it is the central fact of the christian dispensation. Liberty, Milton writes in *Of Civil Power* — 'the state of grace, manhood, freedom and faith' (259) — is 'the fundamental privilege of the gospel' (262); 'our beleef and practise, which comprehend our whole religion, flow from the faculties of the inward man, free and unconstrainable of themselves by nature' (256). It is this, he asserts in *Christian Doctrine*, which makes christians 'GROWN MEN INSTEAD OF BOYS' (537). 'In controversies there is no arbitrator except scripture, or rather, each man is his own arbitrator, so long as he follows scripture and the Spirit of God' (585). 'The pre-eminent and supreme authority . . . is the authority of the Spirit, which is internal, and the individual possession of each' (587). Consequently to deny liberty of opinion within the church is to seek to undo the work of Christ: without it 'there is no religion and no gospel. Violence alone prevails' (123). It is for this reason, Milton declares in *Of Civil Power*, that 'all true protestants account the pope antichrist, for that he assumes to himself this infallibilitie over both the conscience and scripture' (244).

Freedom, then, is not a corollary of christian faith and practice for Milton, but their essence. Hence his identification of authentic christianity with heresy, a word, he points out, which 'only means the choise or following of any opinion good or bad in religion or any other learning' (247). He applies this principle of unqualified liberty even to a christian's relations with God. Discussing the authority of 'testimony' in *The Art of Logic*, he writes:

testimony does not argue anything of itself and by its nature *but rather by the assumed force of some artificial argument* . . .
     So when the exact truth or nature of things is more carefully investigated, testimony has a very meager force. (318)

And, he insists, 'this appears to apply to divine testimony as well as human' (319). Thus he requires proof as well as testimony even from God, and he leaves individuals to make up their own minds, in the Spirit, about the satisfactoriness of those proofs.

4. The very passion with which Milton attaches himself to the notion of freedom, however, can incite him to ride roughshod over the logical difficulties into which it occasionally leads him. Some of these difficulties are connected with his subordinationism. Free acts, he argues, can only take place in time. 'There is certainly no reason', he writes in *Christian Doctrine*, 'why we should conform to the popular belief that motion and time . . . could not . . . have existed before this world was made' (313–14). Milton's God, in other words, unlike the God of the scholastics, is time-bound, a position which makes his unqualified assertion of divine omniscience and creaturely freedom difficult to sustain. A God who exists outside time, after all, can contemplate past, present and future as on a map or landscape laid out before his immutable consciousness. Such a God would appear logically to have certain advantages over a timed God, particularly if he is also deemed to be the creator of free beings. Swinburne (1977) believes that this is why

the scholastics adopted the doctrine of timelessness . . .[:] it allowed them to maintain that God is omniscient in . . . [a] strong sense . . . God outside time can be said never not to know our free actions, even though they may sometimes be future from our point of view. (219)

Like other recent philosophers in this field Swinburne agrees with Milton that the Boethian conception of God is incoherent. He therefore rejects a conception of divine omniscience which includes the future actions of *any* free being; Swinburne's God cannot even make certain predictions about himself. Milton, however, would have found such a conception of God thoroughly offensive. He has therefore to defend both positions, complete divine knowledge of the future and absolute freedom of the will, divine and human.

Another problem arising out of Milton's doctrine of divine freedom in time relates to the first of God's actions. Swinburne's God, and Milton's, has always existed and will always exist. We might find such a life 'tedious, boring and pointless', Swinburne suggests (211), but an omnipotent being could ensure that it was not so. But how? By doing things? A God who has been doing things in time from eternity would always have done an infinity of things already (or infinitely repeated a finite number of things) if doing things were his resource against tedium. This is nonsensical: a backwardly eternal God must have fullness of life in himself, independently of any acts he might perform. This is especially so for Milton since in *Christian Doctrine* he envisages God acting for the first time when he implements his 'first and most excellent SPECIAL DECREE' (166), the generation of the Son. But why does God choose time *t* for the performance of this act? Swinburne has an answer to this, since he includes God's own future choices among the things which he cannot predict in spite of his being omniscient. But Milton requires us to envisage God making a general decree from all eternity, and then, after an eternity of inactive contemplation of these irreformable intentions, suddenly, and at an eternally foreseen moment, acting on the first of them.

A third difficulty connected with Milton's subordinationism was represented by William Empson as a particularly unpleasant component of Milton's theology. Within the Boethian and trinitarian Deity there is presumably a recognition from all eternity by Father, Son and Holy Spirit, of the need for a redemptive intervention in human affairs and an acceptance of how that intervention is to be effected. In Milton's scheme, however, the bloody sacrifice of the Son is the task of a subordinate. It is admittedly a voluntary action, and the subordinate in question has a 'filial', and not a merely 'creaturely', relation to the Father. Nevertheless, he is drawn into a drama not of his making and takes upon himself (as the Father, of course, has always known he would) a brutally painful role to satisfy a rigorous principle of abstract justice. The distinctness of the Son from the Father may be necessary, in Milton's view, to secure the voluntariness of his offer to be that sacrifice, but it considerably increases our anxieties about the moral standing of the Father's choices and providences in the poem.

5. Similar inconsistencies characterise Milton's account of the incarnation. In abandoning orthodox trinitarianism, he also abandons the distinctions between nature, person and substance which had been developed to express it. The 'essence of God', he argues in *Christian Doctrine*,

> . . . allows nothing to be compounded with it, and the . . . word hypostasis, Heb. i. 3, which is variously translated *substance, subsistence,* or *person,* is nothing but that most perfect essence by which God exists from himself, in himself, and through himself. (140–1)

But these distinctions are also important in expressing the doctrine of the incarnation, and Milton's rejection of them makes for difficulties, since he has to argue that there is 'in Christ a mutual hypostatic union of two natures or, in other words, of two essences, of two substances and consequently of two persons' (424). Yet he also insists that 'one Christ, one ens, and one person is formed from this mutual hypostatic union of two natures' (423). But, logically, that person must be identical either with the Son, or with the nature and person of the human being who would have been instantiated had the incarnation not taken place, or with a person constituted in the union of the two natures and so not identical with either. But the first case requires the obliteration of the human nature and person assumed by the Son, the second the obliteration of the Son in the human nature and person united to his, and the third the obliteration of both in a new kind of being and new person, the God-man. But we have seen that Milton rejects the first two cases, while the third means either that the Son's act of becoming man and not the sacrifice of Christ on the cross is the means of mankind's redemption, in which case the Passion and Ressurection are unnecessary, or that the obedience of Jesus unto death is not attributable to the will of the pre-incarnate Son, and he ceases to be the universal mediator. In the light of these difficulties it is not surprising that Milton had to resort to the expedient of asserting that while we cannot explain the incarnation coherently, 'it is best for us to be ignorant of things which God wishes to remain a secret' (424).

11

6. Milton's is thus a confused theology, and it is so largely because of his uncritical commitment to the idea of free will. Why should this have been so? A long line of critics has supplied answers to this and similar questions in terms of Milton's personality, and specifically in terms of what they have seen as his compulsive self-preoccupation. John Carey (1969) puts the matter succinctly: when Milton was agitating for liberty, he suggests, he was really demanding 'liberty for himself' (64). Milton's obsession with free will is thus no more than the theoretical component of a larger preoccupation with his own autonomy and power. Notoriously, Milton seems to have interested himself in such issues as divorce, the liberty of the press and political liberty only when they affected him personally, and numerous figures in his writings — the Father, the Son, Abdiel, Noah and Satan in *Paradise Lost*, Jesus in *Paradise Regain'd*, Samson in *Samson Agonistes* and even Ramus in *The Art of Logic*, have been identified as his alter egos. Particularly significant, perhaps, is his tendency to define freedom in terms of a figure with whom he could easily identify, the modestly prosperous *pater familias*. In *The Reason of Church Government* he even represents God as 'a most indulgent father governing his Church as a family of sons in their discreet age' (837). Political liberty is similarly represented. The English people, he writes in *The Tenure of Kings and Magistrates*, have the right to 'dispose and *œconomize* in the Land which God hath giv'n them as Maisters of Family in thir own house and free inheritance' (237). The power to effect a divorce, he argues in *The Doctrine and Discipline of Divorce*, should be taken from the clergy and church courts and returned 'again to the maister of family' (353).

7. Carey sees this self-preoccupation as the source of Milton's power as a writer. He suggests, for example, that in *Paradise Lost*, 'God and Satan dramatise two powerful elements in Milton's own character — authoritarianism and rebelliousness' (75). Of the Father, Carey writes: 'The irascible eccentric on the mountain top shoots turbulent energies through the whole narrative' (83). Like most critics since William Blake, however, Carey prefers the apparently no less self-reflexive figure of Satan. The 'images of dynamism and magnitude heaped upon Satan', he suggests, 'carry far more conviction' (90). Carey sees Milton as unwittingly divided against himself. On the one hand he finds a 'Shakespearean' intelligence in Milton which is 'deeply responsive to pagan myth' (26); as a christian Milton is seriously committed to 'unworldliness and poverty'; he has enlightened views on the

separation of church and state, on divorce and civil liberty, and his God, at least as he is represented in *The Reason of Church Government*, 'sent Foolishnes to confute Wisdom, Weaknes to bind Strength, Despisednes to vanquish Pride' (824). But there is another Milton, according to Carey, who amputates 'the pagan half of his poetic life' in the early poems, whose constant belief is that most human beings are 'weakly or falsely principled', and for whom nature is 'a purely personal convenience: a respectable front for what his own instincts demand' (68). This Milton indulges in an 'hysterical revenge fantasy' (71) in the anti-prelatical pamphlets, and advocates military dictatorship during the Civil War.

Such self-division, Carey asserts, makes Milton a great poet, permitting the emergence in his work of a spontaneous, and so authentic, play of feeling and image. For Carey, literature is thus a kind of semi-conscious psychodrama, which offers us interesting and possibly improving opportunities to observe the inchoate movements of minds greater but also less controlled than our own. Milton himself, however, would have found such an explanation of his powers both offensive and seriously at variance with his most deeply-held beliefs. The argument implies that the full play of a poet's powers are hampered by, and may even be compatible with, *knowledge*. Indeed, the kind of mental processes which Carey associates with the writing of poetry were likened by Milton in *The Doctrine and Disipline of Divorce* to what happens 'in menstruous bodies where natures current hath been stopt, [and] . . . the suffocation and upward forcing of some lower part, affects the head and inward sense with dotage and idle fancies' (278–9). He would certainly have regarded as pathological the very confusion of inward sense (however caused) which Carey in effect identifies with the energy of inspiration.

8. He would have been no less disturbed by some recent political readings of his work. In important respects all his writings, even the most philosophical or lyrical, are self-consciously drenched with politics. He focuses on the *pater familias*, for example, not just because he saw himself in that role, but also because he wished to challenge the engrossment of patriarchal authority by royalist ideologues before and after the Civil War. If he had been able to foresee the kind of attention he would have been accorded since his death, he would undoubtedly have been most disappointed by the failure of his readers to attend to his politics. But he would also have been shocked by the conclusions

which critics, particularly marxist critics, have reached even in their sympathetic analyses of the political content of his work.

Of these one of the best and most overtly marxist is John Milner (1981). Like a number of other recent critics, Milner applies the doctrine of the material economic base acting as the ultimate determinant of a society's cultural activity with some care. Society, he writes,

> has to be seen as a concentration of many determinations . . . a totality of interrelated and contradictory elements . . . [but this conception] does not, and indeed cannot, allow within itself the notion of art and literature as mechanical 'effects' of some economic 'cause'. (3)

Rather, he argues, we should 'consider' the social system as, in Perry Anderson's words, "a complex totality, *loaded* by the predominance in the long run of one level within it — the economy" ' (5), and so in analysing Milton's writings, he adapts Lucienne Goldmann's conception of 'an ideal typology of possible world visions' (50). The English revolutionary crisis, he suggests,

> gave rise to a rationalist world vision, which contrasted the irrational present with the perfect rational institutions, modes of behaviour, etc., to which the revolutionary bourgeoisie aspired [and] found political form in Revolutionary Independancy (52)

a fundamental rationalist category being freedom, which, with reason, provided the ultimate justification for bourgeois individualism.

Milner cites Milton's analyses of the institution of marriage and of the relations of church and state in support of this view:

> In each case [he writes], society is conceived as consisting of a set of rational individuals, who enter into voluntary, contractual, relationships with each other for their own rational ends, and who are therefore perfectly free to dissolve those relationships in the event of their proving inadequate to the satisfaction of those ends. As Milton himself writes, 'no convenant, no, not between God and man . . . can hold to the deluding or making miserable of both' (108–9)

There is nothing in this, I think, to which Milton would have objected, but he would have resisted Milner's further contention that such rationalism is 'logically *atheistic*' (115) and that this is the real reason why the God of *Paradise Lost* 'never comes to life' (117). Milner finds the God of Milton's theology equally unimpressive.

> Milton [he argues]) rescues the notion of the individual man as rational agent from the clutches of Calvinistic determinism. But only at a price, the price paid by God who is reduced to the level of first cause, an all-knowing spectator, rather than an all-determining participant, in human history. (99)

Milner's Milton, then, like Carey's, does not quite grasp the implications of his greatest utterances. Both critics thus bring into focus the problem of literary consciousness. Carey interprets its component of alienation in psychological terms: Milner's position is more complex. He sees literary consciousness as a special instance of consciousness in history generally. His Milton is 'the intellectual embodiment of the maximum real consciousness of the English bourgeoisie' (53), and so at once typical and special. Intensely aware of himself as a uniquely gifted spokesman for the revolution, he is ignorant of what makes him so, and of the real implications of the position he is taking. Milner's argument also implies that most of those involved in the Independants' enterprise enjoyed an even more limited awareness of what they were about than Milton then and Milner now. It suggests, in other words, that we may all know more (or less) than we realise and say more (or less) than we know. But if this is so, then the central claims that Milton makes about human beings, that they are capable of rationally determining their own lives, falls to the ground. If Milner is right, the idea of self-possession on which Western humanism is founded is an idle and politically tendentious dream.

9. It would be wrong, however, to conclude that marxism necessarily entails a pessimistic epistemology. Milner limits 'maximum real consciousness' to its period: Milton can see as much as is opened up by the projects and practices of his class in a revolutionary situation, and no more. But there are marxist descriptions of literary production which suggest that well-placed minds may be able to escape the limitations of their period. If this is so, something may be saved of Milton's rationalism, though in turn this may provoke a reassessment of some key marxist

assumptions.

'Poets', wrote Percy Bysshe Shelley in the Preface to *Prometheus Unbound* (1820), '. . . are, in one sense the creators, and in another the creations of the age' (174). The marxist notion of ideology can be deployed to justify this optimism. Let us accept that in order to serve the function of maintaining existing modes of economic production and so of class relations, the dominant cultural forms in any society must be sufficiently relevant to the social and economic circumstances of their production as to act as powerful if not necessarily altogether coherent persuaders. But they must also be sufficiently false to conceal current contradictions and conflicts of interest by way of specious, though plausible, explanation. Let us also accept that religion and literature, as major vehicles of cultural expression, help to secure this work of concealment. But in that case, they must also reflect the very contradictions which it is their task to suppress. Those engaged in coping with these pressures might therefore well become aware of them, and so develop insights into how the processes of ideological formation function, even though they lacked a (marxist) theoretical framework in which fully to explain them. In this sense we might conclude that for marxists religion and literature are indeed potentially prophetic.

This seems to have been Milton's case. In *The Doctrine and Discipline of Divorce*, for example, he points out how 'Custome still is silently received for the best instruction. Error suports Custome, Custome countenances Error' (223). In thus grasping one of the ways in which ideology operates, Milton seems also to have glimpsed how some of its limiting effects might be overcome. It is possible, he asserts, with divine assistance — that is, by using one ideological form against another — to 'worke off the inveterate blots and obscurities wrought upon our mindes by the suttle insinuating of Error and Custome' (223–4). How minds might thus transcend, if only partially, the determinations of history, is obviously a question of some importance.

10. We can begin consideration of this question with Blake's dictum in *The Marriage of Heaven and Hell* (1790–3), that 'Milton was a true Poet and of the Devil's party without knowing it' (150). This implies that though Milton's theology was circumscribed by ideological priorities, the intensity with which, as a poet, he established contact with the operations of mind and language enabled him to expose the hidden agenda of concealment and obfuscation required by ideology, and therefore the conflicts and

contradictions in the practical human world which ideology attempted to explain away. With divine assistance — that is, when Milton was working most intensely — his writing could express a double knowledge, sustaining dominant ideological forms on the explicit level, while covertly expressing an alternative range of sympathies released by the knowledge of contradiction to which the poet's special skills had given him intuitive access, or of which they were the register.

Shelley's account of Milton makes this a more conscious process and a collective and historical as well as an individual one, In 'A Defence of Poetry' (1840) he praises Milton for his 'bold neglect' (130) of direct moral purpose in *Paradise Lost*, and for arranging the elements of human nature

in the composition of his great picture according to the laws of epic truth; that is, according to the laws of that principle by which a series of actions of the external universe and of intelligent and ethical beings is calculated to excite the sympathy of succeeding generations of mankind.

Moreover, it is as an historically determined mind that Shelley's Milton is liberated from the limited perspectives which history imposes in other circumstances and on other minds.

We owe the great writers of the golden age of our literature [Shelley (1820) writes] to that fervid awakening of the public mind which shook to dust the oldest and most oppressive form of the Christian religion. We owe Milton to the progress and development of the same spirit: the sacred Milton was, let it ever be remembered, a republican, and a bold enquirer into morals and religion. The great writers of our own age are . . . [similarly] the companions and forerunners of some unimagined change in our social condition or in the opinions which cement it. The cloud of mind is discharging its collected lightning, and the equilibrium between institutions and opinions is now restoring, or is about to be restored. (173)

At certain periods, it would seem, after the Reformation or the French Revolution, for example, the hegemony of the dominant class ideology is weakened, initiating a time of creative, perhaps prophetic, cultural development, if only because in such situations

17

human beings find it easier to grasp the relativity of truth and the malleability of their condition.

11. Milton himself seems to have sensed such possibilities in his own time, and marxist critics other than Milner have suggested that he and other leaders of the English Revolution were accordingly able to envisage their deliverance from the prison of Error and Custom, and the precedents imposed on them by royalist and aristocratic institutions. Eagleton (1976), for example, praises Milton's 'assertion of bourgeois Protestant nationalism' (56) and his 'appropriation of . . . classical modes for historically progressive ends': even if the mode of Milton's 'ideological disinheritance from [his] contemporary historical moment [was] determined in the last instance by the nature of that moment' (59), Eagleton argues, Milton himself did not belong passively to the ideology of his age.

The nature of the historically enfranchised vision which Milton thus enjoyed is indicated by the discovery in his work of symbolic anticipations of the essentials of marxist theory itself, notably in connection with his materialism and his eschatology. Milton's materialism is evident in the account of the creation in *Christian Doctrine*. Since

'action' and 'passivity' are relative terms [he argues], and since no agent can act externally unless there is something, and something material, which can be acted upon, it is apparent that God could not have created the world out of nothing.

There are . . . four kinds of cause; efficient, material, formal and final . . . God . . . unquestionably contains and comprehends within himself all these causes. So the material cause must be God or nothing. But nothing is no cause at all. (307–8)

Therefore, he concludes, matter has existed from eternity as part of God, and 'it is a demonstration of supreme power and supreme goodness that such heterogeneous, multiform and inexhaustible virtue should exist in God.' Thus for Milton matter exists as a constituent of all subjects whatsoever, created or divine. Hence the monumental homogeneity of the celestial and terrestrial worlds of *Paradise Lost*, which so powerfully unifies the poem.

Milton's eschatology has similarly proto-marxist implications. According to Christopher Hill (1977), Milton believed that men such as himself had 'no real need of the state' (263), and that 'the final end of all things [would] be the withering away even of Christ's kingdom'. Moreover, for Hill's Milton, 'Freedom is knowledge of necessity' (267), and Hill accordingly compares Lenin's response to the post-revolutionary period after 1905 with the stance of Jesus in *Paradise Regain'd*, whose

> Suffering, abstaining, quietly expecting
> Without distrust or doubt
>
> (III 192–3)

also expresses, in Hill's judgement, Milton's own position after 1660.

12. But perhaps the most impressive of Milton's anticipations of marxist theory is his dramatisation of the workings of ideology in the Hell of *Paradise Lost* which some critics, notably Empson, have been too ready to take at face value, even while recognising that the behaviour of the leaders of the rebel host is precisely that of ideologues: Empson (1965) compares Mammon to a tycoon, Belial to a lawyer and Satan to 'the spell-binder, Lloyd-George' (27). In fact, Satan feeds his followers with the angelic equivalent of religious ideology as Karl Marx describes it in his contribution of the 'Critique of Hegel's Philosophy of Right' (1844) — a 'general theory of [their] world . . . its logic in a popular form . . . its enthusiasm, its moral sanction, its solemn completing, its universal ground for consolation and justification' (41). The father of lies is thus the father of ideology also, his speeches and those of his subordinates showing characteristic signs of ideological deformation — inconsistency, reliance on obfuscatory myth and suppression of known fact. Satan knows all along, for example, that God is 'matchless' (IV 41); he and Beelzebub continually refer to God as 'Almighty', covering themselves only sometimes with phrases like 'him nam'd *Almighty*' (VI 294); and he keeps changing the grounds on which the rebellion is justified. If God is not omnipotent (as the relatively protracted battle in heaven might appear to suggest) then the angels do have a claim to equality with him. But in Book VI, after line 417, when Satan has in fact suffered defeat, he invites his followers to join him in some morale-boosting chopped logic by openly changing the grounds for their rebellion: glory now takes precedence over liberty, and he proposes that they *stop* thinking of God as omniscient. Later, in Hell, he ignores the fact that the rebellion was

effected in the name of liberty and equality by asserting that his followers had chosen him their king.

To conceal these inconsistencies, he and Beelzebub invent a series of confused myths to divert attention from the truth. They suggest, for example, that God may have been 'upheld by strength, or Chance, or Fate' (I 133); and they think of themselves as self-created beings and of cosmic history in terms of blind process — 'Space may produce new Worlds' (I 650). This is not, however, as Empson claims, evidence 'of Satan's doubt whether God can create anything' (48), since he has already heard of the prophecy that God intends to create another race, less 'In power and excellence, but favour'd more' (II 350) than the angels, a contingency which Satan takes very seriously indeed. No less dubiously he hypothesises 'fixt Laws of Heav'n' (II 18) which would make God at most a constitutional monarch. Finally there is the selective character of his memory. All the rebel angels know that God only deployed half the loyal angels against them, and no one mentions the agent of their defeat — the Son. There can be few defter exposures in literature of the three main devices by which ideology achieves its specious but socially effective coherence.

13. In one key respect, however, the representation of ideology in *Paradise Lost* is at odds with marxist views on the priority of ideology over consciousness. According to Bakhtin (1929), there can be '*no basic division between the psyche and ideology*' (33), at least from the standpoint of content, the basis of this continuity between the psyche and ideology being 'the ideological sign'. Bakhtin admits that 'a dividing line between the individual subjective psyche and ideology' has to be drawn, but the results of doing so, he maintains, would not include but would rather specifically exclude, a prior conception of the individual. This position is based on two important distinctions, between 'outer ideological signs' and 'inner (intercorporeal) signs' and between the individual and the person. Ideology, he maintains, is the ensemble of signs shared by a community. Such signs are external; nevertheless 'every outer ideological sign . . . is engulfed and washed over by inner signs, by consciousness. The outer sign originates from this sea of inner signs and continues to abide there.' But this does not give priority to consciousness or the psyche over ideology, since a 'thought that as yet exists only in the context of my consciousness . . . remains a dim unprocessed thought', which in any case has originated in a consciousness effectively brought into

being by earlier absorption of outer ideological signs. Hence Bakhtin's distinction between the individual and the person. He rejects the common opposition between the individual and the social, together with the assumption that 'the psyche is individual while ideology is social' (34). For him the 'correlate of the social is the natural', and he makes

> a rigorous distinction . . between the concept of the individual as a natural specimen without reference to the social world (i.e., the individual as object of the biologist's knowledge and study), and the concept of individuality which has the status of an ideological-semiotic superstructure over the natural individual, and which is therefore, a social concept.

It is the ideological or sign-sharing community, he believes, which confers personhood on the subject, while the only conceivable notion of individuality, that of the individual as biological specimen, is merely an abstraction, logically subsequent to the notion of a person, and itself a sign and therefore socially determined: 'every sign', Bakhtin contends, 'even the sign of individuality, is social'. Identity derives, not from personal action, as Newman describes it, but from communal life.

Obviously, this is inconsistent with the way in which the community of Hell is represented as being formed in *Paradise Lost*. Satan and his fellow-angels have a sovereign capacity to reject the ideological order into which they are introduced, and consciously to construct an alternative one of their own, knowing it to be false. In one respect at least, therefore, the basic assumptions underlying Milton's representation of ideology in Hell are fundamentally at variance with all but the most vulgar marxist theorising on the topic.

14. To the reader of *Paradise Lost*, however, this may seem more of a problem for marxist theory than it is for Milton, since the effectiveness of the poem remains undiminished by the discrepancy. The pleasure we feel in the naked wilfulness with which Satan improvises a working ideology is just what draws us to him and makes us aware of how ideology sometimes works in our own lives. One of the most exhilarating features of the first two Books of the poem is the skill with which Satan flaunts his falsehoods, while making a show of concealing them. Knowingly to lie, to know that you are known to be lying, to have your lie ecstatically accepted as a lie, to have it enriched and returned to you with

thanks and adulation, to proclaim it with a full consciousness of shared bad faith, of the shared wickedness which it symbolises and conceals, these are the satisfactions which Milton illustrates in the first two Books of *Paradise Lost* and to which we naturally respond. The scenes in Hell have not been compared to a Nuremberg rally for nothing. In effect, Milton captures for us the element of conscious bad faith in ideology, irrespective of its content.

This is why, although the effect of ideology in Hell exactly reverses the effect of Newman's concept of assent, it is not inconsistent with it, for both derive from convictions about the role of consciousness. For Newman assent involves a personal recognition of the true as true which *thwarts* intercourse between people. Assent such as Satan gives and secures from his followers, involves a collective recognition of the false as false and thereby *promotes* a kind of guilty freedom in their relations with one another. Both views are based on traditional notions of intelligence and will deriving from Aristotle. 'Reason also is choice' declares the Father in *Paradise Lost* (III 108), echoing Milton's own affirmation in *Areopagitica* that when 'God gave [Adam] reason he gave him freedom to choose, for reason is but choosing' (527). But it is not only marxists who reject this emphasis. The denial of either the possibility or desirability of deliberate acting has been general almost from Milton's day to our own, and probably represents the greatest single difficulty facing contemporary readers of Milton's poetry. The nature and implications of this widespread and deep-seated anti-aristotelianism need to be analysed further.

15. Among Milton's critics, agreement about the incoherence and distastefulness of deliberate willing has been articulated most forcefully of his virtuous characters. A marxist historian like Hill, for example, and a liberal critic like Carey, are agreed in preferring Comus's vitality to the deliberate goodness of The Lady. The general view has been expressed by Empson:

> The independence of our feelings from our will [he writes], which [Milton] regards as the essence of being fallen, is our basic protection against the lethal convictions which so often capture our brains. If Milton had presented Adam and Eve as 'self-controlled' to this extent they would have seemed like insects and been unable to fall. (169)

Another tradition, initiated by Blake, indiscriminately associates such self-control with both rationalism and empiricism, with

Aristotle and the anti-peripatetic traditions of Locke. Blake calls Aristotle's 'Analytics' 'the skeleton of a body' (157), the pre-occupation of Angels in the service of the usurper Reason whose task is to reduce desire to a shadow. 'The history of this is written in Paradise Lost, & the Governor or Reason is call'd Messiah' (150). F.R. Leavis (1970) argues that this vision of tyrannical self-government by reason exposes what, following Blake and D.H. Lawrence, he calls the 'mechanism of will, idea and ego' (303) against which he sets 'the disinterestedness of spontaneous life, undetermined and undirected and uncontrolled' (292). Blake's distinction between 'identity' and 'selfhood' is very important to Leavis. 'Identity [he writes] is the word with which [Blake] insists, in the face of the ethos of "Locke and Newton", that what matters is life, that only in the individual is life "there", and that the individual is unique' (302).

16. This repudiation of consciousness and choice is by no means confined to English literary critics. Sigmund Freud's conception of a dynamic unconscious, Louis Althusser's declaration (1970) that *'all ideology has the function (which defines it) of "constituting" concrete individuals as subjects'* (160), and Derrida's repudiation (1967(a)) of 'the punctual simplicity of the classical subject' (227) are only instances of a general tendency. Like many other ideas, the reaction against consciousness is continually effected for the first time without ever losing its status as a natural law. It thereby unites schools of thought otherwise opposed to one another. This means that it functions in our culture in a thoroughly ideological fashion, silently determining the thought even of those concerned with demystifying ideology. The real reason why Milton's teaching scandalises nearly all his critics, from Blake and Hill to Empson and Carey, is that it is inconsistent with the ideological priorities of the modern world, and particularly with the need of technologically advanced societies to define individuality in terms of a capacity for change rather than in terms of a continuing essence. In the socialist East, dialectically self-critical class consciousness is supposed to be the vehicle of personal and social development; in the capitalist West, an ideal of private maturity and growth underwrites the disintegration of traditional structures of work and intimate association. All this is a probably inevitable consequence of the massively destabilising effect of a technologically advanced world-economy. In modern society it is no longer practical to think of the average human being as a self-judging, self-determining member of a stable

community of adults. This kind of church congregation envisaged by Milton has ceased to represent a realisable norm.

17. Marxist demystifications of ideology like Bakhtin's have thus to be understood as being themselves thoroughly ideological, but this does not diminish the power of the concept. We certainly may not assume that the defenders of an Aristotelian conception of human beings are any less ideologically determined than their opponents. Newman, for example, may plausibly be said to have written on behalf of the *ancien régime* for a christendom that had been, or ought to be, restored after the unauthorised rationalism of the French Revolution. Milton's ideal of the responsible, autonomous patriarch as the embodiment of rationality and choice is similarly ideologically determined, in his case by the bourgeois character of the English Revolution. This is why the main lines of Milner's account of Milton are so convincing. As Hill notes, in spite of the proto-marxist elements in his writings, 'Milton's is a bourgeois conception of liberty' (263); the virtues that matter to him are 'frugality or thrift, industry, selective rather than indiscriminate alms-giving . . . respect for "the correct market price" (263–4). It is a point of view which commits him to identifying the human essence with the enterprising individualist, a commitment ultimately served by his atomistic and universalist conception of rationality: reason is the universal talent 'which is death to hide' and each of us will be judged on the use to which we put it. Committed to a bourgeois conception of individuality, he thinks of change primarily in terms of individual transformations, that is, of education or conversion. He is compelled to argue in *Second Defence of the English People*, therefore, that 'true and substantial liberty . . . must be sought, not without, but within' (624), and that 'to be free is precisely the same as to be pious, wise, just and temperate, careful of one's property, aloof from another's, and thus finally to be maganimous and brave' (684).

18. We seem then to have reached an impasse. The notion of intelligent voluntariness has been exposed as unreliable in so far as it serves the unacknowledged, historically determined priorities of a particular phase of economic and social history; we cannot trust it because it seems a covertlv self-interested rationalisation of class-determined priorities. But at the same time the instrument that has been developed to identify such rationalisations, the concept of ideology itself, turns out to be similarly exposed as a rationalised explanation of social relations. In the light of this apparently self-cancelling insight, we are faced with a number of

options. We could, for example, adopt a position of radically pessimistic scepticism about both the social process and the performances of individual human beings. Alternatively, we could seize the opportunity for some uninhibitedly pleasurable textual play, happily emancipated from the oppressive constraints imposed on us by our notions of 'truth'. Neither of these options seems to me improper. But neither precludes our going on to examine the notion of intelligent voluntariness in more detail, so long as we continually bear in mind that the fact that an idea has ideological implications tells us nothing about its intrinsic merits. Moreover, having alerted ourselves to the possibility that the spontaneous opposition to the idea of free will, so nearly universal in the modern world, is itself ideological, and therefore possibly less formidable and significant than it seems, there are no good reasons for a merely defensive attitude towards an Aristotelian view of reasoning and willing. So long as we remain conscious of the extrinsic factors working on both sides of the question, therefore, we may examine freely the intrinsic merits of Miltonic humanism, and so discover — if we can — whether or not it is appropriate to see in the average human being, as Milton and Newman do, a '"personalistic" value [which] is prior to and conditions ethical values'. And one advantage of making such an attempt may be to salvage marxist thought from the ideological consequences of its recent clandestine and debilitating alliance with fashionably liberal scepticism about truth and action.

2

The Acting Person

1. My reference at the end of the last chapter to a ' "personalistic" value [which] is prior to and conditions . . . ethical values' is a quotation from *The Acting Person* (1969, 321) by Karol Wojtyła (Pope John Paul II).* Like Newman, the Pope relies on classical and scholastic traditions to analyse the nature of the person as a moral agent. However he also writes in the phenomenological tradition deriving from Edmund Husserl, and this brings his account of ego, will and idea closer to the values of spontaneity,

---

* I depart from normal scholarly practice in not using the Pope's former name when referring to works written before his election partly because he was already Pope when the definitive version of *The Acting Person* appeared in English, and partly because the important similarities between his thought and Milton's throw into striking relief Milton's ferocious hatred of the papacy. The reader should clearly understand, however, that *The Acting Person* is not, properly speaking, a papal document.

26

disinterestedness and creativeness than Leavis might have thought possible. Whatever its intrinsic merits as philosophy, therefore, *The Acting Person* enables the student of Milton's humanism to rediscover the complexity and fullness of the *actus voluntarius* or *actus humanus* of traditional philosophy. For contrary to what Blake and Lawrence have led us to believe, it is possible for men and women, as understood in this tradition, to be, in the Father's words in *Paradise Lost*

> Authors to themselves in all
> Both what they judge and what they choose
>
> (III 122–3)

without ceasing to enjoy what *The Art of Logic* calls 'a corporeal essence replete with life and sense' (311). For whatever reasons, the acts which the Pope analyses and the actions represented in Milton's poems and Newman's writings on assent are based on the same assumptions and draw the same basically optimistic conclusions about human life.

2. It must first be acknowledged, however, that in many ways *The Acting Person* apparently confirms popular distrust of selfhood and willing. The Pope argues, for example, that 'freedom . . . depends on the certainty of truth, . . . on the reference to an authentic value and thus the validity of the judgment about the positive value of the object, concerning which a choice . . . is being made' (233). Often, he suggests, action must be taken in 'the name of *bare truth* about good, in the name of values that are not felt'. He represents human beings as achieving a certain ascendancy over, and aloofness from, the objects of willing simply in the interest of 'truth as a value' (159). Conscience is fundamental to moral activity, but for all its innerness it must be related to objectively valid norms, 'to truthfulness and not only to consciousness' (160) and even though 'the real issue is not just an abstractly conceived objective truthfulness of norms but experiencing their truthfulness' (164), nevertheless, conscience 'does not itself create norms; rather it discovers them' (165). Moreover this reference to truth 'is . . . derived from the will' (137). The person becomes independent of the objects of acting 'through the moment of truth, which is contained in every authentic choice of decision-making' (138); decisions 'which take as their object what is not a "real good" . . . lead to the experience of "guilt" or "sin" (139); and even when they are directed towards objectively authentic

27

values, choices keep the self detached from the willed object and so preserve the inner independence of the ego, for it is precisely when there is 'deliberation of motives' (131), by which the power to suspend willing momentarily is made manifest, that there is revealed in the person what the Pope calls vertical transcendence, a freedom 'in the process of *acting,* and not only in the intentional direction of willings towards an external object' (119). Thus human beings, he maintains, become their own 'raw material' (70), and form themselves by their acting.

All this has parallels in Newman's thought. Newman assigns a role to willing in intellectual activity, for example, which some have found disconcerting. He even suggests (1853) that 'a natural spontaneous act of the mind toward . . . acceptance [of an inference] or the reverse' (14) can and should be subjected to 'the jurisdiction of the will', and that certainty which 'naturally follows upon conviction, is a making up of the mind that a thing is true which is proved, and is therefore under the control of the will' (15). This seems uncomfortably close to what Leavis disliked in ego, will and idea, as well as to the thinking of the Pope.

3. Milton's narratives generate similar discomfort since they are based on similar convictions. There is a note of arbitrariness, for example, like that in the Pope's references to the bare truth about good, in the tests to which many of his characters are subjected, and in the care which is taken to ensure that they understand that eating a fruit or cutting hair is forbidden. In *Paradise Regain'd*, when Satan tempts Jesus with the idea of pagan wisdom, Jesus replies,

> he who receives
> Light from above, from the fountain of light,
> No other doctrine needs, though granted true
>
> (IV 288–90)

Once we have accepted the 'truth' of Scripture and the 'untruth' of pagan literature, apparently, we will regard the reading of Homer and Plato as no more than 'gathering pibles on the shore' (IV 330). But then distinguishing truth from falsehood appears never to be difficult. In *Samson Agonistes*, for example, Samson recalls yielding to Dalila even though he clearly perceived 'How openly and with what impudence' (398) she planned to betray him. But, one wants to ask, why did he do so? Do not complicated wants and beliefs make all the difference in such a case? Similarly it is not enough to assert, as Milton does in the stern opening of Book X of *Paradise Lost*, that Adam and Eve

> ought to have still remember'd
> The high injunction not to taste that Fruit
>
> (X 12–13)

any more than it is enough to demonstrate that what Abdiel is loyal to in his debate with Satan in Book V is indeed true. The mere fact of conscious allegiance or disloyalty to truth cannot justify praise or blame without analysis of the inner workings of each choice. Yet this is how the Father and Samson pass judgement. Like the Pope, in other words, Milton appears to assume the knowability of an objective order of norms, and his characters' capacity to respect them.

He seems too ready also to endorse certain kinds of inflexibility. Whatever the merits of Abdiel's defiance of Satan in Book V of *Paradise Lost*, he is an uncomfortable object lesson for the less clear-cut conditions of ordinary life. On the other hand, we are evidently expected to disapprove of Eve's 'open-mindedness' in her exchange with the Serpent. This is reminiscent of Newman's belief that that 'inquiry' and faith are incompatible. Inquiry, he argues (1870), 'is something more than the mere exercise of inference. He who inquires has not found; he is in doubt about where the truth lies . . . We cannot without absurdity call ourselves believers and inquirers also' (159). But minds seizing on dogmatic truths and refusing as a matter of duty to listen to serious objections to them are precisely what Marx and Lawrence from their different points of view condemned. And to require action in the name of beliefs adhered to as a matter of will, or of values that are not felt, is to come dangerously close to that 'independence of our feelings from our will' so rightly feared by Empson.

4. This view is strengthened by the emphasis which the Pope gives to deliberation. He makes the traditional Aristotelian distinction between willing 'as an intentional act' (110), such as an animal might perform, and what he calls '"I will" in its full content', for which, he suggests, I have to become an object to myself in the sense of imparting 'actuality to the . . . ready-made objectiveness of the ego . . . It is there', the Pope insists (109) — in the I which sees itself as a whole, and the I which knows itself to will — 'that the whole reality of morals . . . has its roots'. This is fundamental to his conception of the place of emotion in

choosing. He recognises that the 'world of sensations and feelings
. . . has an objective wealth of its own' (52), but he also believes
that it can 'have a restraining or even a crippling effect on . . . free
will'. Feelings threaten the 'aloofness' necessary to personal
action; they 'emotionalize consciousness'. However, because I
can form a cognitive relation with my self, 'the meaning of the
emotive facts' (53) can become accessible to consciousness, and
thus it can maintain its 'objectivizing aloofness'. This 'control of
emotions by consciousness has a tremendous significance', in the
Pope's view, for 'inner integration', and it is not achieved, he
insists, 'outside the sphere of the will'.

A similar pattern is evident in his perception of the body, which
cannot be discussed, he writes, without our recognising that the
human being 'is a person' (203), that is, a being who transcends the
self in action: 'self-governance, and self-possession', he suggests,
'may be thought of as "traversing" the body and being expressed
in it' (204). Essential to this dynamism is a capacity to externalise
the self to the self 'by means of the body' (206); indeed the 'ability
to objectify the body and to employ it in acting is an important
factor of . . . personal freedom'. I possess myself 'in the
experience of [my] embodiment precisely because it entails the
feeling of possessing [my] body'. Consequently self-government
consists largely in controlling the body.

Not surprisingly, therefore, the Pope's view of the human
capacities is strictly hierarchical, particularly with regard to the
relation 'between senses and mind' (230). We have, he argues, an
'awareness . . . of our feelings . . . On the other hand, we cannot
assert . . . that we have a "feeling of consciousness".'
Consciousness, therefore, can claim 'precedence' and this brings
with it 'a certain . . . "subordination" of feelings, in particular
the feeling of one's own body', and this subordination, he argues,
'is the condition of self-determination'.

5. Significantly comparable formulations can be observed in
Milton. Satan's suggestion to Jesus in *Paradise Regain'd* that he
might imitate the pagan philosophers is a response to Jesus's
earlier remark that

> he who reigns within himself, and rules
> Passions, Desires, and Fears, is more a King
>
> (II 466-7)

than one who is merely endowed with the public responsibilities of government. The demand is for a division of self into the governor and the governed. Inner weaknesses, however intimate, like Dalila's in *Samson Agonistes* have to be disowned: 'All wickedness is weakness' (834), while physical gifts like Samson's must be subordinated to his wisdom. In itself, his strength is

> vast, unwieldy burdensom,
> Proudly secure, let liable to fall
> By weakest suttleties, not made to rule,
> But to subserve where wisdom bears command
>
> (54–7)

Inevitably, therefore, Milton's model of mind, like the Pope's, is hierarchical. Adam tells Eve in *Paradise Lost*

> that in the Soule
> Are many lesser Faculties that serve
> Reason as chief; among these Fansie next
> Her office holds; of all external things,
> Which the five watchful Senses represent,
> She forms Imaginations, Aerie shapes,
> Which Reason joyning or disjoyning, frames
> All what we affirm or what deny, and call
> Our knowledge or opinion
>
> (V 100–8)

Corresponding to this model of government from above is one of progressive refinement from below, as the material universe is drawn up through the body into the rational life of the spirit:

> flours and thir fruit
> Mans nourishment, by gradual scale sublim'd
> To vital Spirits aspire, to animal.
> To intellectual, give both life and sense,
> Fansie and understanding, whence the Soule,
> Reason receives, and reason in her being
>
> (v 482–7)

Blake's remarks about Reason as Governor in a rigidly structured order of psychic life are thus apparently confirmed.

6. Stated in this way, however, the traditional conception of transcendence is seriously distorted. The Pope's governing conceptions makes this clear. These are: *first*, that the experience

by which I come into a relationship with myself is not by any means exclusively cognitive and far from dividing me against myself, 'is the richest and apparently the most complex of all experiences accessible to [me]' (3); and *second*, that action or choice is the supremely important instance of such self-apprehension. For conscious acting, as the Pope understands it, far from detaching my cognitive powers from the rest of my potentialities, brings them all with it into the action, and there manifests and integrates them. In other words, 'action *reveals* the person' (11). I become myself most fully when I know myself, and I know myself most fully when I apprehend and reapprehend my own continuity and wholeness in deliberate action.

The person thus enjoys experiential unity even in the most self-conscious, agonised acts of willing. We are not divided between 'life' on this side and ego, will and idea on that. Neither threatens nor (necessarily) tyrannises the other. Experientially life lives in willing, and will wills in life. Because of this conviction concerning 'the intrinsic simplicity' (8) of our experience of ourselves, the Pope declares himself an optimist, and repudiates the notion that our capacity to abstract and intelluctualise involves any 'rejection of experiential wealth and diversity' (15). Defining induction as 'the stabilisation of the object of experience' (14), a mental grasping of 'the unity of meaning' (15), he asserts, firstly that this leads to the 'simplicity in the experience' (14) of being human, and, secondly, that it 'opens the way to reduction' (15) by which he means '*to convert to suitable arguments and items of evidence . . . to reason, explain and interpret*' (17). In this he deliberately parts company with the positivist tradition represented by John Stuart Mill, for whom, he sugggests 'induction is already a form of argumentation or reasoning — something which it is not for Aristotle' (14).) But reduction is not an exclusively philosphical exercise: it penetrates

> something that actually exists. The arguments explaining this existence have to correspond to experience. Thus . . . reduction (like induction) . . . is an inherent factor of experience without at the same time ceasing to be, though different from induction, transcendent with respect to it.

Thus, though the Pope writes of 'the will', he does not consider it as a separate faculty coming into play on its own terms. He attributes acting to the person. And just as life is willed and will is life, so what is experienced can be thought about, and thinking about it is intrinsic to the richness of what is experienced. The will may be able to transcend life, and thought may be able to liberate itself from experiential limitations to a knowledge of *bare truth* about good, but neither ceases to be part of experience as well. That is why human self-control, as the Pope understands it, can never be insect-like. Reason and will are never 'lost' in the immanent, but they are never divorced from it either.

7. It follows that there can be no disjunction in the Pope's scheme (though there are distinctions) between the spiritual and the corporeal. In this respect, his catholic humanism comes as close as it possibly can to Milton's materialism. In *Christian Doctrine* Milton argues 'that all form — and the human soul is a kind of form — is produced by the power of matter' (322) and this leads him to the view that death involves annihilation of the whole person — but as his editor, Maurice Kelley, notes (quoting W.C. Curry), Milton does not hold that the form is made out of matter, but that it is produced by material power. Milton writes of 'the breath of life' being 'mixed . . . with matter in a very fundamental way' (325). This does not seem far from the Pope's contention that 'the soul-body relation cuts across all the boundaries we find in experience' (258), nor even from his argument that while 'the somatic dynamism and indirectly the psycho-emotive dynamism have their source in the body-matter, this source is neither sufficient nor adequate for the action in its essential feature of transcendence' (258). The Pope's account is thus close to (but not identical with) Milton's assertion that 'the whole man is the soul, and the soul the man: a body . . . or individual substance, animated, sensitive and rational' (318).

It also bears closely on Milton's descriptions of Adam and Eve in *Paradise Lost*. The Pope holds that the body and the feelings are deeply stirred by the person's 'attitude toward the truth, good and beauty' (227) which, 'with . . . self-determination' effect and constitute 'the spiritual transcendence of the person . . . The resonance', he adds, 'is thoroughly individual'. There is in effect a *'fusion of sensibility with truthfulness [which] is the necessary condition of the experience of values'* (233). Thus though 'the dynamism of the psyche and soma take an active part in integration, not at their own levels, but *at the level of the person*' (198), nevertheless at this 'higher level . . . the dynamism[s] belonging to [the] psyche seem to . . . fuse together' and the body becomes 'the territory where, or . . . the medium whereby' (204) self-expression takes place. The 'autonomy of the body' (211) thus becomes 'a basis . . . for

. . . the structure of the person'.

This is especially true in the exercise of what the Pope calls 'skill' which he equates with 'the Latin *habitus* . . . [meaning] both a skill and a virtue' (213). A related and fuller account of skill is provided by Polanyi (1962). Polanyi distinguishes between 'focal' and 'subsidiary awareness' which he sees as mutually exclusive. I am focally aware, for example, of the words I am typing on the screen and subsidiarily of my fingers moving over the word-processor keyboard. My body and the tools it uses are thus perceived as parts of myself, distinct from the task I am performing, which is outside of me. We 'achieve and practise [such] skills', Polanyi writes, 'without any antecendent knowledge of their premisses' (162), yet subsidiary awareness is an authentic way of knowing, and indeed the foundation of all knowledge. And as the Pope notes, though skill ultimately reaches into the most rarified intellectual and moral activities, it is first developed in the body.

> The presence of skill, [he suggests] makes the whole motor-dynamism, the whole of human mobility so spontaneous and fluent that in most cases we never notice the causative effect of the will in the synthesis of actions and motions. (214)

The powers of the body, then, as the Pope understands them, are not necessarily a threat to freedom, nor even mere instruments of the will. Though 'the person as such repudiates a merely instinctive acting', he writes (123), we may still talk of 'the "instinct of freedom"' (122), for personal values that transcend the body are also integral with bodily life and constitute its perfection. And so it is in the Eden of *Paradise Lost*. The physical experience of Adam and Eve achieves fulness and spontaneity because it is infused by the perceptions and purposes of unfallen intelligence. Their 'sweet gardening labour' is deliberately performed yet it is exactly sufficient

> To recommend coole *Zephyr*, and [make] ease
> More easie, wholsom thirst and appetite
> More grateful

(IV 329–3)

Even Adam's sleep —

> Aerie light from pure digestion bred,
> And temperat vapors bland
>
> (V 4-5)

is expressive of personal values realised in, but not exclusively by, his physical well-being. As he walks to meet Raphael,

> without more train
> Accompani'd then with his own compleat
> Perfections
>
> (V 351-5)

the fluent, decorous grace of his young, naked and upright body is an exact expression of the transcendent values of 'Truth, wisdome; Sanctitude severe and pure' (IV 293). He thus exemplifies that integration of bodily with personal vitality to which the Pope alludes when he describes 'the possibly perfect matching of "somatic subjectivity" with the efficaciousness and transcendent subjectivity of the person' (212).

8. The Pope describes this perfect matching of body and will as the integration of 'action' with 'activation', but this structure also implies a condition of tension and possible imperfection in human beings with which Milton was also concerned. Thus crucial to the Pope's notion of self-government is the possibility of psychosomatic disintegration which has an exact equivalent in the psychology of Milton's later poems. Without integration, the Pope writes, 'transcendence remains . . . suspended in a kind of structural void' (190), for transcendence needs always to be 'accompanied by the subjective unity and wholeness of the structure of self-governance and self-possession' (191). Disintegration, on the other hand, 'signifies a more or less deep-seated inability to govern, or to possess, oneself' (194). The possibility of disintegration, however, is a condition of integration; without instincts and emotions, without all that simply 'happens' in the person and so makes disintegration a possibility for all of us, there would be nothing for the self to realise and control. There is thus a necessary and intimate tension in the person between 'will . . . and . . . bodily potentiality, emotiveness, and impulsions' (123), because the former needs the latter's autonomy in order to act, and the latter needs the former's rational deliberations to come fully into play. Such is the condition of Adam and Eve in *Paradise Lost* before the fall, and even of Jesus in *Paradise Regain'd*, each of whom

operates in a normative condition of increasing integration, but in each of whom also there is a capacity for psychosomatic insurrection, without which their integration as human persons would be meaningless.

This is the point, of course, at which Satan can insert his projects into their lives by trying to convert the 'act' of thinking into something that merely 'happens' in them. 'I will excite their minds', he declares in *Paradise Lost*, 'With more desire to know' (IV 522–3). Hence his use of Eve's capacity to dream,

> Assaying by his Devilish art to reach
> The Organs of her Fancie, and with them forge
> Illusions as he list, Phantasms and Dreams
>
> (IV 801–3)

As Adam later explains, this can only happen when Reason in sleep retires 'Into her private Cell' (V 109) and leaves the lesser faculty of Fancy, which is incapable of choice, to imitate Reason by framing affirmations and denials. Indeed it is only because the rational will can be thus detached from evils perceived by the other faculties that it can remain uncontaminated by what it knows as a consequence:

> Evil into the mind of God or Man
> May come and go, so unapprov'd, and leave
> Not spot or blame behind
>
> (V 117–19)

It can certainly come into the mind of Jesus in *Paradise Regain'd*, who in sleep is quite as vulnerable as Eve. Even without the prompting of Satan, he dreams 'as appetite is wont to dream, / Of meat and drinks' (II 264–5). Later the tempter disturbs his sleep 'with ugly dreams' (IV 408). In Jesus, of course, reason resumes control the moment he wakes, and in any case the fleshly temptations to which he is subjected are peripheral to the real contest between himself and Satan. We must return to Adam, therefore, to examine how far a balancing of what the Pope calls 'man acts' with 'what happens to man' can be convincingly attributed to a full instinctive life.

9. There is no question but that Adam's love for Eve has its origins in pure reactivity.

36

```
    here [he says]
    . . . transported I behold,
Transported touch; here passion first I felt
Commotion strange, in all enjoyments else
Superiour and unmov'd
```

(VIII 528–32)

Raphael describes these feelings as passion, not love, Love, he insists,

```
    refines
The thoughts, and heart enlarges, hath his seat
In Reason, and is judicious
```

(VIII 589–91)

but the distinction does not preclude the integration of passion with self-control, as the celebrated description of Adam and Eve's love-making makes clear. A fundamental aspect of this love-making is that it is preceded by prayer:

```
This said unanimous, and other Rites
Observing none, but adoration pure
Which God likes best, into their inmost bowre
Handed they went: and eas'd the putting off
These troublesom disguises which wee wear,
Strait side by side were laid, nor turnd I weene
Adam from his fair Spouse, nor Eve the Rites
Mysterious of connubial Love refus'd: . . .
Haile wedded love, mysterious Law, true source
Of human ofspring, sole proprietie
In Paradise of all things common else.
By thee adulterous lust was driv'n from men
Among the bestial herds to raunge, by thee
Founded in Reason, Loyal, Just, and Pure,
Relations dear, and all the Charities
Of Father, Son, and Brother first were known.
Farr be it, that I should write thee sin or blame,
Or think thee unbefitting holiest place,
Perpetual Fountain of Domestic sweets,
Whose bed in undefil'd and chaste pronounc't,
Present, or past, as Saints and Patriarchs us'd.
Here Love his golden shafts imploies, here lights
```

His constant Lamp, and waves his purple wings,
Reigns here and revels

(IV 734–41, 750–65)

The syntax and imagery of the opening lines of this passage speak
exactly of the fluency between transcendent rational will and spontaneous instinct and emotion which the Pope also affirms. In a
single sentence the upright posture of naked prayer yields to the
extended intimacy of naked love-making; both are corporeal; both
are rites; both are founded in reason. Even the supreme personal
value of Divine Fatherhood is channelled into the human condition through the act of love, so that all the other 'charities' of
domestic life derive from it. A reference to the patriarchs is
immediately followed by one to the revels of Eros: clearly the
controls of reason do not suppress the potentialities of instinct, but
bring them to full realisation; or as the Pope expresses it, the
necessary tension between 'will . . . and . . . bodily potentiality,
emotiveness, and impulsions' (123) is not to be seen as a kind of
self-cleavage and self-contradiction.

10. Fundamental to this ideal of integration is the interplay
between cognition and consciousness. In 'the Scholastic
approach', the Pope writes, '. . . consciousness was only implied
. . . in "rationality" [and] contained in the will' (30). Properly
understood, however, it is 'an *intrinsic and constitutive aspect of* . . .
"the acting person"' (31) and must therefore be distinguished from
cognition. Cognitive acts 'investigate . . . objectivize . . . intentionally' (32). They do not, however, *'belong to consciousness'* as
such, which 'is restricted to mirroring what has already been
cognized'. Cognition is active, end-directed, consciousness is a
passive mirroring of what 'happens' in the person and of the
person acting. Thus for the Pope cognition seems to suggest 'will'
and 'idea', and consciousness 'spontaneity' and 'disinterestedness'. It also has 'the specific quality of penetrating and
illuminating' (33) whatever becomes the person's cognitive
possession; 'it is entirely dissolved in its own acts . . . in "being
aware"' (34). Thus I enter the world of other people and of objects
in two ways — cognitively, by active directed attention, and
passively 'in the image mirrored by consciousness, which is a
factor in [my] innermost, most personal life. For consciousness not
only reflects but also *interiorizes.'*

Cognition and consciousness can thus each claim a certain
priority — cognition because it intentionally constitutes and

comprehends what consciousness can only reflect, and consciousness in the innerness of its origins and operations. Their relationship is particularly important in their connection with the self. I am capable of cognising myself, my intentional acts of self-knowledge converging upon and in effect constituting my ego, but concurrently with this self-cognition consciousness reflects and interiorises it. What results, in the Pope's view, is a 'coherence of self-knowledge and consciousness' (37), which he sees as 'the basic factor of the equilibrium in the inner life'. Consciousness thus merges with subsidiary awareness as Polanyi defines it, while being both more than it and less: more because it reflects everything, less because it is prior to, and so more 'primitive' than subsidiary awareness.

In any case cognitive self-awareness is more flexible than it seems to critics in the Leavis tradition. It consists, the Pope suggests, 'in the acts of objectivizing penetration of the ego with all its concreteness and its concomitant detailedness, which yields no generalization whatsoever' (40) but is none the less 'real knowledge of oneself as an integral whole' since it 'continuously strives after generalizations . . . opinions . . . or judgments' of the self. Thus the 'singular data' (of cognitive self-penetration) are 'mirrored in consciousness', and 'the continuously developing overall complex that the ego keeps unfolding' is mirrored there also. 'In the opinions about this complex', the Pope insists, 'there is never just one self-knowing theory of one's own ego': my generalising, judgement-forming capacity is always discovering fresh opportunities for self revision and reappraisal.

11. The Pope, then, repudiates the Blakean assumption that 'reason' imprisons us in fixed ideas of 'self'. He sees knowledge and idea as enlarging rather than limiting our potentialities, and he does so on the assumption that consciousness runs concurrently with self-cognition, allowing 'us not only to have an inner view' (42) of our free intelligent choices — '. . . and of their dynamic dependence on the ego, but also to *experience these actions as actions and as our own*'. But consciousness not only *reflects* cognitive (and all other) experience, it is also *reflexive*: 'it is one thing', the Pope writes, 'to *be* the subject, another to *be cognized* . . . as the subject, and still a different thing to *experience* one's self as the subject of one's own acts and experiences' (44). It is this reflexive consciousness that gives us our sense of identity, our ability not simply to cognise the ego (to use Leavis's term) as a 'self', but also to understand ourselves, to experience 'identity'. Thus consciousness, as

well as cognition, plays its part in the constitution of the ego: the individual is 'inwardly disclosed' by it, and thereby revealed as enjoying 'specific distinctness and unique concreteness' (46). Moreover, as long as consciousness

> only mirrors and is but a reflected image, [it] remains objectively aloof from the ego; when, however, . . . experience is constituted by its reflexiveness, . . . objective aloofness disappears and consciousness penetrates the subject shaping it experientially every time an experience occurs. (47)

An important illustration of how reflexiveness operates is provided by Newman's account of an assent becoming a certitude. When I assent to a proposition, I do so, according to Newman, in the light of reasons which are *mine* — reasons which, in Polanyi's terms, derive from my subsidiary as well as my focal awareness and knowledge. Even the most rigorous intellectual activity, Polanyi points out, is dependent on unspecifiable personal coefficients supplied by my mind if only because 'any formal system in which we could assert a sentence, and also reflect on the truth of its assertion must be self-contradictory' (260). Not even the most logical language, therefore, is self-validating; it has to be appropriated subsidarily, as a tool, as an extension of myself. Newman is thus justified in differentiating between an assent and inferences preceding it. Coming to a conclusion must follow the exercise of personal skills which use reasons but are not identical with them; it involves an incommunicable, self-validating and so deeply reflexive approval of its own skilfulness. This is why I can continue to be certain about something even if the inferences leading to the original certitude have been forgotten, or no longer *seem* persuasive. I can still *know* that the original conclusion was indeed conclusively reached. Certitude is thus a fact about the knower as well as the known. It enables me to see myself as the one who is *really* in possession of particular truths, and that this perception is the only possible ground for believing that they are really — unfalsifiably — so.

To be 'objective', therefore, truth has to be profoundly interior, an integral experience of reflexive consciousness. This 'experiential innerness', the Pope (47) suggests, is particularly important in relation to values, for through consciousness I not only recognise good and evil, but appropriate my recognitions into the territory of skilled reflexive responsiveness, and so in a profoundly interior way identify myself with the values I have chosen to know as such.

12. Something very close to this structure of consciousness, cognition and assimilation of values can be discerned in Milton's major characters. Thus the Son in *Paradise Lost* literally becomes the divine attributes of Mercy and Love which he discerns in the Father, and he does so in penetrating his own essence, both cognitively and consciously: 'on me', he declares

> let Death wreck all his rage;
> Under his gloomie power I shall not long
> Lie vanquisht; thou hast givn me to possess
> Life in myself for ever
>
> (III 241-4)

Through this synthesis of free perception of the Good as he perceives it in the Father, and of complete self-awareness, the Son is found 'By Merit more than Birthright Son of God' (III 309). His discernment and choice of divine values, values objective and external to his being, simultaneously constitute and reveal a personal essence by which and in which those values become literally his.

In his exalted state as Son, however, this process is a sublime mystery. We must turn to *Paradise Regain'd*, and his life as Jesus of Nazareth, to see a comparable act of self-discernment and self-realisation described in more assimilable terms. Jesus needs time, as the Son in Heaven did not, to penetrate and govern the 'multitude of thoughts' (I 196) that swarm within him. We then see him constitute himself as a discerned and experienced value in the context of objectively discerned truth. His problem is not to discover what he should 'do' — he quietly recognises that he must perform the part of the Suffering Servant of Isaiah; rather he has to descend 'Into himself' (II 111) in order to act — that is, to resist the temptations offered to him by Satan — by discerning and adhering to truth about good as he discovers it there. In both poems, then, the Son voluntarily, cognitively, consciously and reflexively discovers, expresses and enacts his personal essence and so makes himself, in the words of the angelic Quire at the end of *Paradise Regain'd*,

> True image of the Father . . .
>   still expressing
> The Son of God, with Godlike force indu'd
>
> (IV 596, 601-2)

13. More complex experiences of voluntary scrutiny and self-scrutiny, and of reflective and reflexive consciousness are represented by the early experiences of Adam and Eve in *Paradise Lost*. Both move from relatively primitive self-awareness into a more complex cognitive and conscious relationship with objective values, and experiencing the resulting knowledge as their own enables them to become what they were not but needed in essence to be. Eve, for example, wakes to find herself 'much wondring where / And what' (IV 451–2) she is. She walks to the lake 'With unexperienc't thought' (IV 457), and there sees her own image, to which she is initially attracted as a value outside herself; but she is warned that she is only seeing her own reflection, and at once obeys the internal prompting which directs her to Adam, whom she finds 'Less winning soft, less amiablie milde' (IV 479) but in whom there are values not originally hers, specifically 'manly grace / And wisdom' (IV 490–1), which by loving submission to his authority, she can assimilate without any loss of personal distinctness, since such acts of assimilation are hers, just as the Son's acts and those of Jesus in submitting to the Father's will as value are his and not the Father's.

Adam's coming to knowledge, self-awareness and so to selfhood is more elaborately represented. He is to be

> a Creature who not prone
> And Brute as other Creatures, but endu'd
> With Sanctitie of Reason, might erect
> His Stature, and upright with Front serene
> Govern the rest, self-knowing, and from thence
> Magnanimous to correspond with Heav'n,
> But grateful to acknowledge whence his good
> Descends, thither with heart and voice and eyes
> Directed in Devotion, to adore
> And worship God Supream
>
> (VII 506–15)

The important word here is 'self-knowing' — which in a newly created human being implies an ability to learn. In the first moments of his waking life he is aware only of his body lying 'Soft on the flourie herb . . . / In Balmie Sweat' (VIII 254–5); he then sees the sun and springs up 'By quick instinctive motion' (VIII 259); the world delights him, and he peruses himself 'Limb by Limb' (VIII 267), discovering his own body experientially and experimentally. Finally he speaks, his rationality comes into play and he recognises his origins. Instruction then comes to him in a dream from God, and he confirms his authority over the other creatures by giving them names. Next (like Abraham, Moses and the prophets after him) he has an argument with God, in which he relies on the evidence provided by objectively discerned truth and his own experienced identity to justify his desire for a companion and a mate. This request is based on an assimilation of values he has discerned in the animal world and in God. The animals have mates; God can raise his creatures to what height he will 'Of Union or Communion, deifi'd' (VIII 431); Adam alone is isolated and helpless in his creaturely dependence. But he knows what he needs. The significance of his request for the 'rational delight' (VIII 391) of a wife, however, is that it is an act of deliberate and intelligent self-discovery which is simultaneously a work of self-formation. God's approval of Adam's request is stated in precisely these terms.

> Thus farr to try thee, *Adam*, I was pleas'd
> And finde thee knowing not of Beasts alone,
> Which thou hast rightly nam'd, but of thy self,
> Expressing well the spirit within thee free,
> My Image, not imparted to the Brute . . .
>
> (VIII 437–41)

As his 'likeness . . . [his] other self', Eve is a 'wish exactly to [his] hearts desire' (VIII 450–1). The essence of each is realised and disclosed in the choice of the other. Both engage in a continuous striving 'after generalizations . . . opinions . . . judgments of [the] self'. Neither, therefore, is fixed in 'just one self-knowing theory of [the] ego'. On the contrary, in their choices of each other, they are revealed to themselves and to each other as self-penetrating, self-revising persons.

14. But if the good characters in Milton's world thus become, in body and soul, the values that they embrace through the self-awareness accompanying right action, the obverse is also true: at every level sinners become the evil that they choose. The christian humanist tradition invariably represents such choices as dis-ordered and disordering. 'The lower limit of disintegration', the Pope writes, 'is . . . a total absence of self-governance and self-possession' (193). This is tangibly Satan's fate in *Paradise Lost*:

His Visage drawn he felt to sharp and spare,
His Armes clung to his Ribs, his Leggs entwining
Each other, till supplanted down he fell
A monstrous Serpent on his Belly prone,

(X 511–15)

The effects of a self constituted in a corrupt and contradictory will
are even more impressively suggested in the comparison in
Paradise Regain'd of Satan's fall from the Temple with the rage of
the Sphinx outwitted by Oedipus:

And as that *Theban* Monster that propos'd
Her riddle, and him, who solv'd it not, devour'd;
That once found out and solv'd, for grief and spight
Cast herself headlong from th' *Ismenian* steep,
So strook with dread and anguish fell the Fiend

(IV 572–6)

But like the Son's, Satan's is a special case. His fall seems
irreversible and it is not directly depicted. The process is more
clearly illustrated in the lives of Adam and Eve. Perhaps surprisingly they manifest a perverse kind of integration in their
disintegration. But, as the Pope points out: 'A disintegrated
person is . . . characterized . . . not by a straight forward aboli-
tion or limitation of the transcendent ego' (194) but 'by an
insubordinative and unpossessible ego'. This describes exactly the
effects of sin in *Paradise Lost*. When Eve first eats the fruit she is
initially

Intent now wholly on her taste, naught else
Regarded, such delight till then, as seemed,
In Fruit she never tasted, whether true
Or fansied so, through expectation high
Of knowledg, nor was God-head from her thought.
Greedily she ingorg'd without restraint,
And knew not eating Death

(IX 786–92)

Quickly, however, she manifests a lack of self-governance. As she
tells Adam her story, her countenance is 'blithe' (IX 886), but
'distemper flushing' (IX 887) glows in her cheek. Further disjunc-
tions soon appear: she lies about her motives, and protests that if

44

she thought death would follow from her act she 'would sustain alone / the worst' (IX 978–9). Adam is similarly engulfed by a specious sense of unity when he sins. He and Eve 'swim in mirth' (IX 1009); the 'exhilerating vapour' (IX 1047) of the fruit stimulates them to hectic love-play, and then to 'grosser sleep' (IX 1049); but on waking they are restless, and guiltily aware of being naked, morally as well as physically,

> of Honour void,
> Of Innocence, of Faith, of Puritie
>
> (IX 1074–5)

There is no relief for them, therefore, in merely covering their bodies:

> For Understanding rul'd not, and the Will
> Heard not her lore, both in subjection now
> To sensual Appetite, who from beneathe
> Usurping over soveran Reason claimed
> Superior sway
>
> (IX 1127–31)

'What happens' has usurped the functions of the acting person. The result is not just a series of bad effects at different levels, corporeal, emotional, intellectual and voluntary; we are confronted by woman-fallen and man-fallen, each essentially re-selved in a corruption which removes all further selving from their control but which they none the less understand and feel to be their own.

15. If Milton were a calvinist, this is the point at which *Paradise Lost* and *The Acting Person* would part company. Ideologically and temperamentally, however, he was unprepared to represent the human condition as wholly determined by God, or by 'what happens' in a fallen state. As the Father puts it when he first prophesies the fall:

> I will cleer thir senses dark,
> What may suffice, and soft'n stonie hearts
> To pray, repent, and bring obedience due.
> To Prayer, repentance, and obedience due,
> Though but endevord with sincere intent,
> Mine ear shall not be slow, mine eye not shut
>
> (III 188–93)

The Son's clothing of Adam and Eve with the skins of beasts is also a partial reclothing of their 'inward nakedness' (X 221) and under grace they subsequently work towards a reinstatement of their power to act. They do so, however, in the far more difficult context of the fallen world, and in a sense all the work Milton published from this point onwards is concerned with representing the re-emergence of the acting person from the context of 'what happens' in fallen human beings.

This is certainly so in *Samson Agonistes*. Samson's sin has destroyed his bodily integrity which confirms and reinforces the disintegration of his personality. He is literally deprived of self-possession and self-governance and reduced to the status of 'a fool / In power of others, never in [his] own' (77–8). His blindness —

> Since light so necessary to life,
> And almost life it self
>
> (90–1)

threatens his identity at a very deep level: he has become his own 'Sepulcher, a moving Grave / Buried' (102–3). His thoughts

> like a deadly swarm
> Of Hornets arm'd, no sooner found alone,
> But rush upon [him] thronging
>
> (19–21)

> he lies at random, carelessly diffus'd,
> With languish't head unpropt
>
> (118–19)

an exact reversal of the upright Adam walking to meet Raphael, or of Jesus on the pinnacle of the Temple. Samson's hopes are

> flat, nature within [him] seems
> In all her functions weary of her self
>
> (595–6)

His father cannot console him with the argument that his despairing thoughts

>   proceed
> From anguish of the mind and humours black,
> That mingle with [his] fancy
>
>   (599–601)

because this reminds him of his lack of self-control. His great lament is that

>   torment should not be confin'd
> To bodies wounds and sores
> With maladies innumerable
> In heart, head, breast, and reins;
> But must secret passage find
> To th' inmost mind
>
>   (606–11)

Choice and spontaneity, however, though each a condition of the other's wholeness, are none the less autonomous in their respective spheres. In the Pope's words, 'a human being with a high degree of somatic disintegration may represent a personality of great value' (215). This is the point that Milton's tragedy elucidates, and is asserted in the sonnets on his blindness. Moreover, for both Milton and the Pope, the movement out of disintegration requires, in Samson's words, 'some great act' (1389). Samson is reconstituted in selfhood and so in self-awareness by becoming literally an acting person. And just as the Son is raised to equality with the Father when he empties himself of the Father's glory, and Eve integrates all that Adam represents into her own personal essence by submitting to his loving authority, so Samson liberates himself by becoming 'tangl'd in the fold / of dire necessity' (1665–6). Self-obliteration paradoxically restores him to his identity, that is to his name. In the words of his father

>   *Samson*, hath quit himself
> Like *Samson* and heroicly hath finish'd
> A life Heroic.
>
>   (1709–11)

His act is above all one of conscience, which as we shall see, is the highest level of conscious and cognitive activity in the acting person.

16. In *Of Civil Power* Milton writes:

I . . . mean by conscience or religion, that full persuasion
whereby we are assur'd that our beleef and practice . . . is
according to the will of God & his Holy Spirit within us,
which we ought to follow much rather than any law of man,
as not only his word everywhere bids us, but the very dictate
of reason tells us. (242)

The word 'conscience' has perhaps even broader and move
moving connotations in the sonnet, '*To Mr* Cryiack Skinner *on his*
Blindness', in which he asserts that he is supported in the loss of
his eyes by

The conscience . . . to have lost them overply'd
In libertyes defence, my noble task

(10–11)

In both instances he enlarges the word as far as its semantic range
will allow, to include 'religion' in the first case, and the whole of
his life in the second. Milton's conscience, in other words, is
Milton himself, realised as himself, in the God-created universe he
has discovered through the Spirit.

This corresponds closely with the Pope's thinking. Every act,
he argues, moves outwards towards the object and inwards
towards the subject, where its effects outlast the act itself. 'The
engagement in freedom is [thus] objectified . . . in the person . . .
when through an action that is either morally good or morally bad
. . . the person . . . becomes either morally good or morally evil'
(151). The person is therefore 'a potential and not a fully actual
being' (153). I may or may not seek to make a reference to truth
(to 'the will of God & his Holy Spirit within us') when I form my
values in the moment of choice. Such a 'surrender to the good in
truth', the Pope suggests, 'forms . . . a new moral reality within
the person' (156), which 'manifests itself in the formulation of
norms' and in particular 'norms of ethics' and so contributes to
the formation of conscience. In the action, the person becomes
'somebody' and that 'being "somebody"' (157) is precisely a self-
manifestation.

At first, the Pope writes, conscience is 'an enquiry into the
truth' (160), and it is therefore 'closely related to truthfulness' as
an intention or act of the will; 'the content and the attractiveness
of a value are . . . checked . . . by the conscience, which tests the

truthfulness of the good presented in the value; it is with this test that obligation begins' (167). For the Pope, then, as for Newman, inquiry precedes certitude, which in turn contains an element of willing. However, when linked as the Pope links it to consciousness, this structure is less forbidding than it seems in Newman's account of the role of will in the *maintenance* of certitude. Consciousness, rather than the will, the Pope suggests, 'supplies . . . the subjective experience of truthfulness' (160), and of certitude or incertitude, 'of a faltering conscience, and, at worst, of bad faith' (161), and so it is through consciousness that the conclusions about values are taken into the person. Thus inquiry is not just a matter of theory: its aim is to *grasp* values — both in what is willed and in the willing itself, the latter being precisely the agent's capacity to act freely according to conscience: 'the performance itself of the action by the person is a value' (322). There is therefore value in the act and value in the object and the two come together in a person's 'conviction of the truthfulness of good' (166). The three words, 'conviction', 'truthfulness' and 'good', are constituent of each other, for without conviction and so of conscientiousness, the two other words lose much of their moral significance. This, according to the Pope, relieves the 'tension arising between the objective order of norms and . . . inner freedom', and is the antithesis of mere obedience to a rule which 'overshadows the transcendence of the person or reflects an immaturity in the person . . . [It] would be inhuman', he writes, 'to equate obligation with external pressures.'

17. It follows from this that I have a twofold responsibility in my acting — 'for the value of intentional objects' (171) — my wishes — and 'for the subject' — myself. But, the Pope suggests, 'responsibility has still another aspect' (177) — that of 'responsibility to'. We are 'always responsible to . . . a person . . . to . . . judicial power . . . to God' (172) and to conscience as 'the voice of God'. Milton and Newman also represent conscience as an authority internally constituted in this way. In *Paradise Lost* Milton calls it God's 'Umpire' (III 195) placed within his creatures (not above them); and Newman (1870) writes of 'the phenomena of Conscience . . . [impressing] the imagination with the picture of a Supreme Governor, a Judge, holy, just, powerful, all-seeing, retributive' (101) — again the reference is back to the (imagining) self. For all three, the divine authority of conscience guarantees what the Pope calls 'the intransitiveness of the action' (172); as Newman puts it, the images which are the objects of 'real

49

apprehension and assent . . . depend on personal experience; and the experience of one man is not the experience of another' (82). The person, therefore, according to the Pope, enjoys 'structural "inalienability"' (107) and the ultimate manifestation of these personal powers is revealed in the full play of responsibility for and responsibility to within and between cognition and consciousness. In the Pope's words, 'the creative role of conscience consists in the fact that *it shapes the norms into that unique and unparalleled form they acquire within the experience and fulfillment of the person*' (165). This is why conscience is fundamental to his account of the two ultimately personal conditions 'felicity' and 'despair'.

Felicity is not to be confused with pleasure. The relationship between them, the Pope suggests, is essentially that between activation and action, felicity being the experience of [acting according to the authentic values in which one has become constituted fully as a person. Despair is its opposite. Both arise out of the freedom and intransitiveness of action. This is something which Satan in *Paradise Lost* appears to be fully apprised of. He admits that others with as much reason to glorify themselves as he, have not fallen as he fell. 'Hadst thou', he asks himself

> the same free will and Power to stand?
> Thou hadst: whom hast thou then or what to accuse,
> But Heav'ns free Love dealt equally to all?
> Be then his Love accurst, since love or hate,
> To me alike, it deals eternal woe.
> Nay curs'd be thou; since against his thy will
> Chose freely what it now so justly rues.
> Me miserable! Which way shall I flie
> Infinite wrauth, and infinite despaire?
> Which way I flie is Hell; my self am Hell?
> And in the lowest deep a lower deep
> Still threatning to devour me opens wide,
> To which the Hell I suffer seems a Heav'n
>
> (IV 66–78)

Refusing to repent, in that he willingly anticipates lapsing from repentence, he comes instead to depair:

> So farewell Hope, and with Hope farewel Fear,
> Farewel Remorse: all Good to me is lost;
> Evil be thou my Good
>
> (IV 108–10)

Satan's conscience is evidently still alive, not as an external measure of wickedness, but as a voice nearer to the centre of his being than his ego itself, since it is conscience in the first person which enables him to curse himself in the third, and to call Evil by its own name even as he opts to rename it Good. It cannot be extinguished since that would mean the annihilation of himself. But as his conscience he no longer governs his now ungovernable ego, and in this contradiction he encounters the vertiginous depths of the hell he has become. He is not subject merely to an externally imposed punishment like Prometheus. He is enslaved by himself. As Abdiel points out

> This is servitude,
> To serve th' unwise, or him who hath rebelld
> Against his worthier, as thine now serve thee,
> Thy self not free, but to thy self enthrall'd
>
> (VI 178–81)

The intransitiveness of the action, by which selfhood is constituted in a conscience which is identical with the despair which it evokes, could hardly be given more compact expression.

18. By way of contrast, but along similar lines, we can trace in Adam the process of how conscience and therefore identity begin in a perception of duty, of certitude concerning it, and acceptance of that certitude as truth about good, and are later reconstituted (in part) after the fall. Adam's first speech has been condemned as a somewhat glib argument for the existence of God from causality: 'to speak I tri'd, and forthwith spake', he tells Raphael,

> My Tongue obey'd and readily could name
> What e're I saw. Thou Sun, said I, faire Light,
> And thou enlighten'd Earth, so fresh and gay,
> Ye Hills and Dales, ye Rivers, Woods, and Plaines,
> And ye that live and move, fair Creatures, tell,
> Tell, if ye saw, how came I thus, how here?
> Not of my self; by some great Maker then,
> In goodness and in power præeminent
>
> (VIII 271–79)

In a possible reference to this speech David Hume (1777) writes:

Suppose a person, though endowed with the strongest faculties of reason and reflection, to be brought on a sudden into this world; he would, indeed, immediately observe a continual succession of objects, and one event following another; but he would not be able to discover anything farther. He would not, at first, by any reasoning, be able to reach the idea of cause and effect; since the particular powers, by which all natural operations are performed, never appears to the senses; nor is it reasonable to conclude, merely because one event, in one instance, precedes another, that therefore the one is the cause, the other the effect . . . [In] a word, such a person, without more experience, could never employ his conjecture or reasoning concerning any matter of fact, or be assured of anything beyond what was immediately available to his memory and senses. (60)

What this objection takes no account of, however, is the skill — in Polanyi's sense of the word — implied in Adam's spontaneous use of language, and without which his faculties of reason and reflection could not operate. In any case, the source of these lines is not St Thomas's five ways but St Paul's assertion (Romans I: 19–20) that 'that which may be known of God is manifest in [men] . . . For the invisible things of him since the creation of the world are clearly seen, being perceived through the things that are made, even his everlasting power and divinity.' Thus Adam's 'then' is Adam's, not a rationalist's nor an empiricist's. It registers a personal intuition of finitude, not a logical movement of intelligence, and is no more open analysis than is the 'connoisseurship' or grace of mind by which, according to Polanyi, 'the scientist appreciates a mathematical theory in the abstract . . . and equally the appositeness of such a theory to the appraisal of observed specimens' (60). But a mathematical theory can none the less be judged for its skill by other scientific connoisseurs and Adam's 'then' can be similarly judged by us as an example of ethical connoisseurship — revealing an 'instinct' for worship comparable with the Pope's conception of an instinct for freedom. In the opening moments of his life, Adam constitutes himself as one-who-praises-God (because he ought to do so), and thereby takes the first step towards the felicity he enjoys in the marriage bower with Eve, and which is so different from his later experiences of pleasure and despair because it unites conscience with bodily joy.

19. After the fall, he finds, like Satan, that he cannot break out of his newly corrupted selfhood, but unlike Satan he still adheres to the truth about good which Satan's choice of Evil as Good prohibits. This helps him to achieve a partial reintegration of the self. His problem is complicated, however, by his having to accept responsibility for the sins of others as well as for his own sin, in a way that seems to violate the intransitiveness of the action.

> Ah, why should all mankind [he asks]
> For one mans fault thus guiltless be condemnd,
> If guiltless? But from me what can proceed,
> But all corrupt, both Mind and Will deprav'd,
> Not to do onely, but to will the same
> With me? . . .
>   all my evasions vain,
> And reasonings, though through Mazes, lead me still
> But to my own conviction: first and last
> On mee, mee onely, as the sourse and spring
> Of all corruption, all the blame lights due
>   (X 822–7, 829–33)

In this classic statement of the difficulties involved in the doctrine of original sin as understood by the Western Church, Adam makes two points. First, he states that the depravity he transmits to his descendants will reach beyond the level of what happens, to the level of the person, to 'both mind and will'. His descendants will adhere *as persons* to the corruption of their inherited instincts, feelings and appetites, and so Adam's sin will be truly theirs. Yet in the whole range of its effects it will remain his sin none the less; their responsibility will not diminish his. The speech thus registers Adam's conscientious application of perceived truth about good (and evil) to his own case. His perception of values is such that he not only correctly perceives what he is (Satan does as much) but he also judges himself. This represents a significant move towards reintegration (and is precisely the move Satan refuses to make).

20. All morally reconstructive acts after the fall are necessarily works of Grace, that is, they are made possible by God's free act. But Grace in Milton's work leaves considerable scope for authentically individual choosing, most notably in *Samson Agonistes*. From the first Samson himself insists on his own responsibility for what has befallen him. 'Whom have I to complain of but my self?' (46),

he asks. Later he resists his father's questioning of providence by insisting that he has brought all his misfortunes on himself — 'Sole Author I, sole cause' (376). It is one thing, however, to see oneself as a sinner, and another to be the author of one's own salvation; yet this possibility is sanctioned by the Chorus in a way that is quite remarkable in a Christian poem.

> But patience is more oft the exercise
> Of Saints, the trial of thir fortitude,
> Making them each his own Deliverer,
> And Victor over all
> That tyrannie or fortune can inflict
>
> (1287–91)

This view of both public heroism and private faith is quickly underwritten by events. The Philistine Officer informs Samson that refusal to entertain the Philistine Lords may be very dangerous for him. 'Regard thy self', he says, 'this will offend them highly.' 'My self?' Samson replies; 'my conscience and internal peace' (1333–4). Here 'self', in the sense the word has for the Officer, is replaced by 'conscience', which is promptly identified with Samson's 'internal peace', with his 'self' at a level of felicity altogether higher than the Officer is capable of understanding. We then see Samson deciding to interpret God's Grace as it applies to his special circumstances. The decision to co-operate with his oppressors is deliberate, free and conscientious. In other words, the tension arising out of 'external pressures' and 'the power of injunction or compulsion' is relieved by the only power that can relieve it, Samson's own 'conviction of the truthfulness of the good' perceived in an interpersonal, God-Samson framework. Conscience, precisely in its own intransitiveness, is the necessary condition of his fulfilment of himself in the action, that is, of his movement from despair to felicity. Grace never takes effect *except* in one who is his own deliverer.

21. The formulation of conscience, then, completes individuation and constitutes felicity. It is the culmination of self-making. As such, however, it raises the problem of the possibly competing or even contradictory claims of one's own and other consciences, of the individual and society. Both Milton and the Pope unambiguously endorse the primacy of the former. In acting, the Pope maintains, I create in myself a fundamental or *'personalistic'* (320) value which is prior to and conditions all other ethical values.

Consequently, the social or communal nature of any action 'is rooted in the nature of the person and not vice versa' (319). But the moral life is also dramatic. If the 'cognitive process . . . interiorizes the extra-personal reality' (168), the Pope maintains, obligation introduces me into a drama of which I am the subject, which is enacted in reality, and outside of which I cannot fulfil myself as a person. He distinguishes between our experience of duty with respect to norms which 'may appear to be something derived from without' (163) and the *person's duties* with regard to other people'. If I were involved only with the former my moral life would have the character of a soliliquy. But the latter 'occur in virtue of an interpersonal *nexus* of participation' — of obeying, loving and worshipping others. Thus if social relations ought to be conditioned by the personalistic value at the centre of human acts, the acting person in whom this value is located cannot achieve fulfilment except in the society of others; and just as acting takes precedence over yet requires what happens, so conscientious self-individuation has priority over yet requires socialisation.

22. One consequence of this tension relates to equality. The personalistic value predictates a moral equality between persons, but the principle of conscientious individuation suggests a potential for significant inequalities between them. The tension which results from this infuses the whole of Milton's work. As we have seen, he insists on the principle of equality only so far as it leaves unaffected his predilection for highly specialised claims, sometimes unique to an individual, such as Samson, sometimes vested in a privileged group, such as male heads of bourgeois households. This tension becomes acute in *Paradise Lost* because the uncertainty about freedom and equality to which it gives rise enables Satan to wage war against the Father in the name of both, and yet set himself in glory above his peers. In a sense he is justified in doing so since specific acts do distinguish him from his followers, but he also argues that the rebels know themselves to be

> Natives and Sons of Heav'n possest before
> By none, and if not equal all, yet free,
> Equally free
>
> (V 790–2)

on which ground he claims to be justified in rebelling against the exaltation of the Son. Yet all Abdiel can say in reply to this argument is to confirm the analysis, but to claim for God and for the

55

Son the pre-eminence which Satan claims for himself. What he does not do is show the true relation of equality to order, and so of one individuality to others. This, however, is elucidated in the unfolding action of the poem, as the divine will is made manifest in the history of angels and men.

23. At this point we can usefully turn to the most notorious instance of inequality of Milton's work, that between Adam and Eve, which comes dangerously close to compromising Eve's personal dignity and autonomy. Admittedly in some important ways she is represented as Adam's equal and even his superior. At prayer, for example, they are 'unanimous', and after the fall she is the first to develop the idea of intercessory prayer, thus anticipating the role which the Son already has in prospect for himself. Nevertheless she is repeatedly represented as Adam's inferior by nature and so properly subordinate to him. She herself declares that her love for him is based on this superiority. The obligations arising out of their mutual relationship, therefore, are apparently a requirement of natural hierarchy, and not, as certain of Milton's other writings might lead us to expect, of a personalistic value which is prior to any norms deriving from society.

The parallels between Eve's relation to Adam and the Son's to the Father help to resolve this contradiction, however, at least in principle; for the Son not only becomes himself in his adherence to the values of Justice, Love and Mercy which he discerns in the Father; he also, in an important sense, 'becomes' the Father as well. In abandoning his claim to equality with the Father, and in taking on himself the condition of a slave, he exemplifies the Father's true nature, and takes it into himself. As the Father puts it:

> thy Humiliation shall exalt
> With thee thy Manhood also to this Throne,
> Here shalt thou sit incarnate, here shalt Reign
> Both God and Man, Son of both God and Man
>
> (III 313–16)

To Milton, the Son, as Son, is not-divine; yet the not-divine becomes divine as fully as he becomes man, that is, he becomes not just 'god-like' but truly 'God', in the very act of obedience by which he becomes 'Man' and confirms his status as not-divine. In personally manifesting his own individual and subordinate essence

56

he abolishes that subordination.

The relations of Adam and Eve are similarly structured. In entering free and reciprocal relations of love and duty each 'becomes' the other's 'other self'. Eve's subordination to Adam is thus the basis of her 'exaltation' to equality with him, something he is bound ultimately to acknowledge. But this is incidental to the more important act of joint subordination with which, in the unanimity of prayer, they worship God, and so become in a sense 'divine' also. Creaturely perception of the divine, of course, unlike filial perception, is limited, and must remain so, even for the angels, until the totality of the Father's will is at last revealed in the culmination of the Son's messianic reign by the only Person capable of assimilating, expressing and so mediating it, the Son himself. Then, however, the whole of creation will be able to identify fully with the divine will made manifest in the Son; all power, all subordination, all distinction will consequently be obliterated:

> Then thou thy regal Scepter shalt lay by,
> For regal Scepter then no more shall need,
> God shall be All in All
>
> (III 339–41)

At the same time, an infinite and absolute 'unanimity' will confirm rather than obliterate the distinctiveness of every personal being in the universe, and the order made visible to, and appropriated by, each individual 'conscience'. Consequently, just as Samson frees himself when he becomes tangled in the fold of dire necessity — necessity being the will of God — so the end of the providential plan is not nirvana, or stasis, or absorption into God, but felicity — the plenitude of individual being:

> New Heav'ns, new Earth, Ages of endless date
> Founded in righteousness and peace and love
> To bring forth fruits Joy and eternal Bliss
>
> (XII 549–51)

Righteousness and joy are the prerogatives of personal beings.

24. For Milton, however, a further difficulty remains — the problem of what precisely is meant by equality with God. Throughout both *Paradise Lost* and *Paradise Regain'd* the words 'Divine', 'Godlike', 'Gods', 'Son of God' and even 'God' are freely applied to the Son, to the angels, to Adam, to human beings

57

in general, to the fallen angels and to Satan. Thus the task Satan sets himself in *Paradise Regain'd* of discovering 'In what degree or meaning' Jesus is 'call'd / The Son of God' (IV 516–17), since 'Sons of God both Angels are and Men' (IV 197), is finally a linguistic one: he has to distinguish how literally words and titles are used, in what sense Jesus is 'Son'. Satan's sin in *Paradise Lost* was his 'Affecting all equality with God' (V 763), yet both the Son, as 'True Image of the Father' and Adam himself, as God's image, 'Expressing well the spirit within [him] free', were in some sense godlike, and there was also the possibility, evident to the newly-created Adam, of God's raising a 'creature to what highth' he will 'Of Union or Communion, deifi'd'. What these words mean is fundamental to all three of Milton's later poems, and is inextricably connected with the notion of freedom.

As we have already noted, Satan insists that the angels were all created 'free / Equally free'. He is right. Moreover, in this freedom (precisely understood) the possibility of equality with God is to be found. In tracing the sense in which Milton could have used the word I rely for the present on Kenny's *Will, Freedom and Power* (1975), though I shall consider other works in this field in later chapters. According to Kenny, the weakest of the scholastic theories of free will limits freedom to the absence of external compulsion by which the agent is free to act according to the promptings of his or her spontaneous nature. It is given elegant expression in the thought of Hume:

all mankind have ever agreed [Hume writes] in the doctrine of liberty as well as that of necessity, and that the whole dispute . . . has been . . . merely verbal. For what is meant by liberty, when applied to voluntary actions? We cannot surely mean that actions have so little connexion with motives, inclinations, and circumstances, that one does not follow with a certain degree of uniformity from the other, and that one affords no inference by which we can conclude the existence of other . . . By liberty, then, we can only mean *a power of acting or not acting, according to the determinations of the will* . . . Now this hypothetical liberty is universally allowed to belong to everyone who is not a prisoner and in chains. (95)

A grave limitation in this conception of freedom, however, at least for the reader of *Paradise Lost*, is its evaluation of impulsive

or uncharacteristic behaviour. We can only properly blame
someone, Hume argues, for behaviour which is characteristic or
typical:

> Actions, are, by their very nature, temporary and perishing;
> and when they proceed not from some *cause* in the character
> and disposition of the person who performed them, they can
> neither rebound to his honour, if good; or infamy, if evil . . .
> . . . Men are less blamed for such actions as they perform
> hastily and unpremeditatedly than for such as proceed from
> deliberation. (98)

From this point of view, Adam and Eve can hardly be said have
fallen, because he apparently acted 'hastily and unpremedi-
tatedly', and she, not from rational deliberation, and both
behaved in ways that were uncharacteristic.

25. A second difficulty with the liberty of spontaneity is that it
implies a principle of radical inequality between persons. In exercising it, God would be infinitely the superior of any other being,
and to aspire to equality with him in terms of spontaneity would
be impious and vain. There is no suggestion in *Paradise Lost* that
even Satan does so. However, to the extent that a subordinate
being knows God in the fulness of his spontaneity, and in unconditional acceptance and submission identifies with the life thus
revealed — worships it, in other words — the divine life becomes
integral with the creature's being. This is clearly implied in the
Son's appropriation of the Father's creative power in Books VI
and VII of *Paradise Lost*. Satan's sin, on the other hand, apparently
consists in his resenting the Son's potent intimacy with the
Father's spontaneity and a presumptuous desire to exercise his
own spontaneity independently of the Father's will and in opposition to the exaltation of the Son. Satan cannot accept the indirect
and contingent nature of equality with God in the sphere of spontaneity, that a creature's aspirations to divinity are in this respect
dependent on the Father's gratuitous self-revelation.

A different situation arises, however, with the stronger version
of free will advanced by Scotus and further developed by the Jesuit
theologians, Francesco Suarez and Luis de Molina, the so-called
freedom of indifference, which Hume denies. This envisages a
capacity to act or not when all the conditions required for acting
are present. This is free will as Milton and the Pope understand
it. Unlike the freedom of spontaneity, it is apparently strictly

unquantifiable. Consequently all those who possess it are in that sense equal. On these grounds, I would endorse Kenny's view that we could never 'allot . . . volitional quotients as we allot . . . IQs' (4). The freedom of indifference (provided it is kept distinct from the obviously quantifiable freedom of spontaneity) is thus an appropriate basis for that creaturely equality with God which is so important in *Paradise Lost*.

The distinction between the two freedoms is thus fundamental to *Paradise Lost* and the viability of the freedom of indifference is of no less importance to the humanistic tradition which Milton, Newman and Pope have been represented in this chapter as upholding. The rest of this book attempts a defence of that tradition against the great tide of empiricist and critical philosophy which has dominated Western intellectual discourse since Hume and Kant. In the course of it I shall examine the claims to coherence of Scholastic theories of the will as well as those of a number of modern philosophers. This in its turn will lead to a consideration of literary texts other than Milton's — in particular Henry James's *The Portrait of a Lady* — and problems not strictly philosophical, notably that of evolution. I shall claim that a full, non-reductive theory of freedom is compatible with the latter, and that freedom so understood is entirely consistent with Milton's narratives, Newman's speculations and the Pope's descriptive analysis. When that is done, a re-reading of this chapter will be, I hope, an illuminating experience.

3

Reasons in Eden

1. Knowing a person's future 2. Willing with a body 3. God and evil 4. Descriptivism, prescriptivism and incontinence 5. Aristotle and voluntary actions 6. St Thomas and voluntary actions 7. Voluntary, intentional and free actions 8. Acting at time t 9. Eve acting 10. Difficulties in Milton's account of Eve's fall 11. Davidson on weakness of the will 12. Occasions of sin 13. Adam acting 14. Surdity or sin 15. Unnarratable actions

1. Before looking in more detail at objections to the essentially Thomist account of the will which I attributed in the last chapter to Milton, Newman and the Pope, and which it is the ultimate intention of this essay to uphold, I shall outline some of the issues with which the free will problem tends to be associated, since discussion of them will recur in this and following chapters.

I shall begin with a problem crucial to *Paradise Lost* — the relationship between God and the free actions of created beings. This is an important question even for atheists because it requires us to define our notions of 'person' and 'knowledge'. Kenny (1979), for example, quotes Milton's assertion, 'Future events which God has foreseen, will happen certainly, but not of necessity', and points out that 'Milton does not explain how this certain knowledge is possible in the absence of necessity' (81). In *The Art of Logic*, however, Milton asserts that 'God . . . knows all things equally through their causes' (328), which implies that contingent causes (persons acting freely) are in principle 'knowable'. Kenny questions this. 'But can God really know', he asks, '. . . which world he is creating' (69) if that world is to contain freely acting creatures? Kenny thinks not — unless, somehow, freedom in the full sense can be shown to be compatible with comprehensive physical determinism in consequence of which all our bodily movements could be predicted. Two questions must therefore be clarified in any discussion of divine prescience — whether persons are causes in a sense that the word does not have when we speak of physical causality, and whether certainty about the future is exclusively dependent on the operation of known laws of matter. Both these questions are important to the literary critic, for if persons are causes in Milton's sense, then different kinds of description and explanation will be required in a narrative about their choices than would be appropriate in a narrative which assumes that they are not.

2. Another set of questions associated with the free will problem and affecting our understanding of key words such as 'person', 'identity' and 'acting' arises from the fact of our having bodies. Are we identical with our bodies? Can we sensibly think of a disembodied person? If God is such a person, what is his relation to the physical world? 'Is it possible', Kenny asks, 'to conceive of a being which has no body but which has a mind whose sphere of operation is the whole universe?' (123). We attribute 'intuition, will and choice', he points out, to people but not to animals because of their 'linguistic behaviour' (124).

What makes my thoughts *my* thoughts [he goes on] is such things as that they are expressed by my mouth and written by my hand. If there is a God, who has thoughts, what makes the thoughts *his* thoughts? If God has no body, then there is no divine bodily behaviour to serve as the basis of attribution to him of thoughts and knowledge.

He then takes up Arthur Danto's definition of the body as 'the locus of one's basic actions' (126), and argues that if 'God can act in the world directly . . . then . . . the world would be God's body'. A similar argument is advanced by J.L. Mackie (1982): 'All our knowledge of intension-fulfillment [he writes] is of *embodied* intentions being fulfilled *indirectly* by way of bodily changes and movements which are *causally* related to the intended result' (100). Hence, Mackie argues, it is unreasonable to think of unembodied intentions being fulfilled directly without movement. He therefore dismisses the traditional notion of God as pure spirit whose acts are immediate and none of whose powers is latent. Milton rejects the first of these conclusions — the acts of his God *are* immediate, as Raphael declares in *Paradise Lost*

(VII 176) — but he agrees with Mackie on the topic of intention-fulfilment in that his God is material and the mover of matter.

More is at stake here, however, than questions about God. There are also the problems of the relationships between bodily process and human action and between bodily continuity and human identity. Kenny is particularly interested in the first question, and specifically in reconciling physiological determinism and genuine freedom. The second question is linked with the problem of whether or not persons are free, and whether, indeed, there is such an entity as the self, conceptually distinct from the body. This raises questions about the nature of consciousness.

3. A third area of difficulty associated with free will relates to the responsibilty of God and of human beings for what happens in the world. The problem of evil has obvious importance in the debate about God's existence. If God is omnipotent, omniscient and benevolent, how are we to account for evil in his world, or alternatively for God in a world containing much evil? This question borders on the Miltonic territory of justifying the ways of God to man since he and a number of theologians, as well as some modern philosophers, make use of what is known as the free will defence, the coherence of which other philosophers, including Kenny, question. Kenny believes that the only way God (or anyone else) could have knowledge of the future would be through the operation of known physical laws. But he also argues that even if events at the physiological level (including the physical operations of the brain) were predictable, a person might still be capable of the full freedom of indifference at the level of experience. We will consider this compatibilist position later. For the present we need only consider his contention that if compatabilism is true, then 'the traditional doctrines of omniscience and omnipotence cannot be stated in a way which makes them compatible with . . . divine lack of responsibility for sin, and human freedom of the will' (10–11). For if God is to have infallible knowledge of future actions, Kenny argues, then determinism must be true.

> If God is to escape responsibility for human wickedness, then determinism must be false. Hence in the notion of a God who forsees all sin but is the author of none, there lurks a contradiction. (121)

The issue of God's responsibility for evil, thus raised by Kenny, is given classical expression by Hume.

It may be said [he writes] . . . that, if voluntary actions are subjected to the same laws of necessity with the operations of matter, there is a continued chain of necessary causes, pre-ordained and pre-determined, reaching from the original cause of all to every single volition of every human creature. No contingency anywhere in the universe; no indifference; no liberty . . . The ultimate Author of our volitions is the Creator of the world, who first bestowed motion on this immense machine . . . Human actions, therefore, either can have no moral turpitude at all, as proceeding from so good a cause; or if they have any turpitude, they must involve our Creator in the same guilt. (99–100)

Kenny's arguments differ from Hume's in that Hume accepts the free will defence in principle, whereas for Kenny mere foreknowledge of future contingent actions would involve God in his creatures' wickedness. Mackie goes even further. He suggests that 'the free will defence cannot detach evil from God unless it assumes that the freedom conferred on man is such that God *cannot* (not merely does not) control his choosing' (162).

4. The problem of evil, however, presents difficulties to opponents as well as to defenders of God's existence. If there is a God there is likely to be a divine law. If there is no God, we have to work out our rules of conduct for ourselves: whether we should approach the problem as rationalists or empiricists; whether human beings 'have' natural rights in ways analogous to their 'having' sexual propensities and language-learning capacities; whether 'goodness' is a value distinct from 'happiness'; whether there are rules of conduct which apply to all cases of a given type ('It is always wrong to make a promise to a friend if one has no intention of keeping it') or whether every problem should be decided in terms of the special circumstances attending it; whether moral injunctions can be stated or applied independently of a person's capacity to obey them; and so forth. Because almost any statement about morals implies a view on one or more of these problems, the language of morals seems different in important respects from ordinary language and presents great difficulties for the unwary. I cannot hope to avoid all of them. Nevertheless I shall try to define two problems of particular relevance to the free will debate, that of prescriptivism *versus* descriptivism, and that of *akrasia*, or incontinence, or backsliding.

If, like Hume, I believe only in the freedom of spontaneity, I will probably be a descriptivist, that is, I will hold that the language of morals can do no more than describe the reasons people have for taking certain decisions or sustaining certain habitual behaviours. But in that case I will have no grounds of prescribing for others the values I myself prefer — say, faith, hope and charity, or liberty, equality and fraternity — over those I hate and fear — such as racial purity, strength through joy, and competitive entrepreneurialism. But if I prescribe rules of conduct for humanity at large I run into another difficulty. As a prescriptivist, I am likely to believe that people's moral beliefs will act as reasons for some of their actions. But what if they act against those beliefs? Can they really have held them in the first place? On the other hand, if a real belief that I ought to do something guarantees that I shall do it, can I claim more for myself than the freedom of spontaneity? In other words, is genuine backsliding possible, and if it is not, what basis have I for being a prescriptivist?

5. We will return to all these problems later. We can now begin to consider the origins of the free will tradition in which Milton operated. My account is based heavily on D.J. O'Connor's *Aquinas and Natural Law* (1967) and Kenny's reading of Aristotle and St Thomas in *Will, Freedom and Power*.

Aristotle holds an action to be voluntary, Kenny (1975) notes, 'if there is no compulsion, if there is the appropriate degree of knowledge, and if the originating cause of the situation . . . is in the agent' (15). The cue causes a snooker ball to move, and my right arm moves the cue; but something in me is the originating cause of the sequence, and so the action is voluntary. But such causes can be found in children and even (it seems) in animals and Aristotle accordingly 'includes animals and children among voluntary agents'. The difference between them and adult human beings is that while animals seem to do one thing for the sake of another (a dog apparently scratches at the door in order to go for a walk), clearly determined long-term goals cannot be confidently attributed to them as they can to people. I play a particular shot at the snooker table because, by breaking up the reds as I pot the black, I will set myself up for a good break and bring myself one step nearer to television glory. I thus put into my voluntary action means-end reasoning and a goal deriving from my personal value-system, my moral character: hence Aristotle's assertion, quoted by Kenny, that 'without understanding and reasoning on the one hand, and moral character on the other, there is no such thing as choice' (16).

6. St Thomas advances these conceptions of willing by clarifying the notion of intention and by examining more closely the implications of our reliance on practical as against speculative reasoning in our actions. He holds that the voluntariness of animals is limited by their ability to form intentions and so to act with what he calls perfect knowledge. Kenny quotes him as follows:

> . . . Perfect knowledge of an end involves not merely the apprehension of the object which is the end, but an awareness of it precisely qua end, and of the relationship to it of the means which are directed to it . . . Such a knowledge is within the competence only of a rational nature. Imperfect knowledge of the end is mere apprehension of the end without any awareness of its nature as an end or of the relationship of the activity to the end. This type of knowledge is found in dumb animals (19).

We know that a dog has unsatisfied needs when it scratches a door, but we do not know whether it is aware of them as such, still less whether it is capable of entertaining the prospect of going for a walk. The sensations of going for a walk (whatever they may be for a dog) may only occur on the walk itself. A dog-owner, on the other hand, can pick up her walking stick in order to excite in her dog the bundle of desires which lead to door-scratching.

The Thomist account of action, then, emphasises intention and therefore practical reasoning. O'Connor identifies the four things we can do with practical reasoning as follows:

> (1) apprehend a given end as a good to be pursued; (2) consider what can be done to attain that end; (3) decide what is to be done for this purpose; (4) direct ourselves to a certain course of action in the light of (1)–(3)
>
> (2) and (3) [he suggests] are tasks which even Hume agrees to assign to reason in moral questions. (34–5)

The important questions, therefore, relate to (1) and (4).
I shall consider (4) first. O'Connor writes:

> When the speculative reason considers a demonstrative argument, our assent to the conclusion of the argument is forced by understanding the necessary logical connections

involved in the relations between premisses and conclusion. (35)

The conclusions of practical reasoning, however, are not equally decisive. They could only be so, O'Connor points out,

> if it were *logically inconsistent* not to perform a right action, once we have adequately considered reasons for doing it. And . . . this . . . is certainly not the view of Aquinas. Indeed he says explicitly that 'the practical intellect is not about necessary things but about things which may be otherwise than they are, and which may result from man's activity'. (36)

Or as Kenny (1975) puts it,

> The only way to avoid defeasibility in practical reasoning would be to insist that the premiss setting out the goal should not only be correct but also complete; that *all* the wants to be satisfied by one's action should be fully specified. (93)

It follows from this, according to St Thomas and to Kenny, that practical reason cannot determine action and that the will is accordingly free.

But what of the first of the uses for practical reason identified by O'Connor — apprehending 'a given end as a good to be pursued'?

> When St Thomas says that it is in virtue of reason that we appreciate that something is good [O'Connor writes], he has in mind his metaphysical doctrine that good is an end and that the end of a given thing is what is suited to its nature . . . Goodness is not a simple and unique quality, but the perfection of a nature. Particular goods are, therefore, as varied as the different natures which they perfect. It is thus not difficult to see why for St Thomas the apprehension of good is the work of reason. Different natures work in different ways, and it is the part of reason to understand this working and so to understand the good which is the appropriate end of each. But the doctrine is plausible only on the assumption . . . that there really are essences or natures of things, and that it is part of the work or reason to understand them.

St Thomas's is thus a universe in which the essences of things disclose their ends or are disclosed by them. Values are systematised in nature and so are accessible to reason. To act reasonably, therefore, is to act well and to sin is knowingly to act against reason. Sin is possible because we may not like the ends towards which we and other things in the world are directed. Thus Davidson (1980) quotes St Thomas to the effect that a sinner is one who

> has knowledge of the universal [but] is hindered, because of a passion, from reasoning in the light of that universal . . . [and so] reasons in the light of another universal proposition suggested by the inclination of passion, and draws his conclusions accordingly. (33)

7. We can now distinguish important (possible) differences between voluntary, intentional and free actions. An action is voluntary if it is directed to an end of the agent's, as when a dog scratches to get out. An action is intentional when the agent is capable of identifying the ends towards which its acts are directed (the wants they will meet) and to distinguish between those ends and the means by which they are to be achieved. There are philosophers who hold that it is enough for an action to be intended in this sense for it to be properly described as a free action, provided only that the agent is not also subject to external coercive force. However some determinists regard an action as intended without believing in freedom at all. (William Godwin, whose work I will be considering later, is one such.) On the one hand it is possible to distinguish between intentional actions which exemplify only the freedom of spontaneity (when I pick up a knife to open an egg, for example) and intentional acts which represent a completely free choice between competing value systems and the range of performable actions relating to them. To say that an action is intentional, therefore, is not necessarily to say that it is free. Nor does it follow that all free actions are intentional: as we shall see, Kenny holds that the freedom of indifference can be attributed to the actions of animals.

For Milton, however, and for the Pope, the *actus humanus* is voluntary, intentional and free — it is end-directed; it is the outcome of an exercise of practical reasoning; and, in the words of the Pope, it is not 'determined in advance by the object in the intentional order' (132). It 'is not the objects and values that have a grip' (135) on the person, he asserts; on the contrary, self-government is achieved 'in . . . relation to them'. The acting person is thus always capable of acting or of refraining from action in the light of the reasons currently under consideration. If it can be shown, therefore, that the actions of Adam and Eve in *Paradise Lost* are wanting in any one of these three characteristics — voluntariness, intentionality or two-way choosing — then the structure of freedom, and with it the possibility of backsliding or sin, to which Milton is committed will apparently be invalidated, and Milton's task of vindicating the ways of God to man will have been undertaken in vain.

8. Consideration of two-way choosing will only be possible later. For the present I shall confine myself to the problem of voluntariness and intentionality in *Paradise Lost*. This will require identifying particular choices by locating them in time. As Kenny (1975) points out, the word *actus* in Scholastic usage can refer to 'an *inclinatio*, a tendency or disposition rather than an episode' (24), but Milton insists that even God's acts must have taken place at some clockable time *t*, and the Pope shows a similar bias, at least in relation to human acts. He refers to the action as 'the specific moment whereby the person is revealed' (11), to 'the moment of efficacy' (66), to the 'moment of creativeness which closely accompanies the moment of efficacy' (70) and to 'the proper moment of freedom . . . freedom and efficacy together' (99) determining whether the person as a person becomes morally good or bad. When 'the will is presented with more than one object', the Pope suggests, 'a separate process . . . precedes and conditions the decision and is sometimes defined as the deliberation of motives' (130). There is thus 'a momentary suspension of the process of willing'. This is followed, or fused with, 'the moment of truth' (138) in which the person's independence of the object of willing is made manifest, and which under another aspect can be seen as the 'somatic moment' (206), the moment of self-possession and self-governance made manifest on one's control of one's body.

9. From this it would seem that voluntariness and intentionality form a temporally structured sequence, and that Milton's project in *Paradise Lost* depends on his successfully presenting two such sequences in the sin of Eve and the sin of Adam.

As we have already noted, his theory of action locates the moment of efficacy either in the will or in the judgement. Eve sins in her judgement because as a woman she is intellectually more susceptible than Adam. This is why Satan's speech beginning 'O Sacred, Wise and Wisdom-giving Plant' (IX 679), finds 'too easie entrance' (IX 734) into her heart. By its end, she has entered what the Pope calls 'a momentary suspension of the process of willing' or the state 'sometimes defined as deliberation of motives'. What happens in this state is relatively uncontrolled, which explains why the fruit seems so appetizing to her at this point. However, from the first line of her response to Satan's speech, 'Great are thy Vertues, doubtless, best of Fruits' (IX 745), it is clear that she has not yet succumbed to temptation, in so far, at least, as she holds back from the somatic moment. Nevertheless, in the first five lines of her speech only the word 'doubtless' suggests a willingness to consider the claims of obedience against those of experimentation, and when she refers to God's having forbidden the eating of the fruit, she does so in a subordinate clause, thus giving syntactic precedence to the 'praise' of the fruit implicit in God's having named the tree the Tree of Knowledge over the dangers inherent in his having prohibited the eating of its fruit. Even when she refers to this prohibition in a main clause — 'Forbids us then to taste' (IX 753) — the word 'then' indicates that the authority of the divine imperative now depends on its viability within an argument and the sequence of sentences, following the important 'but' in 'but his forbidding' suggests that she has made up her mind. A second 'But', however, — 'But if Death' (IX 760) — counteracts the first, though again a reference to the divine warning in a conditional clause seems quasi-blasphemous. Thereafter she argues exclusively in favour of eating the fruit. Perhaps the crucial lines are

What fear I then, rather what know to feare
Under this ignorance of good and Evil,
Of God or Death, of Law or Penaltie?

(IX 773–5)

which explicitly make mere ignorance a ground for acting. In any case she proceeds to the conclusion of her argument, from which arises the 'somatic moment' first envisaged, then effected:

what hinders then
To reach, and feed at once both Bodie and Mind?

(IX 778–9)

Eve has thus apparently reasoned herself into sin.

10. The precise moment when she does so, however, and thus the act itself have still to be identified since the syntactic game just analysed hides the action it might have been expected to reveal. Yet the sequence of events seem to be clear enough. Until she meets the Serpent, Eve has kept to her plan of life without engaging in the deliberation required by a conflict of motives. She then experiences uncertainty about her priorities and finally acts in defiance of them. But when does she sin? When she first allows herself to be tempted? In her two speeches (IX 646–54 and 659–63), she shows a clear and adequate knowledge of divine law. By the end of the Serpent's final speech, however, that knowledge has ceased to operate decisively in her thinking. If this happens in consequence of a clear-headed decision on her part to let it happen, then she has sinned already — by wilfully failing to avoid an occasion of sin. But knowing what she so clearly knows and states between lines 647 and 663, *how could she possibly allow herself to do so?*

This question also presents itself even in Eve remains sinless until the end or near the end of her last speech, and I shall therefore postpone consideration of it until I have examined how she might innocently have entered temptation. The latter seems the preferable option since the poem's working assumption is that the somatic moment is the real moment of her fall. At this point we have to remember her alleged intellectual weakness. It seems she may have lost her grip involuntarily on her plan of life under the spell-binding influence of the Serpent. In such a case, her decision to listen to his arguments would be intelligible in terms of reasons, and so an intentional and voluntary act but not a sinful one; it would have been the consequence of an involuntary forgetfulness. But if that were still her state when she ate the fruit, her fall would not be a proper case of deliberate backsliding at all; there would be an absence of voluntariness in one vital respect; and since she does in fact sin we must assume that at some point she regains her grip on her plan of life before doing so. Her references to it in her last temptation speech, syntactically cautious though they may be, show this to be a possibility. We have therefore to explain how it comes about that an unfallen mind, fully cognizant of known truth about good, can first contemplate and then perpetrate an act inconsistent with that truth.

11. In *Essays on Actions and Events* (1980), Davidson attempts to

resolve this difficulty. I turn to his account of backsliding, not because I think Milton would have agreed with it but because it is so impressively consistent with the syntactic tactics of Eve's temptation speech and because it clarifies why it is so difficult for Milton to represent the voluntariness and intentionality entailed in Eve's guilt.

Davidson's argument is based on a distinction between prima facie judgements and all-out unconditional judgements. An all-out unconditional judgement, he maintains, always accompanies an intentional action. Prima facie ('pf') judgements, on the other hand, that, for example, some 'actions are desirable in so far as they have a certain attribute' (98) are conditional; they say what would count as a reason, but they 'cannot be directly associated with actions for it is not reasonable to perform an action merely because it has a desirable characteristic'. To have a reason for acting, therefore, to make an all-out unconditional judgement, one must add something to such a 'pf' judgement. Davidson then suggests that all-things-considered judgements, based on one's rationally considered plan of life, are 'pf' judgements of this kind and so need something extra to become reasons for acting.

In Davidsonian terms, then, Eve's all-things-considered judgements when her temptations begins include all the reasons that her plan of life suggests for resisting temptation — obedience to God, love for Adam and fear of 'death'. Her speeches beginning 'Serpent, we might have spared our coming hither' (IX 647) and 'Of the fruit' (IX 659) are decisive on this point. Nevertheless she succumbs to the Serpent's persuasions. This is possible, Davidson suggests, because of the double-think inherent in our capacity to use the conditional mood, to adopt the syntactic strategy of Eve's temptation speech. Eve knows that *all things considered* she should respect the divine precept, but hearing these words, with these sensations of hunger, she prefers to linger, she prefers to deliberate, she prefers to eat. These preferences, however, do not diminish her certainty that, if all the reasons she believes to be good were in play, she would do otherwise.

12. If Davidson is right, then, the logical problem in Eve's fall is resolved. But that by no means ends the matter. I have argued that to be guilty of sin she must at some point be restored to a full sense of her plan of life in relation to the Tree of Knowledge, that is to a memory of that (very recent) state of mind in which those 'pf' judgements were linked to the something extra which made them all-out unconditional judgements in her speeeches at IX 647

and 659. Her willingness to over-ride these memories, to let her plan of life remain as a body of 'pf' judgements only, must therefore be understood as an intentional act in its own right, distinct from the act of eating the fruit. In Davidsonian terms she must have had all-out unconditional reasons for remaining in, or for returning to, a state of deliberation (Newman would have called it a state of inquiry) about the divine command. We know her all-out unconditional reasons for attending to the Serpent in the first place: his speech was

> impregn'd
> With Reason, to her seeming, and with Truth
>
> (IX 737–8)

Besides it was mid-day and she was hungry. We also know her all-out unconditional reasons for eating the fruit, because she states them in advance. But we do not know her all-out unconditional reasons for deciding to *inquire* into a course of action which she remembers holding in an all-out unconditional way, to be utterly wicked and stupid *because* of its incompatability with her plan of life, and we do not do so because she does not put them into words.

This does not mean that her lingering in the conditional mood cannot have been intentional. Neither Scholastic nor modern notions of intention require reasons to be formulated linguistically in advance of the action. As Kenny (1975) observes, 'a rational agent may . . . act for a reason without giving . . . any account of the reason' (20). Kenny only requires that actions should be capable of explanation later. It is entirely possible, therefore, for Eve *deliberately* to have entered a state of inquiry without stating her reasons for doing so, even to herself. In fact, logically, there was nothing else she could have done: it makes sense, after all, to ask why one allowed oneself to be tempted but none to wonder whether one should do so, since to ask the question is to answer it in the affirmative. Thus the psychologically convincing grammatical games which Eve plays in her temptation speech are informed by a necessarily murky inexplicitness about her intentions as she makes it. This means, however, that at least in Eve's case, Milton's desire to describe sin runs into a serious difficulty. Her fall can only be accounted for in terms of reasons if she explains after the event why she decided to contemplate a course of action inconsistent with her plan in life. But the outcome of her deliberations precludes her doing so, since she now has a new plan of life, a new set of priorities, chief of which is to persuade Adam to sin with her. After the fall she is not interested in telling the truth about herself, and in any case probably lacks the intellectual discrimination (by virtue both of her sex and her fallen state) to do so. It follows that even if Milton, as omniscient author, were able to explain her decision to become (or remain) an inquirer, his account could not be tested against the dramatised action. Eve necessarily remains enclosed in her own reasons. Milton cannot *show* that hers was not after all a genuine case of confusion in which she involuntarily lost her grip on her original plan of life, but was rather a clear case of deliberate collusion with an occasion of sin. He cannot even specify the moment of her acting. The full content of Eve's incontinence is thus in principle unavailable for narration and analysis. Consequently, God's ways in her case can only be justified on the hypothesis that she acted in one way and not another; the best Milton can do is to show that the ways of God to Eve might have been just.

13. What he needs, it seems, is a more clear-cut example, involving, in Davidson's words, 'an unclouded, unwavering judgement that [an] action is not for the best, all things considered, and yet where the action . . . has no hint of compulsion or of the compulsive' (29). Adam's fall appears to meet these requirements. As a man his weakness is not one of intellectual confusion but masculine wilfulness. Milton, therefore, allows no protracted deliberation in Adam's fall. His speech — 'O fairest of Creation, last and best' (IX 896) — is grammatically very different from Eve's. It begins with an exact description of her original splendour — 'Holy, divine, good, amiable . . . sweet' (X 899) — but she is then seen no less exactly as fallen:

How art thou lost, how on a sudden lost,
Defac't, deflourd, and now to Death devote?

(IX 900–1)

The brutal alliteration does not admit of any blurring of the consequences of Eve's act. Adam sees all the moral and theological causes, implications and consequences of what has taken place:

Rather how hast thou yeelded to transgress
The strict forbiddance, how to violate
The sacred Fruit forbidd'n! som cursed fraud

74

Of Enemie hath beguil'd thee, yet unknown

(IX 902-5)

This is unmistakably the language of an uncorrupted intellect, gazing in horror at the known truth about good and what follows, all things considered, from disobedience to it. Yet in the next line Adam sins:

And mee with thee hath ruind, for with thee
Certain my resolution is to Die

(IX 906-7)

The moment of Adam's fall can thus be precisely located — yet it too is invisible. It is in the word 'with', which unites Adam to Eve and confirms that the awaited transitive verb which puts him into the accusative case (me) will bind him to her in sin.

All this occurs without any explicit reasoning on Adam's part, without any rehearsal of his conditional 'pf' judgements. The remainder of his speech, however, beginning 'How can I live without thee, how foregoe' (IX 908) rationalises his decision in Kenny's and Davidson's sense, and this ought to be enough to explain it. Unfortunately Adam also rationalises in another sense, disingenously justifying rather than explaining his decision. This adds considerably to our difficulties: in a case like Adam's, it seems, we need to examine his reasons for rationalising before we can judge the adequacy of the reasons adduced for the original action, just as in Eve's case we needed to examine her reasons for inquiring. This need not involve a vicious regress: I can state my intentions in advance of an act of rationalisation as when I examine my conscience or engage in self-analysis; but the rationalisation of an act of apparent backsliding which is not preceded by such an explicit act of good faith is inherently suspect. Consequently the 'reasons' for Adam's fall are as mysterious as the 'reasons' for Eve's, in spite of its being so precisely timed and so eloquently justified. We do not even know for certain that his action is a voluntary one. He might have acted under compulsion and without any adequate reasons at all. Once again Milton's project seems to have foundered. He cannot justify God's ways to men, because he cannot show what the first man and woman did.

14. Davidson's account of intentional action thus highlights a serious difficulty in the way of any attempt to describe the kind of *sinful* backsliding required by Milton's argument. It seems that

some inexplicitness about one's intentions is a condition of backsliding: in the case of a protracted internal debate like Eve's, this inarticulateness is only partial, but none the less necessary to the crucial step of intentionally keeping one's 'pf', all-things-considered judgements in their conditional state so that temptation can continue; in a case like Adam's, whose backsliding does not involve a lingering divorce between all-things-considered judgements and all-out unconditional judgements, the inarticulateness in advance of the action must be complete. Such inarticulateness does not preclude later rationalisation, but rationalisation is only unproblematical when it is predicated of propositions, not when it is attributed to agents. In particular, backsliding agents (or those with irrational fears that they might be such) cannot be relied upon to give true reports of the practical reasoning which preceded their actions. Among human beings, therefore, backsliding is a logical possibility only. Individual instances of it are not susceptible to detailed and reliable report and analysis.

Davidson's own arguments strongly reinforce this conclusion. As we have seen, he holds that we carry around with us a body of wants and beliefs with which to direct out lives — our 'pf' all-things-considered judgements.

> Every judgement [he writes] is made in the . . . presence of and is conditioned by that totality. But that does not mean that every judgement is reasonable, or thought to be so by the agent. There is no paradox in supposing that a person sometimes holds all that he believes and values supports a certain course of action . . . The akrates does not . . . hold logically contradictory beliefs, nor is his failure necessarily a moral failure. What is wrong is that the incontinent man acts and judges irrationally. (40–1).

Thus Adam can judge that in principle he ought *not* to eat the fruit, yet what he actually believes and values as he looks at his fallen wife can in practice over-ride that judgement without his withdrawing his intellectual consent from it. He thus finds himself performing acts which he judges he should not perform. 'What is special in incontinence', Davidson concludes, 'is that the actor cannot understand himself: he recognizes, in his own intentional behaviour, something essentially surd' (42). *Surd* derives from a translation of the Greek *alogos* (thoughtless or wordless) into the Latin *surdus* (silent, mute). But wordlessness is incompatible with the notion of sin as Milton writes of it, and with the notion of rational explanation which the project of making a case about free will by means of a narrative evidently requires. Thus Adam's sin, no less than Eve's, apparently resolves itself into undescribable irrationality. Certainly if Davidson is right neither can sin in the scholastic sense at all: they can only, more or less intermittently, go mad.

15. It would seem, then, that cases of choosing in the scholastic sense cannot be described. This conclusion is perhaps unintentionally confirmed by P.T. Geach (1958), as quoted by Kenny (1975):

> If a physical description of some set-up is given, we cannot coherently say that an effect E *and* the opposite effect would equally fulfil the tendencies involved in that set-up. Now for contrast let us consider . . . action after deliberation. However carefully we describe a man's weighing of the pros and cons, we may end the story with 'and then he did it' or with 'and then he didn't do it' and *equally* make sense, equally have shown what led up to the man's action. In scholastic language, natural tendencies are one-way, *ad unum*: voluntary tendencies are two-way, *ad utrumque*. Of course if the man did it we shall say he did it because of the pros and in spite of the cons, and vice versa, if he didn't do it — but either story will be a coherent account. (110)

But will it? Won't *both* be equally incoherent in accounting for the action? Geach's argument in fact suggests that free choice can never be expressed in language.

Kant makes a related point in *Critique of Pure Reason* (1787), when he presents the arguments against free will in his exposition of the Third Antinomy:

> every beginning of action [he writes] presupposes in the acting cause a state of inaction; and a dynamically primal beginning of action presupposes a state, which has no connection — as regards causality — with the preceding state of the cause . . . Transcendental freedom is therefore opposed to the natural law of cause and effect, and such a conjunction of successive states in effective causes is destructive of the possibility of unity in experience. (271)

But narrative requires such unity. Davidson, of course, has no need to hypothesise a break in the causal chain because he rejects the ideal of transcendental freedom. But he secures its continuity in the case of backsliding by introducing a principle equally 'destructive of unity in experience' and so of narrative — that of pure irrationality.

It would seem, then, that any account of free will which requires that free actions should also be demonstrably voluntary and intentional, cannot even be called a fiction of thought, since not only full descriptions of voluntary *ad utrumque* tendencies but also rationalist accounts of backsliding appear to be incompatible with linguistic coherence and experiential unity. They are *alogos* and cannot be fictionalised at all. This conclusion obviously has serious implications for Milton, since if it cannot be countered, his great argument collapses. In the next chapter we shall examine a more up-to-date version of the *actus humanus* in the hope of restoring to it the vital characteristic of narratability on which so much apparently depends.

4

Reasons in Europe at the End of the Nineteenth Century

1. Language and intention 2. Reasons as causes 3. The defeasibility of practical reasoning 4. Kenny's compatibilism 5. James's technique 6. The relevance of The Portrait of a Lady *7. Isabel's self-understanding 8. What happens to Isabel at t 9. Two-way abilities and body language 10. Dennett's decider-switch 11. Dennett's robotic self-controller 12. Necessitarianism in the world of James 13. The final chapter 14. Isabel's fear 15. Kenny and Freud 16. Isabel's logic of goodness*

1. The more up-to-date version of the Aristotelian view of acting to which I referred at the end of the last chapter is that developed by Kenny in *Will, Freedom and Power*. I shall identify four elements in this account and test them, not against *Paradise Lost*, but against a text more conscious of the problems of the post-Kantian world, Henry James's *The Portrait of a Lady*. I shall then consider an alternative view of action proposed by Dennett in *Elbow Room. The Varieties of Free Will Worth Wanting* (1984).

As we have seen, St Thomas differs from Aristotle in predicating intentionality of human acting. According to St Thomas, personal action is distinguished from animal voluntariness by the agent's awareness of ends-means reasoning. Kenny (1975) agrees with this view but his version of action 'assigns a very special place to linguistic behaviour' (23): 'an animal, lacking a language, cannot *give a reason* [for its actions] . . . intentional action presupposes language in the same way as self-consciousness presupposes language' (20). For Kenny then, intentionality is intrinsically linguistic. If he is right, actions for which stateable reasons cannot be given before or after the event must be regarded as unintentional. It will not be possible to claim that Adam and Eve could have had reasons for acting as they did even though those reasons were inherently inexpressible. By definition intentions are expressible, and what cannot be expressed cannot be counted as contributing to the humanness of acting. On this general point Davidson and Kenny are agreed.

2. Kenny differs from Davidson, however, in denying that reasons can be causes as that word is understood in the Humean tradition. Hume identifies *experience* as '*the foundation of all our reasonings and conclusions*' (32) about causality: we conclude that B follows A only on the basis that we have found that it invariably does so; we know nothing of causes in themselves. But we do know that all change, including change in the mind, is caused and that causality is law-governed.

> The same motives [Hume writes] always produce the same actions . . . Ambition, avarice, self-love, vanity, friendship, generosity, public spirit: these passions, mixed in various degrees and distributed through society, have been from the beginning of the world, and still are, the source of all the actions and enterprises which have been observed among mankind. (94)

The task of the historian is to illustrate this consistency, 'to discover the constant and universal principles of human nature, by showing men in all varieties of circumstances and situations'. Inconsistency in human behaviour may seem evident to the unthinking observer.

> But philosophers, observing that, almost in every part of nature there is contained a vast variety of springs and principles, which are hid, by reason of their minuteness or remoteness, find, that it is at least possible the contrariety of events may not proceed from any contingency in the cause, but from the secret operation of contrary causes. (86–7)

Consequently, the

> most irregular and unexpected resolutions of men may frequently be accounted for by those who know every particular circumstance of their character and situation. A person of obliging disposition gives a peevish answer: But he has the toothache, or has not dined. A stupid fellow

discovers an uncommon alacrity in his carriage: But he has met with a sudden piece of good fortune. (88).

It is an illusion, therefore, to think that our own volitions are not necessitated: when we examine the behaviour of others we can readily explain their actions in terms of their motives and dispositions, yet in performing actions ourselves 'we are sensible of something like' (94n) the freedom of indifference. 'We feel that our actions are subject to our will . . . and . . . the will itself is subject to nothing.' But such indifference cannot be demonstrated, Hume argues, and the philosopher is justly inclined to prefer the judgement of the external observer.

A Humean narrative is accordingly plausible almost by definition. It acknowledges the difficulty of accounting for everything but assumes that everything can be accounted for, and so works towards a clarification of what was originally obscure through a series of discoveries about matters of fact and motivation. Its coherence depends on how well, in Davidson's sense, it rationalises the behaviour of its characters and identifies reasons as causes of action, directly in the case of those who scrutinise their own acting, indirectly in the case of those who scrutinise the actions of others and the passions revealed in their manners. Anyone seeking to sample a narrative controlled by the causes Hume mentions — 'Ambition, avarice, self-love, vanity, friendship, generosity, public spirit' — has only to read the work of Hume's great contemporary, Henry Fielding, whose perception of himself as a historian is very much in the Humean mould. What Fielding and Hume ignore, however, is that, as we saw when analysing the fall of Adam in *Paradise Lost*, rationalisation may itself by an intentional action for which reasons need to be given. The Humean narrator characteristically assumes that the discourse of explanation is transparent and unrelativised and so does not need to account for itself.

3. Kenny, however, denies that reasons are ever sufficient causes of voluntary action on the different ground that practical reasoning is inherently defeasible. For St Thomas the indeterminacy of the practical reasoner's situation derives from the openness of the logic of goodness which the mind discovers when it examines the essence of things as revealed by their ends and the ends of things (and so what is good for things of their type) as indicated by their essences. Kenny, however, discovers in the structure of practical reasoning itself, intellectual or not, an

inherent defeasibility, so that for him even spontaneous animal voluntariness exhibits the full freedom of indifference. In his view, a dog with an inchoate urge for exercise might scratch at the front door, or at the back door, or it might fetch its mistress's walking stick. There is no necessary connection between the particular want and the means available to satisfy it. It follows, Kenny believes, that if the defeasibility of practical reasoning is the basis of freedom, it applies to all voluntary actions and not just to those that are also intentional.

Kenny also rejects St Thomas's logic of goodness made manifest in terms of the ends for which things were created. The Thomist model envisages all such goods (except the beatific vision itself) as being open to alternative modes of evaluation. Of finite goods, O'Connor quotes him as saying,

in so far as they are lacking in some good, [they] can be regarded as non-goods; and from this point of view they can be set aside or approved by the will which can tend to one and the same thing from different points of view. (51)

There is, however, a truth about good which is discoverable by reason, and which systematically relates action to the last ends of the agent and the objects of willing, but it cannot compel the will, since other evaluations of the good — those of passion in particular — are always available. Kenny (1975) rejects this scheme because he finds it 'alien to contemporary philosophical fashion' (94). O'Connor agrees: 'we have . . . reason to doubt', he writes, 'that there really are essences or natures of things, and that it is part of the work of reason to understand them' (35). For Kenny it is 'the universality of the postulated major premisses . . . [that establishes] the theory's inadequacy' (94).

For the logic of goodness proposed by St Thomas, Kenny favours substituting a logic of satisfactoriness to 'ensure that in practical reasoning we never pass from a fiat which is satisfactory for a particular purpose to a fiat which is unsatisfactory for that purpose' (81). The question that needs to be answered, in this view, is not 'What rules must I follow to ensure that I act according to known truth about the final end of things?' but 'What rules must I follow to ensure that the acts I perform will have results that I deem satisfactory in the light of my present wants?' And just as St Thomas holds that goods can be seen from different points of view, thus leaving the will free, so Kenny holds that satisfactoriness is 'a relative notion: something is not satisfactory *simpliciter*, but satisfactory relative to a given set of wants' (93). But no statement of wants (which serve as premisses in this kind of argument) can ever by self-evidently and indefeasibly complete. Consequently not even the most rigorous application of a valid logic of satisfactoriness to a particular set of wants would compel me to act in the way that comparably rigorous theoretical reasoning would compel me to come to a theoretical conclusion. Kenny is careful to note that the logic of satisfactoriness

> needs to be supplemented with a logic of description of action . . . to take account of the differences of fiats and directives . . . [and] to represent adequately . . . the weighing up of the pros and cons of a particular course of action (95)

but since the *logical* input into such reasoning is inherently defeasible, the intentionality which is added to voluntariness by mankind's language-using powers does not diminish the freedom of indifference which attaches to all genuine voluntariness. Kenny is thus able to retain in a modern context the specific feature on which the Thomist theory of free will is based — 'the contingency of the conclusions of practical reason'. Not even stateable or stated reasons can operate as Humean causes.

4. The fourth plank in Kenny's free will platform is his defence, in principle, of compatibilism. Compatibilism in its modern form begins with Kant, whose argument that determinism, universal Humean causality, is a condition of thought in the world of appearances, runs alongside the claim that in the world of pure reason an uncaused cause at the beginning of every causal chain is no less a condition of thought. Since we are bound to regard ourselves as moral agents, Kant argues, we must regard ourselves as the free and so responsible initiators of such chains; nor is there any contradiction in our doing so since intuitions about the world of appearances cannot logically contradict those deriving from that of pure reason. Freedom and determinism are therefore compatible with one another.

Kenny (1975) transposes this conception of co-extensive but independent modes of thought into a modern key. The post-Kantian compatabilist, he writes, introduces

> a distinction between levels of description and explanation. He can agree that freedom and [determinism] are

incompatible at a single level, while denying that there need be any incompatibility at a different level. He can agree that we know at the psychological level we are free and therefore at the psychological level undetermined. But he can deny that we know anything about determinism at the physiological level.

The relevance of this to the issue between free will and determinism is as follows. The concepts and vocabulary of physiology are totally different from those employed in the everyday description in human behaviour. It is only actions described in terms of human behaviour that libertarians claim to be free. Even one hundred per cent predictability at the level of physiology need not by itself involve any increase in predictability at the human level . . . [From] an action described in human terms a further action described in these terms may well be predicted . . . But it would be impossible for prediction in these terms to achieve one hundred per cent certainty, since the everyday language of intention and motive . . . presupposes a structure of freedom and limited unpredictability. (149)

Kenny, it should be noted, is not *committed* to determinism at the level of physiology, only to the contention that freedom at the 'human' level does not preclude the operation of deterministic laws in our bodies, and vice versa, in the event of physiological determinism being shown to be the case.

His argument proceeds as follows: 'given that A ϕd at t, in order to show he enjoyed liberty of indifference we have to show four things' (150). These he lists as follows:

1 A had at t the ability to ϕ
2 A had at t the ability not to ϕ
3 A had at t the opportunity to ϕ at t
4 A had at t the opportunity not to ϕ at t (151).

Kenny then describes the conditions under which such an action could be said to be compatible with physiological determinism, these being: '(a) that A ϕd at t because he wanted to ϕ at t; (b) that the physical movements which constituted A's ϕing at t were in accordance with a deterministic physiological law'.

It will have been noted that two of Kenny's conditions for the liberty of indifference do not conclude with the words 'at t'. This is because he believes that 'the ability to ϕ and the ability not to ϕ . . . is something which can be settled independently of the circumstance obtaining at t'. He sees human beings as language-users with long-term goals and complex skills more or less effectively related to those goals. Such abilities, he contends, are not bound to moments of action; they are 'powers' but not 'occult powers'. Thus even quite trivial abilities, such as my capacity to suppress a yawn, may be linked to significant goals, such as a commitment to listen attentively and open-mindedly to a friend's paper at a conference, but my ability to perform such actions, and to refrain from doing so, are not dependent on my being motivated on and by particular occasions.

Kenny's argument continues. If A ϕs at t, it is clear that he had the opportunity to do so. But did he have the opportunity not to do so? He did, Kenny claims, provided 'the reason that he is [not] not-ϕing is that he wants to ϕ. For . . . an opportunity is not removed simply by the presence of a contrary want' — in this case the opportunity not to ϕ by the presence of a *wish* to do so. But, Kenny continues, how can it be that A 'is ϕing because he wants to if . . . the antecedent physiological conditions were such that no event answering to the description predictable from them could be described as not ϕing?' (151–2). Only, he argues, 'if one of the features on which the physiological prediction is based is a factor which would not have obtained unless the agent had *wanted*' (152) to ϕ at t, for in that case 'the physiological prediction [would] not remove opportunity, and thus [would] not negative freedom'. Thus if one of the features leading to a prediction that I will yawn during my friend's paper is a factor which would have obtained even if I had not wanted to do so, such as the onset of flu, then I would not have had a genuine opportunity not to yawn and consequently my yawning would not have been a free act. However, if it were based on a change in my wants in consequence of signs of boredom in the distinguished audience and growing disloyalty on my part, the physiological feature making the yawning predictable would not be inconsistent with my having yawned freely.

5. The coherence of this argument has been challenged and defended. I propose to examine its adequacy in the light of a post-Kantian literary text, James's *The Portrait of a Lady*. In doing so I shall make occasional references to how the novel illuminates differences between Kenny and Davidson. Some caution will be necessary, however, in following this procedure. The character with whose freedom James is most explicitly concerned is the novel's

heroine, Isabel Archer, and he warns us that his intentions with respect to her are 'To awaken on the reader's part an impulse more tender and more purely expectant' (I 69) than would be consistent with making her a 'victim of scientific criticism'. Explanations in terms of Humean causes are thus insufficient for James's purposes; instead his writing suggests the need for a continual revision of view; what is said may not be what is meant; what is meant may have to be qualified by other meanings which the words used will bear; the assured convictions of a character may have to be qualified in James's apparent lack of them. The demands he thus makes on his readers are emotional and moral as well as intellectual. We are expected to compare, reappraise and trust. James is above all a writer who perceives rationalisation and self-scrutiny as intentional acts which will require rationalisation in their turn.

6. Nevertheless the relevance of his novel to the present discussion is clear. It is literally about an experiment in freedom, the subject of which is Isabel, a young American, who is brought to Europe by her aunt, Mrs Touchett, and who unexpectedly inherits a fortune from her uncle, Mr Touchett, at the instigation of his son, Ralph, who is in love with her, and, being mortally ill, has no use for the money himself. He wishes to observe the consequence of so fine a person enjoying the vast increase in spontaneity, in opportunity, which great wealth brings. One of the questions which the novel addresses, therefore, is whether freedom is identical with spontaneous action. At one point in the novel Isabel herself comes very near to thinking that it is. Walking alone through the London streets, and thinking of her plans to spend winter travelling wherever she wants in the company of her new friend Madame Merle, she has a vivid sense of 'the absolute boldness and wantonness of liberty' (II 35).

But she is preoccupied also with the question of how she *ought* to act. 'A large fortune', she remarks, 'means freedom, and I'm afraid of that. It's such a fine thing, and one should make good use of it' (I 320). Her situation thus highlights two very relevant problems, that of forming a plan of life and sticking to it, and that of identifying the appropriate premises for doing so. On the one hand, Isabel feels justified in treating her own wants as premises, since she has 'an unquenchable desire to think well of herself . . . a theory . . . that one . . . should move in a realm of light, of natural wisdom, of happy impulse' (I 68); but on the other she has intimations of an objective moral order and a fear in consequence of doing 'anything wrong'. At first she is confident that she can readily identify the wrong — it is 'to be mean, to be jealous, to be false, to be cruel' (I 68–9) — but as her situation develops, everything becomes more problematical.

In particular, the difficulties of forming and being faithful to a plan of life, on whatever premisses, are increased by the fact that she is doubly deceived. In the first place, she is not told of Ralph's role in securing her fortune, so that almost until his death her relations with him are not on an entirely open footing; but far more seriously, she is deceived by Madame Merle into marrying the latter's former lover, Gilbert Osmond — 'a sterile dilletante' (II 71), Ralph calls him — whose daughter, Pansy, ostensibly the child of his first marriage, is in fact Madame Merle's. In principle neither of these deceptions affects Isabel's freedom, but they do make it difficult for her to understand the motivations of those closest to her, and therefore to base her own plans and expectations on a realistic appraisal of her world.

7. The difficulties confronting Isabel, however, are not just external. There are forces at work within her which considerably complicate her understanding and ours of how and why she makes the decisions she does. James's extreme reticence in this area does not help things either. She receives three proposals of marriage. Two she rejects, one she accepts. None is directly reported — we learn about them after the event. The first occurs before she leaves America. The man in question. Caspar Goodwood, is, we are told 'quite a splendid young man' (I 47), who inspires her 'with a sentiment of high, of rare respect'. We are not told why she refuses him. Later, in England, but before coming into her money, she rejects in some ways an even more eligible lover, Lord Warburton, and again the grounds for her doing so are far from plain. Her acceptance of Gilbert is equally mysterious: we learn about it in the course of a conversation she has with Caspar. The few clues we are given about her feelings on these occasions only add to the mystery. It seems Isabel is afraid of something.

> Deep in her soul [James tells us] — it was the deepest thing there — lay a belief that if a certain light should dawn she could give herself completely; but this image, on the whole, was too formidable to be attractive. Isabel's thoughts hovered about it, but they seldom rested on it long; after a while it ended in alarms. (I 71–2)

Is this fear sexual? A lover, we are told, might have described her reluctance to think about marriage as 'something cold and dry' (I 71), but it is only at the end of the novel that her most impassioned suitor, Caspar, seems dangerous to her.

A stronger clue is given in her reaction to Gilbert's first declaration: she begs him to stop

> with an intensity that expressed the dread of having, in this case too, to choose and decide. What made her dread great was . . . the sense of something within herself, deep down, that she supposed to be inspired and trustful passion. It was there like a large sum stored in a bank — which there was a terror in having to begin to spend. If she touched it, it would all come out. (II 18)

There are sexual connotations here, but the indications of a fear of choice itself are stronger. Isabel, it seems, is afraid of what she and Lord Warburton call her 'remarkable mind' (I 154) — not least because she finds it so difficult to explain her actions. She does not 'know why' (I 160) she rejects him, and she is 'surprised' (II 50) by her acceptance of Gilbert, yet years later she says of the latter decision that it was 'perfectly free; it was impossible to do anything more deliberate' (II 284).

8. Isabel's is thus a very problematical study of freedom not least because James is initially so careful not to narrate what happens 'at t'. He begins to do so only after Isabel has married and set up house with Gilbert and Pansy in Rome. Her relations with Pansy are complex. At an early stage in Gilbert's pursuit of Isabel — he is a suitor whom Ralph's mother heartily dislikes — the subject of Pansy arises in a conversation between Mrs Touchett and Madame Merle. Madame Merle thinks Isabel likes the child.

> 'Another reason then for Mr Osmond's stopping at home! [says Mrs Touchett] 'Otherwise, a week hence, we shall have my niece arriving at the conviction that her mission in life's to prove that a stepmother may sacrifice herself — and, that, to prove it, she must first become one'. (I 398)

Isabel's tendency to sacrifice herself on Pansy's behalf, which this remark so lightly predicts, becomes a dominant motif in the novel.

In Rome Pansy falls in love with an apparently feeble young dilettante called Rosier. However, she has been educated to strict obedience in an Italian convent and is fearful of her father. Mr Rosier's chances are extinguished, therefore, when Lord Warburton, still haunted by his feelings for Isabel, shows an interest in marrying Pansy. Isabel is no longer happy in her marriage, and she has become Pansy's protector and friend. But she remains committed to 'the idea of assisting her husband to be pleased' (II 177), and when Lord Warburton calls one evening, she is 'on the point of taking the great step of going out of the room and leaving her companions alone', but finds that she cannot 'rise to it; something held her and made this impossible . . . a vague doubt — a sense that she was not quite sure' (II 177–8).

The occasion is a slight but significant one. In a series of later incidents we see Isabel similarly 'unable' to act on her professed intentions. Having sworn she will 'never make another promise' (II 304), for example, she promptly undertakes to visit Ralph on his deathbed if he summons her to it. The summons duly comes and she decides to leave for England even though Gilbert sees such an action as 'the most deliberate, the most calculated, opposition' (II 354) to his wishes, and a violation of their marriage. 'How can you call it calculated?' Isabel protests, 'I received my aunt's telegram but three minutes ago'. 'You calculate rapidly', Gilbert (convincingly) replies. Her decision to leave Rome is thus explicitly a decision to leave her husband, yet within hours of making it she promises Pansy (immured in her convent for loving Mr Rosier) that she will return. By the time she reaches London, however, she claims to have forgotten her reason for making this considered undertaking. 'Perhaps I shall find another' (II 398), she tells her friend, Henrietta Stackpole. 'You'll certainly never find a good one', Henrietta replies.

9. Anyone who finds this account of Isabel's behaviour convincing must, I think, have reservations about both Kenny's and Davidson's theories of intention. As we noted, Isabel is conscious of considerable deliberation in her decision-making particularly in accepting Gilbert and in promising Pansy to return to Rome — yet she continually 'loses' her reasons and finds herself unable to rationalise her actions. Equally disturbing is her inability to stick by intentions articulated in advance. Both tendencies suggest an inability to develop a medium-term stability in her plan of life, and so to achieve an adult identity. This makes it difficult to rationalise her choices. Her actions never seem 'out of character', yet one has little confidence in adducing adequate and convincing reasons for them. On the other hand, for all their apparent

'surdity', one would hesitate to dismiss Isabel as neurotic or disturbed.

As inconsistent with the account of intention advanced by Kenny and Davidson are James's descriptions (so long delayed) of what happens to Isabel at t. An important element in Kenny's argument is his suggestion that one's ability to ϕ or not to ϕ can be settled independently of the circumstances obtaining when one ϕs. This is obviously true of physical acts, such as walking through a door. But what of speech-acts? The words 'I love you', for example, are specific to the occasion on which they are uttered and one's capacity to say them (and not just to use them in other contexts) is untestable apart from those times when the opportunity to do so occurs. Kenny concedes that not everything I do is free. If I yawn during my friend's lecture, for example, because a hypnotist has instructed me to do so every time I hear the word 'epistemic', my yawning is not free. If a longer and more deeply rooted conditioning process makes me stutter every time I am sexually aroused, I am not free either, in those particular circumstances, to speak as I want to. But an even subtler conditioning process may make me involuntarily tongue-tied about my feelings in the presence of one person only, or perhaps only when I detect in that person a desire for me to be emotionally open. On the other hand I may find myself unable to keep silent when I want to do so: this happens to some people quite regularly at meetings. In the matter of speech-acts, then, it seems that the ability to ϕ or not to ϕ cannot be settled independently of the circumstances obtaining at t, the circumstances which both determine the content of what I say and (possibly) my capacity to say or not to say it.

Kenny's account of long-term abilities would not be seriously affected if this difficulty involved a few speech acts only. But does it? Why for example, does Isabel find it 'impossible' to leave Pansy and Lord Warburton alone together, even though she thinks she wants to? Is her sense that she is not quite sure sufficient explanation? Such a feeling could certainly be a want in Kenny's sense, and so rationalise her action, but according to Kenny it could not operate as a Humean cause and her remaining in the room is said to be determined: she finds it 'impossible' to rise to her intended action. We may reasonably interpret this as an inability to utter a highly specific non-verbal signal, but if this is so, it considerably extends the range of those two-way abilities which are not testable independently of the circumstances obtaining when we perform them. If we speak with our bodies as well as our tongues, the most casual movement may be a sign as well as the action it seems to be. Even when we are alone we may be signalling to ourselves when we scratch, when we yawn, when we turn over in bed. Most of this signalling, like most of our speaking, may be voluntary and intentional, but like our speaking it must, by definition, be specific to the (inter-personal) context which determines its meaning. It follows that our ability to engage in this rather than that meaningful movement cannot be testable independently of the circumstances obtaining at t, and since there seem to be no criteria for determining which of our movements say something while effecting something else there is no way of deciding which of our physical actions are involuntary, and which are not.

On two counts, then, Kenny's arguments seem to be inadequate. First (like Davidson's), they exaggerate the importance of language, of what Newman (1870) calls Formal Inference which allows 'language [to] have a monopoly of thought; and thought [to] go for only so much as it can show itself to be worth in language' (211). As 'a test and a common measure of reasoning' (212), Newman suggests, such linguistic thinking

> will be found partly to succeed and partly to fail; succeeding so far as words can in fact be found for representing the countless varieties and subtleties of human thought, failing on account of the fallacy of the original assumption, that whatever can be thought can be adequately expressed in words.

Secondly, Kenny's arguments are too optimistic about the testability of two-way abilities. Taken together, these two objections point to a third. One of the distinguishing characteristics of Jamesian narrative is its sensitivity to the way in which non-verbal signalling — the raised eyebrow, the shrugged shoulder, the shudder and the blush — merges with the verbal and makes all speech, all meaning uncertain. The accounts of willing we have so far considered have assumed that such convergence implies and constitutes unity, but in Isabel's case, we are confronted with evidence of disunity — with speeches and actions that happen independently of stateable reasons and yet appear deliberate, and even with a disturbing independence of action and speech, as if they were in contention. In order to explore this situation further, it will be useful to consider the altogether different theory of

91

willing proposed by Dennett, which I mentioned at the beginning of this chapter.

10. Dennett bases his account of willing on the reported behaviour of his dog. This dog, he tells us,

> loved to fetch tennis balls, but faced with two balls on the lawn and unable to hold them both in his mouth at once, he would switch rapidly back and forth, grabbing one and letting go of the other, mesmerized by his preference for getting over keeping — for perhaps several dozen cycles — until *something* clicked and turned off the behaviour. (30)

The deterministic vocabulary here is appropriate. We could say with Kenny that the dog has the power to go on grabbing the tennis balls and the power to stop doing so, and the opportunity to do one or the other, and that consequently his stopping the grab-and-drop routine (the bringing of different wants into play) exemplifies the freedom of indifference; but it makes better sense to say '*something* clicked'. And it may make better sense also to say the same of Isabel's decisions, especially those made against her conscious wishes and expressed intentions. But in that case, what happens to the notion of reason as Davidson understands it?

Before answering this question we need to look more closely at the implications of '*something* clicked'. It suggests that decisions happen as follows: I discover a problem requiring a practical solution. I dwell on it, using my language-related powers and also what Newman calls non-inferential thinking and Polanyi my subsidiary awareness, so that even after I have acted, I may not be able to put all my reasons into words. At a given moment I decide — like a golfer deciding to strike a ball — but the part of me that plumps for action is not the part of me that dwells on problems. Precisely because practical reasoning is defeasible, Dennett argues, my automatic pilot has to over-ride it at a moment of *its* choosing. My long-term skills and two-way abilities, the possession of which can be settled independently of the circumstances at t, depend on those two-way abilities becoming strictly one-way abilities at t.

A Kennyan might argue that the something which clicks is simply that physiological factor which would not have obtained had I not wanted at t to act as I did. But suppose I want to do something for some reasons and to refrain from doing it for others. I refrain from doing it. To suggest that I do so because I do not *really* want to act otherwise, or that my reasons for refraining are stronger than my counter-reasons, would be to treat my reasons as Humean causes. Besides, I regret my decision as soon as I make it, but it is irreversible as I knew it would be. What has happened? Dennett's explanation seems eminently satisfactory: a factor has come into play at *t* which 'decides' for me, or rather for my consciousness, and which accordingly negatives freedom in Kenny's sense. This is not a case of Davidsonian surdity, however, that is, of an all-out unconditional judgement conflicting with a prima facie 'all things considered' judgement. Instead, judgements of all kinds are forced to sink their differences by a power of mind that in principle cannot be rationalised.

In discussing the relations between will and intellect as St Thomas understands them, O'Connor follows precisely this logic. St Thomas, he writes,

> considers an objection quite in the manner of Professor Ryle: Do not the mutual influences of will and intellect result in an infinite regress, each act of will requiring a preceding act of the intellect, which in turn requires an earlier act of the will and so on? His answer is that the regress is unnecessary since will and intellect influence each other by a different kind of causation. Intellect moves will as a final cause by proposing the end to which it tends; but will moves intellect as an efficient cause. Intellect guides will, in other words, but does not control the moment of its operation. But this leaves the operation of the will basically mysterious: it justs acts when it decides to. Freedom of exercise is a spontaneous and indeed capricious act; only freedom of specification is under rational control . . . But freedom of specification can at most explain *what* we choose; it cannot explain *when* we make the choice. And since freedom of exercise [Dennett's decider-switch] can always anticipate or cut short rational deliberation, it is, in the last resort, unexplained and opaque to reason. (55–6)

As Dennett puts it: 'We must relinquish control over the very process that generates the incomplete set of considerations on which we act, and hence we are always somewhat at the mercy of that process' (87).

11. He clarifies this point by comparing the sort of failure attributable to a well-programmed robot with the failures of

human beings. He images his robot or Deterministic Deliberator exploring an uninhabited planet. This robot has been 'designed to make the most of its opportunities' (115), an opportunity being

> an occasion where a self-controller . . . is informed about . . . a situation in which the outcome of its subsequent 'deliberation' will be a decisive . . . factor. In such a situation more than one alternative is 'possible' so far as the . . . self-controller is concerned; that is, the critical nexus passes through its deliberation. (118)

By and large the robot performs well, but sometimes it fails, not through malfunction or systematic confusion about its environment, but by making the sort of mistake which, if made by a human being, would invite the response, 'he blew it'. Such mistakes are possible in robots, Dennett maintains, because 'a well-designed, real-time self-controller . . . makes use of heuristic procedures, and hence is designed to "take chances" by relying on some "random" generation of considerations' (117); and they are possible in human beings for the same reasons: like robots, we rely on a shut-down device which acts without reasons and without which we would be locked into permanent indecision. Robotic deliberators sometimes shut deliberation down too soon, or let it go on too long, but they can also be designed to 'learn' from such errors. One may assume that biological deliberators, animal and human, are similarly equipped. Do we need more? Dennett asks. Traditional accounts of action, he maintains (such as Kenny's, Davidson's and the Pope's), rest on the 'illusion of . . . an ultimate center' (78). His model envisages two interacting systems, understanding and wanting on the one hand, deciding on the other. Each may adapt more or less satisfactorily to the performance of the other, but neither is responsible for the performance of the whole organism, and the question, 'Which is me?' is meaningless. I am the synthesis of their combined operations.

12. In thinking of the relevance of this account to *The Portrait of a Lady* it is important to resist any prejudice against comparing human beings with robots. When Ralph arranges Isabel's inheritance, after all, she is effectively set up as a self-controller under test. This is not surprising. The novel was written in the context of a heavily deterministic intellectual culture. Writing fourteen years before its publication, in what was to become the final chapter of *The Renaissance* (1873), Walter Pater had argued

that the

> chief factor in the thoughts of the modern mind concerning
> itself is the intricacy, the universality of natural law, even in
> the moral order. For us, necessity is . . . a magic web woven
> through and through us, like that magnetic system of which
> modern science speaks, penetrating us with a network,
> subtler than out subtlest nerves, yet bearing in it the central
> forces of the world. (218)

'Can art', he wondered, 'represent men and women in these
bewildering toils, so as to give the spirit at least an equivalent for
the sense of freedom?' It may be well in this spirit that James
warns us against making Isabel a 'victim of scientific criticism' —
we should make the effort — tenderly and expectantly — to find
in her life something that even in a modern situation can at least
pass for freedom. A similar demand was made on behalf of other
heroines of the period by the authors of *Daniel Deronda*, *Diana of the
Crossways* and *Jude the Obscure*. In the novel, above all, Pater
believed

> this entanglement, this network of law, becomes the tragic
> situation, in which certain groups of noble men and women
> work out for themselves a supreme *dénouement*. Who [he
> asks], if he saw through all, would fret against the chain of
> circumstances which endows one at the end with those great
> experiences? (219)

In her cheerfully un-Paterian way, Dennett answers this question as Pater does.

> What we want when we want free will [he writes] is the
> power to decide our courses of action, and to decide them
> wisely, in the light of our expectations and desires. We want
> to be in control of ourselves . . . We want to be agents,
> capable of initiating, and taking responsibility for, projects
> and deeds. All this is ours . . . as a natural product of our
> biological endowment, extended and enhanced by our initia-
> tion into society (169).

Deliberation, verbal and non-verbal signalling and decision-
making may not be controlled from a single centre, but together

they operate as the personal life. James would have agreed. Isabel has to be understood as the complex functioning of her whole organism — what Dennett calls the 'inscrutable tangle of microcausation' (77n) — and this includes, yet is not exhausted by, all that she knows about her feelings, and all that she does not know about them, all that she governs from the centre of her consciousness and all that she does not and so finds fearful. Of one notable decision — to marry Gilbert — we may say, as Ralph effectively does, that she 'blew it', but all her other decisions, as we have so far examined them, are really hers and ultimately defensible on rational and moral grounds, however mysterious and divided the processes involved in making them may have been: in the last analysis, *she works them out for herself*.

13. In a number of ways, then, Dennett's account makes better sense of Isabel's case than either Kenny's or Davidson's, but there are none the less difficulties in his model of action which a close reading of the penultimate scene of the novel brings into focus. The circumstances of this incident are as follows. Ralph has died. Isabel is staying at his home in England, uncertain about her future. One evening in the garden she is unexpectedly confronted by Caspar, whom she has not seen since Ralph's funeral. His effect on her is a powerful one, 'a new sensation . . . he had never produced . . . before . . . a feeling of danger' (II 430). He tells her that he learnt from Ralph about the unhappiness of her marriage, and that Ralph asked him to do everything for her that she would let him do. He cannot bear seeing her pay for her error, and he begs her to think of him. This forcibly reminds Isabel of the 'idea of which she had caught a glimpse a few moments before' (II 433), and when he asks her why she should 'go through [the] ghastly form' of returning to Gilbert, she replies 'To get away from *you*!' But this expresses 'only a little of what she felt. The rest was that she had never been loved before.' He presses his case: she has no children — 'nothing to consider' (II 434); the world is all before them and it is very big. 'The world's very small', Isabel replies, 'at random' (II 435) — she has 'an immense desire to appear to resist'. At this point James intrudes briefly into the narration. 'I know not [he writes] whether she believed everything he said; but she believed just then that to let him take her in his arms would be the next best thing to her dying. This belief, for a moment, was a kind of rapture'. But the next moment Caspar makes a passionate demand on her — 'Ah, be mine as I am yours' — and his voice seems 'to come harsh and terrible'. Isabel realises this is

'but a subjective fact' (II 436) and pleads with him to go away. In response he kisses her.

> His kiss was like white lightning, a flash that spread, and spread again, and stayed; and it was extraordinarily as if, while she took it, she felt each thing in his hard manhood that had pleased her, each aggressive fact of his face, his figure, his presence, justified of its intense identity and made one with this act of possession.

The next moment she is free and in flight through the darkness. She reaches the house. 'She had not known where to turn; but she knew now. There was a very straight path'. She subsequently returns to Rome.

14. An important feature of this episode is the recurrence in it of the theme of Isabel's fear in a way which is relevant to the arguments of Kenny, Davidson and Dennett. Kenny, for example, argues that an agent has the opportunity not to ϕ at t 'if he is ϕing because he wants to' (151). But suppose my reason for ϕing at t is that I am frightened of not ϕing because of a feeling in myself that I neither like nor understand. Does this mean that I want to ϕ in Kenny's sense? If my fear is the only significant want in play, it may, but what if my wants, the premisses of my practical reasoning, are subject to unpredictable in-rushes of emotion which consciousness cannot understand or control? Kenny might argue that such occasions do negative freedom, but that they are pathological and so do not affect his general argument, Dennett that in such circumstances the functioning of the decider-switch becomes obvious and useful: in a crisis emergency action *is* after all taken — blindly, in panic, but (perhaps) effectively. The problem with both these explanations, at least for the reader who is moved by the ending of James's novel, is that they diminish its possible significance. If Isabel's consciousness and the most important act of her life are not significantly related, her tragedy has no meaning. To assimilate the final chapter of *The Portrait of a Lady* we will need to take the territory of the inchoate and the unconscious far more seriously than Kenny and Dennett seem prepared to do.

At a certain level, it is true, both make gestures towards unconscious mental processes. Dennett's decider-switch is an unconscious process by definition, but he ignores possible difficulties in this assumption. He writes of our 'naturalistically conceived selves' (100) as portions of the physical universe [that] have the property of being designed to resist their own dissolution . . . of being caused to have reliable expectations of what will happen next . . . [of having] the futher capacity of significant self-improvement (through learning) . . . [and] the open-ended capacity (requiring a language of self-description) for 'radical self-evaluation'.

But this assumes what needs to be shown, namely, that the effectiveness of the human organism's operations as a self-preserver and self-duplicator are consistent with the values which a language of self-description makes available to it for making judgements about itself. The problem is that the consciousness which describes itself linguistically, by Dennett's own argument, cannot be the whole of that part of the universe endowed with the properties which Dennett lists. Biologically, my ego is not the whole of me. It is not an end in itself, but a functioning part of a larger whole, and it is that whole which is designed to resist dissolution. It may well be designed to do so in the teeth of the priorities of consciousness if this should prove necessary. I must certainly assume that it *uses* consciousness for its own ends, not those of consciousness. Dennett cheerfully implies that this is no problem. James's narrative of Isabel's agonised decision-making, above all in his enigmatic last chapter, suggests that it may be.

15. Kenny is equally untroubled by the possible operations of unconscious mental processes since, in his view, the defeasability of practical reasoning remains unaffected whether it is consciously or unconsciously conducted. But this is to ignore the problem of why conscious reasoning chains should be supplemented from time to time by unconscious ones. Why, for example, is it so difficult for Isabel to account for her behaviour and to rationalise her fear? The simplest explanation is that she does not want to think about what frightens her because it frightens her so much. Freud suggests that it is possible to have fears so intense that one needs not only to keep their causes out of sight but the consequences of those causes as well — the fear itself. If we assume that consciousness could not do this on its own, we may have to posit a suppressing mechanism to effect it, comparable with Dennett's decider-switch. Alternatively we may account for fear like Isabel's in terms of a fixed unwillingness on the part of consciousness to give attention to its entire content. Granted the feasibility of either of these two descriptions, we can examine the implications of Kenny's suggestion

that unconscious practical reasoning may be possible.

I shall do so by examining a case-history reported by Freud to which Kenny (1975) laconically alludes. It concerns a young man who embarks on an unnecesary slimming programme because he is convinced he is '*zu dick*' (too fat). Analysis reveals that he is sexually jealous of an Englishman called Dick, and wishes to get rid of him. How could he possibly try to achieve this end by such absurd means?

To an analyst the man's problem is not jealousy but fear and shame of being jealous. This is why he suppresses (or turns his attention away from) the entire experience. But obviously this does not solve his problem. It simply hands it to the unconscious to be dealt with. The unconscious, however (or the patient's power of unconscious practical reasoning), dislikes the fear and shame every bit as much as the conscious does, and also wants to get rid of them. Its mode of practical reasoning, however, is not subject to the reflexively disciplined good sense which operates in consciousness — that is its freedom as well as its limitation. It therefore changes 'Dick' to *dick* and invites consciousness to get rid of *dick* in this new form, a task consciousness finds far less objectionable than that of coping with its feelings about Dick. Indeed it has a vested interest in accepting the suggestions of the unconscious, though it needs to structure them into a superficially sensible plan of life. Such a process may be compared with the collusive interactions in a stable but unhappy marriage, or the unspoken agreement of the fallen angels in *Paradise Lost* never to mention the Son. Freud's patient accordingly rationalises his slimming programme but not surprisingly he finds no relief in it. Freud's solution to his patient's difficulties is to unify his practical reasoning by bringing his suppressed feelings into the open, or, if you will, by enabling him to attend to memories and experiences from which he had diverted his attention.

It is not inconsistent with Freud's theory if English-speakers find this story amusing. That, however, is beside the point. What is interesting is the possibility of double chains of practical reasoning to which the case-history points and which Kenny regards as possible. We may plausibly suppose that such chains operate in Isabel's life, if not in this or that psychoanalytical report. Nor do we have to believe in the punning capacities of the unconscious, or in the therapeutic efficacy of analysis, to see this as a problem for Davidson as well as for Kenny. If we could be sure that conscious and unconscious chains of reasoning always operated independently, each resulting in separable actions, there would be no problem. The difficulties begin once we accept that consciousness may need to explain actions promoted by the unconscious in terms satisfactory to itself. The situation becomes more acute if we envisage a collusive arrangement between them, as Freud does. In either case we are faced not with one but two chains of unconscious practical reasoning, the second being the 'bad faith' with which consciousness controls its relations with the unconscious, (or, if you like, keeps unwanted memories hidden) particularly with respect to intentions and rationalisations. The want which would be the premiss of this second chain of unconscious practical reasoning would be that all things should *not* be considered. If we recall the extent to which our wordless, corporeal sign-making would also be subject to such a complex of autonomous and semi-autonomous lines of practical reasoning, the possibilities of reason-governed behaviour which Davidson envisages, or of freedom based on the defeasibility of practical reasoning favoured by Kenny become remote. Surdity could be the rule, and action the outcome of the play between sub-systems within the person, each of which might separately enjoy the freedom of the practical reasoner as Kenny understands it, yet none of which would necessarily be in sole control of a particular action, so that freedom, or more specifically voluntariness and intention, could never be confidently attributed to the person as a whole.

16. Kenny, Dennett and Davidson fail, then, to account for all the tendencies in human behaviour which are represented by Isabel's fear. They ignore the hell below consciousness. But they also ignore the possibility of a heaven above it, a possibility recognised in the closing pages of *The Portrait of a Lady* by the suggestion that after all Isabel may be operating according to an authentic logic of goodness. The scene with Caspar reverses that of the fall in *Paradise Lost*. In it a man in a garden tempts a woman to abandon her duties in a fallen world and fly with him to paradise. It even contains an allusion to the closing lines of the poem, but Isabel's reply to Caspar's suggestion that the world lies all before them is that the world is small. Perhaps she means that it is morally small. In any case she ends on the straight path that leads back to Pansy and marriage. But if Isabel is really choosing a higher good here, her action cannot easily be adjusted to Kenny's conception of wants as the premisses of practical reasoning, or to Dennett's notion of what is 'Worth Wanting'. Is James

really suggesting that it is possible to act for the sake of *bare* truth about good?

Davidson's account of incontinence (1985) suggests one way in which this might be. Isabel's flight from Caspar's arms can be understood as exemplifying a special kind of *akrasia*, as Davidson understands it, in which 'reason' wins a perverse victory over 'passion'. He gives the following example:

> I have just relaxed in bed after a hard day when it occurs to me that I have not brushed my teeth. Concern for my health bids me rise and brush; sensual indulgence suggests I forget my teeth for once. I weigh the alternatives in the light of the reasons: on the one hand, my teeth are strong, and at my age decay is slow . . . on the other, if I get up, it will spoil my calm and may result in a bad night's sleep. Everything considered I judge I would do better to stay in bed. Yet my feeling that I ought to brush my teeth is too strong for me: wearily I leave my bed and brush my teeth. My act is clearly intentional, although against my better judgement, and so is incontinent. (30)

If Isabel in her final scene acts on a logic of goodness which is truly independent of wants, then her flight may be an action of the same type as that described in this passage. In such a case what she and others have feared for so long may be a form of what Davidson perceives as 'weakness of the will', though terribly intensified. The problem with Davidson's account, however, is that it can only represent such irrationality as 'wrong'. James, on the other hand, leaves open the possibility that, in spite of everything we long for on Isabel's behalf, the totally unsatisfying, the manifestly surd, may, after all, be right.

It would seem, then, that *The Portrait of a Lady* raises important questions about the unity of the self and the nature of moral action which the philosophers we have so far considered are unable to resolve satisfactorily. These are problems which we will need to explore further in subsequent chapters.

5

Cor ad cor loquitur

*1. The causes of action 2. Robots and consciousness 3. Identifying
with others 4. The mental and the physical 5. Laplace's mistake 6.
What it is to be a person 7. Swinburne and Parfit on personal essences
8. Personal uniqueness 9. God's knowledge of hearts 10. Predicting
the actions of the Son 11. Trust and knowledge in Newman and
James 12. The example of David and Jonathan 13. The heart as a
condition of freedom*

1. Two questions of great importance to my argument emerged
from my analysis at the end of the last chapter of the climactic
scene of *The Portrait of a Lady*. Are there personal essences to which
freedom might be attributed? And are there moral values which
can serve as premises of moral arguments in place of wants? I
shall begin to answer the first of these questions by attempting to
syncretise certain ideas so far considered, and then by examining
the legitimacy and importance of the notion of personality. In
Chapter 6, however, I shall look at some difficulties involved in
that notion. This will lead to a discussion first of social conditioning, then of evolution, and so to a consideration of the second
question.

One of the more important disagreements between Kenny and
Davidson concerns the relation of reasons to actions. The evidence
of James's novel suggests strongly that Kenny is right on this
issue, and that reasons do not function as causes of action. It
seems to be impossible after an action to determine whether any
reasons which might account for it did in fact operate as its determinants. Davidson himself (1980) concedes the possibility of
'lunatic internal causal chains' (79) in consequence of which an
action 'was not performed with the intention that we could read

from the attitudes that caused it', and cites the example of a climber who believes that it would be in the interests of his own safety to let go of a rope which supports a companion, and who is so unnerved by the thought that he lets go of the rope. Davidson would recognise, I think, that this kind of difficulty is one reason why the last chapter of *The Portrait of a Lady* is so difficult to interpret. But Kenny's argument avoids this problem: it establishes that no statement of reasons in advance of Isabel's flight could ever be full enough to make all but one outcome of her encounter with Caspar impossible. Reasons are thus inadequate as evidence after the event, and as predictors before it.

That such looseness might provide a basis for free will as Kenny understands it, however, seems doubtful. Dennett's suggestion that human beings do not have a centre of knowing and willing, but semi-autonomous procedures of deliberation, decision-making and action which are adequately integrated for practical purposes has evident plausibility. The decider-switch programmed to intervene 'blindly' but not arbitrarily in the deliberating process in order to determine the moment and so the determinants of action solves the problem raised by St Thomas and by Kenny of the defeasibility of practical reasoning rather better than his identification of the freedoms of spontaneity and indifference does.

2. The difficulty with Dennett's account, however, is that in explaining decision-making by means of convincing analogues with semi-independent sub-systems in robots he stumbles against the problems of consciousness. Consciousness reveals a principle of unity in people, and possibly in animals, based on a *fusion* of synchronic two-way interactions between periphery and centre with which comparisons of brains with machines cannot easily cope. Consider Dennett's account of the evolution of intelligence on the basis of what happens in

Artificial intelligence . . . programs . . . that model in considerable depth the organizational structure of systems that must plan 'communicative' interactions with other systems, based on their 'knowledge' about what they themselves 'know' and 'don't know', what their interlocutor system 'knows' and 'doesn't know,' and so forth. (39).

The quotation marks register evident unease about what 'knowing' might mean in an AI system, an unease not resolved by a subsequent attempt to fit the robotics analogue into a hypothetical account of evolution. 'We may suppose', Dennett writes, 'that our imagined progenitors in the thought experiment were no more conscious than AI robots would be — whatever that comes to.' But then we must also assume that consciousness is not entailed in the kind of deliberating in which amoebas, worms and perhaps even Dennett's dog engage. It seems likely that consciousness — responsiveness to an internally constituted picture of the world which is in turn continually reconstituted in the light of the reactions it elicts — comes functionally into play only at a relatively late stage in the thought experiment, and it is by no means clear that the same vocabulary is appropriate to mental processes before and after that event.

Dennett skirts around this difficulty. He writes sentences such as: 'when one of these creatures was stymied in a project it would "ask for help", and in particular it would "ask for information". Sometimes the audience would respond by "communicating" something.' This description could apply to a computer linked to other computers, to a computer being operated by a person, to a startled deer looking for evidence of comparable alarm in other members of the herd, or to a young child in a nursery school; but it is not at all clear that the words 'ask', 'help' and 'information' have even comparable meanings in each case. The climax of Dennett's argument is reached in the following remarkable paragraph:

> Then one fine day an 'unintended' short-circuit effect of this new social institution was 'noticed' by a creature. It 'asked' for help in an inappropriate circumstance, where there was no helpful audience to hear the request and response. Except itself! When the creature heard its own request, the stimulation provoked just the sort of other-helping utterance that the request from another would have caused. And to the creature's 'delight' it found it had just provoked itself into answering its own question!

Reading this I can imagine an isolated deer looking up, startled, in order to receive an indication from its companions' reactions that all was well or not well, and not finding it being effectively pacified by its own return to grazing, though I do not know whether the word 'delight' has a place in this account. On the other hand, I have no difficulty in imagining a gorilla similarly placed being genuinely delighted and showing it. It may well be, therefore, that deer are indeed like robots, and that gorillas are not. The problem of consciousness, in other words, is not solved by my showing that a system *might* be able to send signals to itself. I also need to understand the implications of a capacity for delight, for self-awareness, in deliberating systems.

3. This argument is based on intuitions I have about deer and gorillas, and to that extent is perhaps whimsical, but Davidson (1980) indicates why I have such intuitions. He too offers an account of communicative interaction between deliberating systems and illustrates his views by examining that it would mean to model a perfectly humanoid robot, to which he gives the name Art.

> in building Art [he tells us], we used circuits of the sort we would use if we wanted to build a machine that could process information, and so forth. But of course we must not jump to the conclusion that when those circuits come into play, Art is processing information. Much of what is at stake is whether what would be information for us, if Art were merely an extension of our own faculties (as a computer is), is information for him. But this we can decide only by seeing how such assumptions fit into the total picture of Art's behaviour. (250–1)

By definition Art is physically predictable; a knowledge of his circuitry and the encoded in-put from his information-gathering systems would allow us to predict the future of his circuitry and the physical movements of his body. But, Davidson argues, we would still need 'to know whether a particular one of these would be interpretable as an action or response' (251), and we could only do so by ignoring his circuitry and interpreting his action 'as we would a human movement'. But unlike physical states and changes of physical state, he argues, mental states and changes of mental state are not law-determined. Two people, for example, may have the same sensation, say of yellowness, but they may be differently wired up, so that circuits in very different states may be associated with identical experiences. And just as there need not be any systematically invariable correlations between specific behaviours and specific experiences, so there are no systematically invariable correlations between specific behaviour and specific beliefs and wants. We cannot assign

> beliefs to a person one by one on the basis of his verbal —
> behaviour, his choices, or other local signs no matter how

plain and evident, for we make sense of particular beliefs only as they cohere with other beliefs, with preferences, with intentions, hopes, fears, expectations, and the rest. (221)

In short, we can only make sense of other people by identifying with them. We assume that they have developing internally constituted worlds just as we do, and that their actions, like ours, are significantly related to these worlds and in turn have effects on them. Unknowable in terms of laws, other people are understood by means of imaginative analogy:

> we could not begin to decode a man's sayings if we could not make out his attitudes towards his sentences, such as holding, wishing, or wanting them to be true. Beginning from those attitudes we must work out a theory of what he means, . . . a theory that finds him consistent, a believer of truths, and a lover of the good . . . Life being what it is [however], there will be no simple theory that fully meets these demands. Many theories will effect a more or less acceptable compromise, and between these theories there may be no objective grounds for choice. (222)

This, after all, is why Isabel's is so effective a characterisation for those of us who find it so. We are left at the end of the *The Portrait of a Lady* believing that her behaviour in the climactic scene of the novel really does add up to something, while recognising the legitimacy of conflicting interpretations of it. Isabel's is thus quite as good an example of what Davidson calls the anomalousness or lawlessness of the mental as she is of Dennett's conception of blindly operating decision-making. But there is nothing in the AI systems which Dennett hypothesises which suggest that they are capable of enclosing subjectivities analagous to our own in this living way, still less of their being capable of enclosing all the problems of the unconscious with which we were concerned in the last chapter.

4. Internal anomalousness, as we have seen, is something that Kenny holds to as much as Davidson, and for essentially the same reason as Davidson does: both believe that it secures the compatability of determinism with their respective (but differing) versions of freedom. Admittedly Kenny is only concerned with determinism as one of the hypotheses of compatibilism. His arguments, however, assume that 100 per cent prediction of events could only

be based on the systematic operation of blind physical laws, and specifically (1979) that if 'human actions are determined by human physiology' (86), and if 'physiological laws . . . form part of a total system of deterministic laws governing the whole universe,' then it must be possible for an omniscient God to 'predict what each human being will do simply in virtue of know-ing the initial conditions and the deterministic laws governing the whole universe'. However his arguments also suggest (as do Davidson's) that such a God could not *know* (with 100 per cent accuracy) what believing, wanting and intending might be taking place in any human being at any stage of this process.

Davidson describes the relation of the mental and the physical which this distinction implies as one of supervenience. He denies that there are psycho-physical laws, and maintains (1985) that

mental characteristics are in some sense dependent, or supervenient, on physical characteristics. Such super-venience might be taken to mean that there cannot be two events alike in all physical respects but differing in some mental respect, or that an object cannot alter in some mental respect without altering in some physical respect. (214)

Three claims are made here: that exactly the same physical states are related to exactly the same mental states, but not vice versa; that mental changes cannot take place without related physical changes taking place concurrently; and that mental events can be the cause of physical changes and vice versa. Thus even though Davidson (1980) believes psychological events are in the strict sense anomalous, he is no less confident that they '*are identical with* . . . physical events' (248) and that consequently they do not compromise the law-determined character of the physical universe. Whether supervenience so stated is logically coherent or not has been disputed. In any case, Davidson (1985) describes his as only a 'broad rude version' (243) of it. It seems to me, however, that the difficulty with his position is really less logical than doctrinal. He is committed to it in consequence of a dogmatic conviction that the 'physical' is the locus of law. Neither he nor Kenny is prepared to regard consciousness as an empirically observable property of matter organised in certain complex ways, just as being soluble in water is an observable property of some solids and was so even before solubility as a process was understood, and when it might have been thought to be in some respects anomalous. What may be needed, in other words, is not a revision of our view of mind but a revision of our view of the nature of matter.

5. Such a reappraisal is offered by Polanyi, specifically in his response to P. Laplace's frequently refuted argument that an intelligence (such as Kenny's God) which at a given moment in time had knowledge of

> all the forces by which nature is animated and the respective positions of the entities which compose it . . . would embrace in the same formula the movements of the largest bodies in the universe and those of the atom: nothing would be uncertain for it, and the future like the past would be present to its eyes. (quoted in Polanyi, 140)

This view of physical predictability is evidently the same as Kenny's and Davidson's. Polanyi, however, argues that if by 'forces' Laplace means only what are usually taken to be 'physical' forces, then prediction even of future physical states would be impossible in any case involving conscious organisms. 'The tremendous intellectual feat conjured up by Laplace's imagination [he writes], has diverted attention . . from the decisive sleight of hand by which he substitutes a knowledge of all experience for a knowledge of all atomic data' (141).

Polanyi, in other words, denies that the facts of movement in conscious beings could ever be stated as 'physical' laws, not because quantum theory rules out prediction at the sub-atomic level, but because they are subject to the integrated, synchronic two-way interactions which constitute consciousness and are therefore anomalous even with respect to 'physical' causality. Thus on the one side Davidson (1980) argues for the anomalousness of the mental on the grounds that, unlike the physical, 'the mental does not . . . constitute a closed system' (224); that too much happens 'to affect the mental which is not itself a systematic part of the mental' for mental or psycho-physical interactions to be stateable as laws; but that mental events are identical with physical events and as physical events they can be described nomologically. On the other side, Polanyi contends that in conscious bodies the physical (as Davidson, Kenny and Laplace understand it) does not constitute a closed system either, and that too much happens in such organisms to affect the *physical* that is not a systematic part of it for the physical events in conscious organisms to be describable in terms of exclusively physical laws.

Davidson argues (quite coherently) that the 'principle of causal interaction deals with events in extension and is therefore blind to the mental-physical dichotomy' (215) which is of course synchronic; physical states are not, therefore, causes, of concurrent mental states, or vice versa, though either can be represented as causing subsequent physical or mental events. But it surely makes better sense to follow Polanyi, and represent mind-body states as causes of subsequent mind-body states, so that neither has indefeasible predictive value in the absence of the other. There is certainly no language of the purely mental in which laws of mental process have been stated; and since no experiment for the prediction of future brain-states has yet been designed, the assumption that the language of the purely physiological is capable of such prediction is mere hypothesis anyway.

6. We can now sketch a preliminary answer to the first question posed at the beginning of this chapter. Human beings are individuals at least to the extent that the exchanges of the central nervous system are centred in consciousness. This results in the *whole* psychosomatic complex being anomalous — i.e. not subject to the kind of description from which predictive laws could be formulated; but anomalousness need not mean that human behaviour is merely random, only that no language can express human kinds of consistency. Actions can be rationalised, but it is not clear that all the reasons we have for acting can be stated either before or after an action, nor that reasons are causes of acting. Lunatic causal chains may be in play, or multiple lines of conscious and unconscious reasoning, producing mysterious, but not necessarily pathological results. Besides, moments of decision seem impervious to introspective analysis: there is evidence of a radical disconnection between deliberation and action.

It would seem, therefore, that the possibilities for free and responsible action in human beings are limited. In the sense which the word has for Dennett and Davidson and which corresponds to the traditional freedom of spontaneity, freedom may be attributed to many human activities, but the degree to which past conditioning by oppressive external factors may induce present compulsion makes its extent unspecifiable. It is certainly more divided and blinder than philosophers who rest content with it usually admit. Spontaneity is 'worth wanting', but understandably we want more — not as we run for trains, or open an egg, but at moments comparable with key moments in the life of Isabel Archer, and possibly as a perceptual resource in our relations with others. This is why, even in Kenny's identification of the freedoms of spontaneity and indifference were sound, it would leave us dissatisfied. We need to feel capable of rising to fully conscious acts of indifference, to transcend the hell below us, and to aspire, perhaps, to a heaven above.

7. The task with which this summary confronts us is thus that of reconciling the unity implicit in consciousness with the arbitrariness haunting action. To do this we must re-examine the idea of personhood. I shall first consider ideas on the subject advanced by Swinburne, Parfit and Plantinga. This will lead to discussion of a key problem, whether free acts are predictable.

Like Polanyi, Kenny and Davidson, Swinburne (1979) argues that the 'correlations of mental events and intentions with brain events are too "odd" for science to explain' (172). I shall not repeat his arguments. He also questions the coherence of defining personal identity in terms of bodily and/or experiential continuity. He argues (1977) that 'bodily continuity and similarity of memory and character are [no more than] evidence of . . . personal identity' (122–3) and do not constitute it. A

> man . . . in his late fifties [for example] who does not remember most of the events of what we would ordinarily call 'his' childhood, has a very different character from the character which, we would ordinarily say, 'he' had when he was young, and has very few of the same brain cells as those which, we would ordinarily say, 'he' had fifty years before (121)

cannot sensibly be described as 'only somewhat the same person as the boy he is ordinarily said to have been . . . he is the same person *simpliciter*' (121–2): identity is 'something ultimate' (122).

Is this a valid and significant conclusion? Parfit (1985) illustrates his objections to it by describing a science-fiction system for 'transporting' people through space.

> I enter the Teletransporter . . . When I press the button, I shall lose consciousness . . . The Scanner here on earth will destroy my brain and body, while recording the exact states of all my cells. It will then transmit the information by radio . . . to . . . the Replicator on Mars. This will then create, out of new matter a brain and body exactly like mine. It will be in this body that I shall wake up. (199)

But will what wakes up *really* be me? Or will it be someone else, who will proceed along the life path that I would have followed had my body been sent physically to Mars in a 'frozen' state and woken up in the Replicator? In a rare allusion to his anti-trinitarian convictions in *The Art of Logic*, Milton in effect roundly answers this question in the negative: 'things which differ in number', he writes, 'also differ in essence, and never do things differ in number without also differing in essence. *Here let the Theologians take notice*' (233).

Parfit is not so sure. He goes on to envisage a more advanced transporter which sends the same information to Mars without destroying my brain and body on earth. There would thus be two autonomous versions of me indistinguishable in time and space but not in other ways. One might, however, develop the story further. Suppose the Earth-me were to sustain a serious brain-injury that destroyed all personal memories and seriously altered its character: which would have the better claim to my 'identity' — the Mars-me, with all 'my' memories and character intact, and with an unqualified conviction of his right to use my name, or the Earth-me, with nothing but a sad remnant of my consciousness to console himself with? Swinburne, I suspect, would decide in favour of my really being the latter. Parfit argues that what the Teletransporter fiction really points to is that there is no 'deep further fact' (309) about any of us — nothing is or could be added to my utterly individualised 'nature', that is, to the human system of inter-related phenomena which has been successfully replicated on Mars, to make it personal, and that this is why my 'special concern' should focus on the continued rational functioning of my nature or natures, since that is all there is to be concerned about. In other words, he agrees with Milton that the terms nature and person are indistinguishable. I believe both positions are inadequate. Swinburne's 'something ultimate' is exposed by the story as elusive to the point of nonenity, but neither Milton nor Parfit are justified in denying the distinction between nature and person.

This can be shown by means of a sequel to Parfit's science fiction. Suppose that after it sustained its brain-injuries, the Earth-me was sent to the Moon in a body-destroying transporter for treatment which proved unsuccessful. The Moon-me died, and so, eventually, did the Mars-me. There were thus three versions of me, the Earth-me (whole and brain damaged); the Mars me (whole) and the Moon-me (brain damaged). Some years later, a new Replicator is developed which reconstitutes 'bodies' from computer records out of the original matter of which they were composed, and which repairs substantial injuries to bodies so resurrected. I am revived in all three versions, the two brain-damaged versions recovering their facu'ties but finding themselves unable to recall their brain-damaged lives, though retaining a sense of inchoate misery such as persists after a forgotten nightmare. In the brave new world into which the three of us have been resurrected two further technologies have been developed — experiential recall and alterity penetration. With the former I can 'relive' past experiences, with the latter I can experience someone else's thoughts and sensations as if they were my own, and in combination the two technologies enable me to 'live' the past experiences of others and afterwards compare them with my own. What would happen when the various versions of myself were thus put in touch with their past selves and with each other?

It is clear, I think, that if on coming round from recall of their brain-damaged state, the Earth-me or the Moon-me were to declare, 'The creature who went through that nightmare was a horribly distorted version of me', or alternatively 'simply was not me at all', their verdicts would have to be accepted: the brain-damage was or was not such as to destroy *me*. It is not plausible, I suggest, to imagine them coming to different conclusions on this matter. More interesting is the question of how alterity penetration between the various versions of me would compare with alterity penetration of someone other than myself. I suggest that the latter would be interesting, that I would find someone else's life more or less like mine, but that the former would involve recognition of the other lives as 'mine'. I would accordingly recognise my alter egos as consubstantial with me, as separate persons, with whom I shared, not just the generic abstraction, human nature, but the nature or substance of *me*. Thus if Parfit's fictionalising is a valid procedure it can be used to distinguish between the terms nature and person in spite of his arguments to the contrary.

But that still leaves us with the question of what it is that makes the resurrected Earth-me, Mars-me and Moon-me different persons? Apparently nothing more than the fact that three identical natures are materially and so spatially separate from one another. This distinction, however, is not as unimportant as Parfit's conclusions might be taken to imply. (Here Milton's argument in *The Art of Logic* comes into its own.) More is entailed in difference in number than mere difference of location. Each of my resurrected selves can relate to the other; each would have a distinctive relationship with my resurrected wife and children; my resurrected parents would have to decide if they were mother and father to one or all of us. Each of us would have separate futures, and it is by no means certain that after, say, twenty years of separate living, we would feel as uncontentiously one in nature when we met up once again for a session of total recall and alterity penetration as we once did. This suggests that the 'deep further fact' about a specific human nature by which it is constituted as a person is not a fact *in* it, but a fact (at any rate in the first instance) *about* it. I am what I am by virtue of my place in the inter-personal nexus, just as a word means what it means by virtue of its place in an inter-verbal nexus.

8. But would this 'deep further fact' *about* me mean very much? To answer this question we will need to look at some arguments of Plantinga's (1974) based on possible world logic. 'An object x has a property P essentially', Plantinga suggests, '. . . if and only if x has P in every [possible] world in which x exists' (60). He defines a possible world as 'a possible state of affairs — one that is possible in a broadly logical sense' (44). There are trivial essential properties, he argues, such as *'being something or other'* (60), and properties which are essential to me but which I do not have in the world that obtains. For example, there is a possible world in which I am a champion snooker player. Being a champion snooker player in world S is thus a property of mine in the world that obtains and in every other possible world, nor is it a trivial essential property because it means that I am the kind of thing that can have a plan of life which involves bodily skills. But can we go further? Plantinga asks. Do I 'have an *essence*, or *haecceity*, or *individual nature?*' (79). Such a property would be an essential property, exclusive to me, not only in this but in every possible world, nor could there be a possible world in which something other than me had this property.

To show that I could have such a *haecceity*, Plantinga tells the story of a Mayor of Boston, Curley Smith by name, who is offered a bribe at 10 a.m. on 10 November 1973. For Plantinga's purposes, we have to assume that Curley is 'significantly free' to accept or reject this bribe. He accepts it. Logically there is a possible world in which he rejects it. But, Plantinga asks, could an omnipotent God have created such a world? He thinks not: Curley would have stopped him. But suppose Curley is such that in every possible world in which he enjoyed significant freedom he would freely evince a depravity like that he exhibited in the world that obtains on 10 November 1973. That would mean, Plantinga suggests, that Curley has the essential property of transworld depravity. In other words, Plantinga holds that it is possible to think of people exercising their freedom in a way that is *characteristic* of their individual essences.

Does this argument make sense in terms of the distinctions between nature and person which Parfit's fiction suggested to us? Specifically, could an individual essence constituted by a unique placement within the inter-personal nexus entail specific essential properties involving action? I think it could. In this view, for Curley to be Curley, he would have to have Curley-specifying relationships as well as the nature or substance of Curley. In consequence of his thus being the person Curley, there would be a Curley-type consistency in the ensemble of the internal operations of his life and their consequences in action. This consistency would include not just his consciousness or sense of himself, but his unconscious practical reasoning also and the mechanisms outside consciousness enabling him to decide when to act. His personal unity would not necessarily be threatened, therefore, by his enclosing what seem to be self-contained unconscious mental processes like those proposed by Freud and Dennett. Curleyness would be the mark of Curley as a whole and could include (but would not be identical with) what christians and others might wish to call his soul (assuming he has such a thing). What such Curleyness most emphatically would not presuppose or require, however, would be a Cartesian ghost in the Curley machine.

Its existence could never, of course, be positively demonstrated, but there is nothing illogical in declaring it to be a possible — indeed a likely — outcome of the action on Curley's particular human nature of key personal relationships in his life. These would not include all the people he ever met by any means — his experience of the nurse who helped deliver him, or of the janitor in City Hall to whom he nods of a morning would probably not be essential to it: in practice, the defining relationships contributing to Curleyness would be his genetic relationship with his parents and certain crucial influences upon him in the early months and years of life, culminating in his earliest rational activity involving other people, out of which would develop over the years an increasingly individual style of choosing. Curley's life could ultimately make sense — from its rudimentary beginnings to its vigorous maturity to its possibly rambling conclusion it might constitute a whole. In Newman's words (1870), Curley could logically exercise 'the prerogative of completing his inchoate and rudimental nature . . . out of the living elements with which his mind began to be' (349). I do not deny that in principle events could so turn out that Curley stopped being Curley, that his relationships with the world and other people could become so incoherent that his actions in 1978 might not be attributable to the bribable Curley of 1973. It has yet to be shown, however (reported cases of multiple personality notwithstanding), that a truly new person could take over Curley's nature. In general we find ourselves and other people unfolding in a way that makes sense, that we can 'identify' with.

But would this 'deep further fact' about Curley, arising out of his being thus placed in the inter-personal nexus, be sufficiently stable and specific to be given a proper name? If it were a consequence of divine providence, the answer is clearly yes. A God's-eye view of possible worlds would see which relationships were necessary for the realisation of Curley's *haecceity* and which not, so that if God wanted to make Curley, either for Curley's own sake or because his life was essential to the life of someone whom God *did* want to make, then God would have to give him Curley-specifying relationships and all that they might entail, when linked to Curley's nature and the opportunities for action possible in a Curley-containing world.

Let us suppose, however, that the universe is godless. If it is wholly determined and there is no free will, then whether my life has or has not sufficient coherence to be properly regarded as a whole is a matter of chance and it is not clear that any one could reach a firm conclusion on the matter. On the other hand, if there is a free will but freedom is as blankly unpredictable as Swinburne argues it is, the actions of the shapers of my personality before it becomes capable of acting for itself must be inherently unreliable and my *haecceity* radically contingent. Had there been a God, in other words, he would have been unable to create *me*. But what if, as Plantinga maintains, it makes sense to hypothesise a certain-to-be-corrupted Curleyness at Curley's core, or in his 'heart', even if he is free? In such a case it would also make sense to think of there being a certainty of response to Curley in the hearts of those persons whose action on his consciousness is a precondition of Curleyness being instantiated. In other words, personal and inter-personal stability would imply each other. This would not guarantee me the absolute *haecceity* consequent on a relationship with God, but it would make the notion of true identity a practical

115

and interesting one. In other words, unless there is a God, the coherence of the notion of true personal identity depends on it being possible in principle to predict the actions of the 'heart', in the sense that word has in the motto on Newman's coat of arms and in the title of this chapter. Only if we are free and stable in our relationships can we be free and stable in our personalities, and vice versa. It is necessary for heart to speak to heart.

9. But does it make sense to speak of the anomalous actions of someone with a heart being predictable either by God or by other similarly anomalous beings? Swinburne thinks that if anomalousness implies genuine freedom it does not. Hence his definition (1977) of omniscience.

> A person *P* is omniscient at a time *t* if and only if he knows of every true proposition about *t* or an earlier time that it is true *and* also he knows of every true proposition about a time later than *t*, such than what it reports is physically necessitated by some cause at *t* or earlier, that it is true. (175).

Swinburne thus denies God foreknowledge of his own future free actions, but this is surely to go too far. For if God is omniscient he must know himself; he must know whether he is capable of acting stupidly, or wickedly, or unlovingly. He must know his own preferences — whether, in a given world, he would wish to punish Curley for his turpitude, or tolerate him, or forgive him and grant him eternal joy. He must also know what possible state of affairs he could bring about, and every possible contingency that might arise from such states of affairs, and what decisions he would make in the light of every possible free choice which any possible freely-acting creature might make. In short, it is impossible to imagine how a God with the kind of omniscience Swinburne predicates of him could ever surprise himself, unless he were indeed 'heartless', unless the 'further deep fact', the 'something ultimate' that constituted him as a person, were merely a principle of wilfulness, a capacity to act without regard to what is the case. But that would be to make divine freedom radically irrational, which is inconsistent with the idea of God and with the idea of freedom. As Aristotle taught, freedom requires the agent to have a character and a plan of life — in God's case a heart and providential intentions.

Does that mean, however, that God is *determined* by his heart? Certainly, if, as Kant (1783) held, God has no criteria for acting except those of reason, for then he would be 'determined in his eternal reason' (109). But we may think of God as 'choosing' in a far more radical sense, if we hold him to be capable of preferring this possible creaturely *haecceity* to that (though both are equally good), or if the instantiation of one creaturely *haecceity* required an interpersonal nexus which precluded the instantiation of a second, equally good creaturely *haecceity*. In such cases God's heart would choose. But if God has a heart, and in consequence can be certain how he will choose in advance of doing so in a given contingency, and if he instantiates the hearts of his creatures in one of the highly specific sets of circumstances which their developing as persons requires, will he not have as good a knowledge of their hearts as of his own, and will he not therefore have the same kind of advance knowledge of their future actions as he has of his own, even in the absence of physical causality in such cases?

10. The experience of reading *Paradise Lost* and *Paradise Regain'd* suggests (though of course does not prove) that an affirmative answer to this question would be appropriate. In Book III of *Paradise Lost* the Father prophesies the fall and mankind's subsequent redemption — 'Man shall not quite be lost, but sav'd who will' (173). He then states the requirement of Justice for 'rigid satisfaction, death for death' (212). Finally the Son offers to meet this requirement by offering up his own life. Unlike the prophesy of the fall which (possibly because it refers to a distant event) seems to determine Adam and Eve's behaviour in advance, the Father's certainty that mankind will be redeemed does not seem to compromise the Son's freedom in the least, nor does the confidence shown by the Father and the Son in the latter's success in fulfilling his promise. Swinburne's arguments, however, suggest that we should have anxieties on both counts. I believe that we do not do so because of a spontaneous intuition that the Father really could know the Son and the Son really could know himself well enough for both to be confident about the future choices of the latter.

Both poems are thus predicated (convincingly I believe) on the heroic steadfastness of the Son's heart. We have noted the difficulties which Milton encounters in *Christian Doctrine* as a consequence of his denial of any distinction between nature and person in his account of the incarnation. For reasons of political prudence as well as literary tact, he avoids discussion of this problem in *Paradise Regain'd*. Instead he lights on the simple concept of transworld identity to suggest that the Jesus of the later poem is properly called 'Son of God' in the exact and unique sense which that title has when attributed to the Son in the earlier one. Objectively, of course, only one world obtains in both poems, but the relation of Jesus's world to that of the pre-incarnate Son in the two poems is for a time the subjective equivalent of the relation of one possible world to another. The Jesus of *Paradise Regain'd* has no memories or direct knowledge of his pre-incarnate state, yet he is readily understood to be one and the same person as the Son in *Paradise Lost* because in an apparently completely different interpersonal context he evinces that transworld holiness of life which characterises the Son's heart. In both poems Messiah-Jesus defines himself as a person by freely discovering, accepting and honouring in his heart the terms of his uniquely filial relation with the Father.

11. The self-knowledge and anticipatory powers of the Father and the Son in Milton's poems, however, do not carry the argument all that far forward, since their relationship is a sublime mystery. More analysable examples are needed to flesh out our understanding of the predictability on which personhood and free will seem, paradoxically perhaps, to depend. I suggest that such examples can be found in the treatment of friendship in the writings of Newman, *The Portrait of a Lady* and the Second Book of Samuel. Even with these examples, however, the results of such an analysis can only be very tentative at this stage.

In an early description of the cast of Isabel's mind to which reference has already been made, James writes:

> She had a theory . . . that one should be one of the best, should be conscious of a fine organisation (she couldn't help knowing that her organisation was fine), should move in a realm of light, of natural wisdom, of happy impulse, of inspiration gracefully chronic. It was almost as unnecesary to cultivate doubt of one's self as to cultivate doubt of one's best friend: one should try to be one's own best friend and to give oneself, in this manner, distinguished company. (68)

A related remark on the theme of knowing and trusting a friend occurs in some jottings of Newman. The passage, quoted by Ferreira (1980) reads:

> On revelation being directed to a person and devotional and how this affects the question. You may examine with your *will* determinedly fixed. As when a friend is accused, you do

118

not let yourself doubt him *at all,* till he is found guilty. (114
— epigraph)

If we bear in mind Newman's belief that knowledge is personal,
much as it is for Polanyi, and that such intimate and subjective
states as 'devotion' are for him powerful 'subsidiary' sources of it,
the closeness of his position to Isabel's is quite striking. Both kinds
of conviction, about a friend or a belief, are also convictions about
one's self, about the legitimacy of making up one's mind with the
resources made available by a constitution more or less 'fine', and
they are held independently (if necessary) of such evidence as
might be presented scientifically or forensically — until, of course,
one discovers that Madame Merle is vile or one's friend is guilty.
The question we need to address, therefore, is whether convictions
about other people held in this way may properly be regarded as
knowledge, since in the last analysis they seem to be falsifiable, as
the history of Newman's convictions about his brethren and of
Isabel's about her husband seemingly confirm.

The fact that mistakes are sometimes made in this area,
however, is not evidence that they are invariably so. Nor is it clear
that I cannot distinguish after the event between what it felt like
to believe what proved to be an error, and what it felt like to
believe what proved to be the case. Indeed we may suppose that
Newman's misjudgements of Frederick Faber, and his subsequent
recognition of them as misjudgements, may properly have
confirmed rather than weakened his certitude concerning
Ambrose St John's loyalty and affection. In the same way, it may
well be that Isabel's faith in herself is ultimately vindicated. Fuller
discussion of the final scene has to be reserved for a later stage in
the argument. However, there is an important earlier passage
which might support such a claim. Isabel has married Gilbert, and
is beginning to think that she may have done so 'on a factitious
theory' (II 193) and that he is not, after all, 'better than anyone
else'. At this point, Gilbert suggests to her that she has too many
ideas and that she ought to get rid of them; but James is quick to
assure us that it was not her opinions Gilbert objected to — she
had none. 'What he had meant had been the whole thing — her
character, the way she felt, the way she judged. This was what she
had kept in reserve; this is what he had not known until he found
himself . . . set face to face with it' (II 195). This suggests that
Gilbert may have discovered Isabel's heart and learned to fear it.
The upshot of her mistake in marrying him would thus be to

119

confirm her original 'theory' about the fineness of her own constitution and the appropriateness for her of ultimate self-trust. Whether such a reading of her self-awareness is justified or not depends, of course, on how we assess the final scene. All we can say at this stage is that it seems Isabel does have a heart, that in an important way it may centre her life, and that she and Gilbert may have truly understood it.

12. The radical ambivalence of James's writing, however, makes discussion of all the issues involved in this problem very difficult. In order to clarify at least some of them in this necessarily provisional treatment of my topic, I turn now to a simpler narrative mode, namely the account of the friendship of David and Jonathan in the Second Book of Samuel, chapter 20.

It is clear from this narrative that Jonathan has the opportunity and the power to betray David into the hands of Saul, that David trusts him not to do so, and that that trust is vindicated. Let us suppose Jonathan's actions to be free in the fullest sense. Can we say that therefore David's trust must fall short of knowledge? Provided that we confine discussion to knowledge of Jonathan's heart, I think not. David can know Jonathan would never willingly betray him even though Jonathan is genuinely free to do so. But does that mean that David can predict how Jonathan will act in the detailed circumstances of their plan to effect David's escape, supposing, that is, no unforeseen circumstances arise to complicate its implementation? Kenny would suggest not, that no specific bodily movements in Jonathan could be predicted from a knowledge of his desire to help David and his decision that those wants could best be fulfilled by his signalling to David in the manner agreed between them. Thus, according to Kenny, David would never be able to predict the exact moment when Jonathan would send his young attendant in search of his arrows. But this is to suppose that we must move either with machine-like regularity or with random unpredictability. But if Polanyi is right, the exercise of every skill is informed by 'unspecifiable personal coefficients supplied by the . . . mind' (262). Such personal coefficients make us recognisable to each other as properly functioning (and not malfunctioning or eccentrically functioning) individuals: 'we experience another person's similar [but not identical] faculties', Polanyi suggests, 'as the presence of that person's mind' (263). Thus David in his hideout, watching Jonathan with his young attendant walking across the country, might indeed be able to anticipate his friend's every move — subsidiarily — just as tennis players can sometimes anticipate each other's strokes with perfect accuracy.

13. It is entirely plausible, therefore, to think of the mind-body complex as both anomalous in terms of known physical laws and predictable in action as well as in disposition. For this reason I question Swinburne's contention that the future free actions of human beings must be unknowable in principle even to an omniscient God. If there is such a God we may logically suppose him capable of knowing his creatures by all the means that David could know Jonathan, Newman Ambrose St John and Gilbert Osmund his wife — but with infinitely greater fullness. He would know them perfectly in terms of the unspecifiable personal coefficients, the skills, the wants and the inter-personal relationships which constitute their hearts. He could therefore anticipate perfectly all that they freely do as voluntary and intending agents, in the details of their bodily movements and in the evolution of their personal being.

It is important to clarify what I have attempted to achieve in this chapter. I have not shown that human beings are in fact free; I have only attempted to specify the conditions required for their being so. These are that they should be individuated in terms of a nature and further in terms of personal specifity arising out of their relations with others and in consequence of their actions. If the actions arising out of such a complex cohere and suggest a wholeness of life, we have evidence of what, following Newman, I have called a 'heart'. What that ultimate personal reality is objectively depends on the kind of universe in which we live. If it is a God-centred universe, then my personal essence is determined finally in terms of my individual relationship with God, and through him with other persons. But even if we inhabit a godless universe, two kinds of partial knowledge may be possible, knowledge arising from the operation of known laws and knowledge of hearts. Provided the latter are stable, provided, that is, as co-definers of each other's hearts, we are each of us capable of acting with sufficient wholeness to allow the lives of others similarly to cohere, then personal *haecceity*, while not an absolute, may be regarded as a working reality. If, however, freedom is such as to preclude effective knowableness, as Kenny alleges of the level of mind and as Swinburne alleges of all action, divine or human, then the notion of personal essence either ceases to be viable or is reduced to a meaningless abstraction. But in that case, there is nothing to which freedom can be attributed. Fortunately that would not seem to be an obvious conclusion. At the very least we may look for evidence of sufficient stability and sufficient knowledge between persons to examine further the potentialities of the human heart.

6

Social Determinism and Moral Laws

*1. Social determination of personality 2. Bakhtin on introspection 3.
Ideological subjectivities 4. Godwin's Satan 5. Godwin on self-denial
6. Parfit on self-denial 7. Social contexts in James 8. Three sets of
wants 9. Wants and norms in Isabel's practical reasoning 10.
Freedom as a value 11. The drift towards norms 12. Norms and the
sense of self 13. Selfhood and back-sliding*

1. In the last chapter I examined what Parfit derisively calls the
'deep further fact' which some philosophers hold must be added
to this or that human nature to constitute it as a person. I
suggested that the action on such a nature of key elements in its
interpersonal situation *might* be sufficient to constitute a uniquely
self-developing human 'heart', an essence to which 'characteristic' actions could be attributed. In a God-centred universe such
a personal essence would be providentially anticipated and
brought into being, it would be absolute. In a godless universe, its
stability and wholeness would be a consequence of chance interactions in early life and its stability and long-term coherence
would be conditional, but at least in the generality of cases more
than a merely continuous and variously unfolding nature would
unite the adult of fifty to the child of eight. It is not irrational,
therefore, to hold that a heart made specific by it place in the inter-
personal nexus constitutes identity in its full sense.

It does not follow, however, that if there is a personal element
in what we are and do, it will be identifiable as such to introspection or external observation. On the contrary, if the heart is
constituted essentially by factors external to it, as a word's meaning is constituted by its context, and if those factors include (as
they must) much that is impersonal, then nothing a person is or

does can ever be purely personal. *Haecceity* might be no more than an effect. This is the conclusion which Bakhtin reaches when he asserts that there is no real dividing line between psyche and ideology and attacks phenomenological analysis (to which the Pope is indebted and which has the affinities with the thought of Polanyi and Davidson) on the grounds that the human subject cannot be discussed apart from the world in which it comes into being. The functional psychology on which phenomenologists 'take their stand' (31n), he argues, takes for its object 'not the *what* of experience but its how' (30), and so distinguishes between '*the content of experience*' which deals with 'nature, culture and history' on the one hand, and the functions of such contents in '*the closed system of individual psychic life*' on the other. This means, he suggests, that in phenemonological discourse 'everything regarded as meaning ends up being excluded without trace from the scope of the psyche', since nothing is regarded as pertinent to an account of its operations but 'the functioning of separate referential contents arranged in some sort of individual constellation called "the individual soul"'.

The Acting Person seems to make just this mistake. The Pope insists, for example, that his book is not concerned with 'moral values as such, this being the domain of ethics' (12), and that his subject is the 'actual dynamic involvement' in actions, that is the *structure* of morally significant events in the mind, not any specific instances of them. At the end of his book he admits to finding the question of 'man's "existential status", the status of his being or existing, the whole truth about his limitations and his ontic contingency' (356) a 'disturbing' one. All this suggests a tendency in his thought towards what Bakhtin calls 'ontologizing ideological notions, providing them with an autonomous sphere of ideal being' (31n). Effectively the Pope ignores (as Swinburne, Plantinga, Kenny, Davidson and Dennett do also) what for Bakhtin is crucial — the determining action of ideology on conceptualisation, and in particular on the *sign* of the person. Unless this is understood, he contends, all discourse about 'the person' is deficient in self-awareness.

2. This applies particularly to the most deliberate manifestation of self-awareness — introspection. Bakhtin admits that '*to understand* means to refer a particular inner sign to a unity consisting of other inner signs, to perceive it in the context of a particular psyche' (35), and that an 'outer sign expression, an utterance' (36), can give 'outer sign expression to inner signs', and require

'the receiver of the utterance to refer to an inner context, i.e., . . .
a purely psychological kind of understanding'. He acknowledges,
therefore, that in 'its pure form, the inner sign, i.e. experience,
is receivable only by self-observation (introspection)'. But, he
contends, 'inner sign as such can also be outer sign'. Indeed the
'results of introspection in its process of self-clarification must
necessarily be expressed outwardly . . . Introspection, functioning
as such, follows a course from inner to outer signs'. Precisely as
a mode of understanding it places experience in 'a context made
up of other signs we understand' (since a 'sign can be illuminated
only with the help of another sign'). It follows that as 'a kind of
understanding' (37) even introspection 'inevitably proceeds in some
specific ideological direction', for the other signs will be necessarily
composed into an ideological frame of reference. In any case
introspection invariably 'aims at elucidating [the] inner sign, at
advancing it to the highest degree of semiotic definiteness': in effect,
we clarify our introspection by putting it into words. 'This process
reaches its limit', Bakhtin argues, 'when the object of introspection' becomes an object also 'of ordinary, objective, ideological
(semiotic) observation'. In any case, the 'understanding of any sign,
whether inner or outer', is inseparable, he claims, from the '*situation in which the sign is implemented*'. Even the inner sign is always
illuminated by, irradiated with 'an aggregate of facts from external experience', that is, of 'a *social situation*'. 'Complete disregard
of social orientation [he concludes] leads to a complete extinguish-
ment of experience . . . *the sign and its social situation are inextricably
fused together.*'

3. This is a difficult argument to counter because at the level
of signs it seems impregnable. A pure, theoretically general signification of subjectivity does not seem possible and must therefore be
regarded as undiscussable. Just as James alerts us to the intentionality relativising all rationalisation, so Bakhtin requires us to
see the sign of the person as being determined by the impersonal,
historical order in which it is made. And against which it is made,
since in marxist theory all social relationships and therefore all sign-
making are inherently combatitive. Analysis lends support to this
general contention. Thus Hume's urbane philosopher, James's
interrogatively self-conscious rationaliser, the Pope's acting person,
Dennett's deterministic deliberator, Swinburne's 'something
ultimate', Plantinga's *haecceity*, Davidson's rationaliser and Kenny's
hypothetical self slipping poison into his son's porridge, are none
of them the neutral examples of thinking and willing they purport

to be. Neither the self-effacing humour of some of the examples, nor the relentless abstraction of others succeed in concealing this. The Pope's scholastic and phenomenological terminology, for example, which so carefully avoids the politically or socially specific, can be read as a measured challenge, in its uncompromising universalism, to the social determinism of the official ideology with which he had to contend as Archbishop of Kraków. Dennett's deliberator, on the other hand, is exposed in the metaphor of elbow room: like honest American individualists, making their own way in the world, his self-controllers are not crowded out either by nature or by other deliberators. By way of contrast, Kenny's is an ambience in which reference to elbows would be inept: his characteristically modest irony guarantees the propriety of conduct premissed on wants. Or so each can be made to appear. What at any rate is clear is that neither the uses philosophers find for the word 'person', nor individual human minds, are ever demonstrably neutral in ideological terms: generalisation is always a locally relevant tactic.

4. The only way of countering this argument would be to establish that the human heart might be able to act in its own way, that personal *haecceity* is not necesarily like the *haecceity* of a great painting, which may be properly regarded as supervening passively on the material conditions of its existence, but in its own right can make a difference to reality. The value of being able to show this is illustrated in the work of William Godwin, a social determinist like Bakhtin, who also wrote during a period of revolutionary transformation, and like Bakhtin was eager to establish significant relationships between mental life and history.

In *Enquiry concerning Political Justice and Its Influence on Morals and Happiness* (1798), Godwin proposes a strictly determinist account of human existence, explicitly and repeatedly denying the possibility of transcendence in action. For him the crucial question about action is not whether it is free but whether it is 'voluntary', by which he means intentional, that is, performed for, and so determined by, reasons thought out in advance on the basis of an empirically acquired knowledge of causes and effects. He accordingly represents character as being virtually entirely the product of social conditioning, and human relationships as amenable to indefinite improvement from generation to generation through education in the truths revealed by reason. This unyielding rationalism was notoriously to cause some of his contemporaries (notably Wordsworth) much pain, and it now appears aridly naive. It also tends to confirm Bakhtin's arguments about the inherently ideological thrust of the sign of the person: Godwin's reasonable human being is able to absorb revolutionary into mental change, and so bypass the challenge of French revolutionary practice by affirming the ends of a radical social programme without willing the political means.

The starkness of Godwin's system, however, has the virtue of exposing the implications of his premisses. His account of social conditioning is entirely uncompromising, and at one point is illustrated by a highly relevant example:

> poetical readers have commonly remarked Milton's devil to be a being of considerable virtue. It must be admitted that his energies centered too much in personal regards. But why did he rebel against his maker? It was, as he himself informs us, because he saw no sufficient reason, for that inequality of rank and power, which the creator assumed. It was because prescription and precedent form no adequate ground for implicit faith. After his fall, why did he still cherish the spirit of opposition? From a persuasion that he was harshly and injuriously treated. He was not discouraged by the apparent inequality of the contest: because a sense of reason and justice was stronger in his mind, than a sense of brute force; because he had much of the feelings of an Epicetus or a Cato, and little of those of a slave. He bore his torments with fortitude, because he disdained to be subdued by despotic power. He sought revenge, because he could not think with tameness of the unexpostulating authority that assumed to dispose of him. How beneficial and illustrious might the temper from which these qualities flowed, have been found, with a small diversity of situation. (I 323-4)

The last phrase is particularly telling. Godwin wishes to represent Satan as an intelligent and impassioned figure, potentially heroic, yet it needs only 'a small diversity of situation' to make him what he is. His Satan is thus far less robust a *person* than Plantinga's cheerfully venal Curley Smith. There is no *haecceity* in this Satan's acting because he is wholly determined. In consequence he is prey *essentially* to every wind that blows.

5. Bakhtin's is a subtler position than Godwin's but, as the deconstructionist extentions of formalist arguments which I referred to in the Introduction have shown, the problem of radical instability does not disappear when transposed into the order of

signs. Marxist theory attempts to resolve it by subordinating theory to practice, and individual consciousness to class consciousness. The sliding of signifiers in theoretical discourse, and the radical instability of consciousness are thus allegedly anchored in the material specificity of history. I shall address the problem of centrelessness inherent in both formalism and determinism in a different way in the penultimate chapter. For the present, however, I wish to focus on the significance of Godwin's response to it, and of Parfit's important recent revival of some of Godwin's arguments.

Godwin introduces *Political Justice* by listing the principles he thinks his book establishes. He identifies 'pleasure or happiness' (I xxiii) as the 'true object of moral and political disquisition', and distinguishes between the primary pleasures of the senses and 'certain secondary pleasures, as the pleasures of intellectual feeling, the pleasures of sympathy, and the pleasures of self-approbation'. The latter, he suggests, are 'probably more exquisite' than the former. At any rate, the 'most desirable state of man, is that, in which he has access to all these sources of pleasure, and is in possession of a happiness the most varied and uninterrupted'. Government, Godwin maintains, was introduced to control 'injustice and violence' (I xxiv), but 'as it was forced upon mankind by their vices, so has it commonly been creative of their ignorance and mistake', offering 'new occasions and temptation' for the perpetration of the injustices it was intended to suppress. Specifically government threatens the 'pleasures of self-approbation, together with the cultivation of all our pleasures' by suppressing personal independence. An unjust, authoritarian society — the *ancien régime* — is thus to blame for the false sensibilities and perceptions of those subjected to it.

There are some gratuitous assumptions here but no seriously inconsistent arguments. It is not obvious, for example, that sampling the range of pleasures makes for more happiness than concentrating on one or two of the most vividly enjoyable, or that primitive societies are necessarily 'unjust'. But Godwin's belief that a reduction of state power and a redistribution of wealth would offer more scope for rational voluntariness and so for sustained improvement in the human lot, while optimistic, has never been tested and is at least arguable. The real difficulty confronting him is that his determinism apparently supports a descriptivist morality with which he feels uncomfortable. The problem of social determinism, with which I am chiefly concerned in this chapter, is thus linked to a second, that of moral relativism.

Like many Humeans, Godwin feels the need for norms, for 'a rule of the utmost universality' (I xxv), in spite of his determinist principles, and he claims to have found one in a utilitarian version of the golden rule. 'Justice', he writes, 'is a rule of conduct originating in the connection of one percipient being with another' (I 126). It provides the 'true standard of the conduct of one man towards another' (I xvv) and 'proposes to itself the production of the greatest sum of pleasure or happiness'. In 'a loose and general way' (I 126), it entitles each to 'equal attention'; but since the highest, completest forms of happiness include the intellectual, sympathetic and self-approving pleasures, those who are capable of enjoying or bestowing the latter have rights to more consideration than the rest. Godwinian justice thus requires considerable powers of disinterested self-detachment in those who pursue it. 'I am bound to employ my talents', Godwin writes '. . . for the production of the greatest quantity of general good' (I 135). To this end I should act not just as my feelings direct but in the light of reasons, for reason 'though it has no tendency to excite us to action' (I xxvi), being 'merely a balancing of different feelings', enables us to make valid comparisons between 'different excitements' and to act as it suggests is to achieve full voluntariness:

> the perfection of the human character consists in approaching as nearly as possible the voluntary state. We ought to be upon all occasions prepared to render a reason of our actions. We should remove ourselves to the furthest distance from the state of mere inanimate machines. (I 68)

Habit and impluse are thus the enemies of voluntariness and therefore of the ideal state: for Godwin, the theoretical is indeed the only genuine human attitude.

6. Parfit provides an interesting modern parallel to these arguments. Godwin, he points out, presents 'Utilitarianism as a theory about rights' (366), the fundamentally arbitrary element in *Political Justice* being its assumption that those with a greater capacity for contributing to the 'sum of pleasure and happiness' either by giving or enjoying such pleasure and happiness, simply have the *right* to do so at the expense of those with a lesser capacity for giving or enjoying them. Godwin argues, for example, that in the event of a fire, Fénelon's butler — objectively speaking —

would be under an obligation to sacrifice his own coarse life for the intelligent and sensitive life of his employer. But how is such an obligation to self-sacrifice entailed in the world as Godwin understands it, that is in a deterministic world? Parfit claims to have solved this problem — he is contemptuous of non-Humean free-will theories — by showing that attempts to act self-interestedly, or to make the outcomes of action as good as possible, or to act on the basis of common-sense morality, are logically self-defeating, and that the only non-self-defeating plan of life is a strictly rational utilitarianism based on a radical reconsideration of the notion of the importance of personal identity.

Parfit holds (more or less as I do) that 'a person is distinct from his brain and body, and his experiences' (275). But he also argues that

> persons are not separately existing entities. The existence of a person, during any period, just consists in the existence of his brain and body, and the thinking of his thoughts, and the doing of his deeds, and the occurrence of many other physical and mental events.

As we noted earlier, he believes that it follows from this that

> physical continuity is the least important element in a person's continued existence. What we value, in ourselves and others, is not the continued existence of the same particular brains and bodies. What we value are the various relations between ourselves and others, whom and what we love, our ambitions, achievements, commitments, emotions, memories and several other psychological features. Some of us would also want ourselves or others to have bodies that are very similar to our present bodies. But that is not the same as wanting the same particular body to continue to exist. (284)

If I were a rational being, therefore, and, having injured an eye in an accident, I found that immediate treatment in a Moon clinic was the only way of saving it, I would willingly allow myself to be transported there in a Mark 1 (body-destroying) Transporter, and so obliterate the consciousness that is currently me so as to sustain at its optimum level the ensemble of relations between myself and others which I really value: my present consciousness would in effect act towards that ensemble as Fénelon's butler was expected to act towards Fénelon. On comparable grounds, Parfit argues that my attitude to the past should be the same as my attitude to the future. If I rightly regard my non-existence in 1938 with equanimity, I should be capable of feeling the same about my non-existence in 2038, or even 1990. It is no less irrational to prefer the near at hand to the distant, my own children to possible future generations of children, and so forth. What Parfit purports to demonstrate is all that what follows from the Godwinian principle 'I should not act just as my feelings direct but in the light of reasons' is the only non-self-defeating plan of life open to us, provided we disabuse ourselves of everything except what reason shows to be the case about ourselves, our relations with other people and the knowable consequences of action.

It is impossible to do justice to the ingenuity of these arguments in so short a space. Nevertheless they can be quite quickly disposed of in principle. Parfit's error is to ignore the conclusion attributed to Tarski by Polanyi, 'that any formal system in which we could assert a sentence and also reflect on the truth of its assertion must be a self-contradictory' (260). In other words if I accept the injunction to be reasonable, I cannot look to reason to justify my acceptance: logically my reasons for being reasonable must be in me, not in reason. It makes no difference, therefore, that Godwin makes a self-evidently illogical leap onto the raft of justice while Parfit takes command of the supertanker of reason with far greater formality, for not even supertankers are self-loading, self-directing systems; they have to be informed by purposes from the bridge. As Ferreira notes, in a passage to which I have already alluded (quoting Harman's discussion of the rules of inference, and in particular of *modus ponens*):

> Individual assessments of P and *if P then Q* are necessary: there is no impersonally compelling rule which will relieve us of intellectual responsibility. What logic provides are the relations that obtain between propositions; this will not, however, tell us what to accept nor will it provide an invariable legitimation. Toulmin's observation that 'in logic as in morals, the real problem of rational assessment — telling sound arguments from untrustworthy ones . . . requires experience, insight and judgement' applies here as well. (45–6)

It does not follow, in other words, that I should not pursue a plan of life because it is self-defeating. Recognising that it is so, I might still 'instinctively' prefer it: I might judge that it was 'better' to fail in one way than to succeed in another, and my instincts might be 'right'.

7. For this very reason, however, Parfit's arguments can still make a claim on us, for if Newman, Tarski, Toulmin, Harman and Polanyi are correct, rationalism, or at any rate some of its conclusions, even the most extravagant, may prove viable on non-rationalist grounds. Godwin and Parfit rely on their experience, insight and judgement, after all, to develop their arguments; counter-intuitive as some of their conclusions may seem, therefore, they may be worth holding on to, even if for 'reasons' which reason itself cannot supply and which neither Godwin or Parfit would be prepared formally to take account of. This has a particular relevance to the present discussion because *The Portrait of a Lady* apparently takes us by a similar route to similar conclusions. Isabel, for example, makes the interestingly Godwinian claim that she wants 'to be treated with justice' (I 318). She wishes also to treat others so. Like Godwin and Parfit she too needs 'a rule of the utmost universality', and like them she appears ready to commit herself to a life of the utmost self-denial for its sake. Moreover, as a text which invites us to relate sympathetically and not just scientifically or critically with its characters, *The Portrait of a Lady* may take us closer to Godwin and Parfit's 'instinctive reasons' than their own writings do.

Isabel's is a relevant case because, as we have seen, the world of *The Portrait of a Lady* is as susceptible to a determinist reading as Parfit's or Godwin's. Moreover the determinants in which James is especially interested are in effect the cultural ones to which Bakhtin attaches such importance. This is why James is so interested in the minds of expatriate Americans, for becoming an expatriate may involve a degree of emancipation from the powerful social determinations of one's native culture. We are told, for example, that Ralph came to England as child and

> became at last English enough. [But his] outward conformity to the manners that surrounded him was . . . the mask of a mind that greatly enjoyed its independence, on which nothing long imposed itself, and which, naturally inclined to adventure and irony, indulged in a boundless liberty of appreciation. (I 49)

For some of James's characters, however (if not perhaps for

Ralph), the fact that the American ethos is allegedly highly individualistic complicates this issue; by demonstrating their independence of character in Europe, they may merely be affirming their Americanness, and perhaps also illustrating the relative vulnerability of American values in a stronger and older culture. (Such are the possible implications of the characterisations of Henrietta Stackpole and Caspar Goodwood.)

Isabel is involved in these ambiguities from the moment of her arrival in England. She tells Ralph's father that she is 'sure the English are very conventional' (I 78) and he agrees they are, but when she remarks that this cannot leave much room for unexpectedness, Mr Touchett is less sure. 'You can't tell what they'll like', he says to her. 'They're inconsistent; that's their principal interest' (I 79). Isabel is delighted with this prospective variety, yet when Lord Warburton proposes to her, she finds herself instinctively resisting 'his system' (I 144), partly on the grounds that she has 'a system and an orbit of her own', and partly because Caspar has just arrived from America and he has 'no system at all'. The word 'system' here is, of course, thoroughly ambiguous. Is the 'system', which Isabel regards as being in some sense hers, American as against European or is it (either in fact or in her opinion) special to her?

The reference to Caspar further complicates the matter, because we are subsequently told that one of the reasons for Isabel's not being in love with him is that he is so predictable in his uncompromising individualism. When he is alone with her, he talks 'too much about the same subject' (I 165) — presumably his love for her, and he always dresses 'in the same manner . . . the figure, the stuff [is] so drearily usual'. He can therefore be variously interpreted as an entirely individuated non-conformist — with no system at all — or as the nugatory bearer of the unsophisticated individualism of his native country. An exactly complementary ambiguity attaches to Lord Warburton. Is he a sign of a profoundly 'systematized', socially determined upper-class English ethos, or an emancipated nobleman, who can act unpredictably in contrast to the unrelieved predictability of his American rival? In any case what does 'predictability' imply — conditioned inflexibility or a mature fidelity to a clearly perceived plan of life? And would such a plan of life result in deliberate and deterministic 'voluntariness' of a Godwinian kind, or impassioned, existentially self-justifying faithfulness?

8. Clearly, what needs to be shown in this situation is that it

is possible for men and women first to establish a plan of life for themselves, and not simply in consequence of their inheriting a particular culture, and then to act on it. I shall focus on three such plans, the first two of which seem to be premissed in a thoroughly modern fashion on the wants of those who form them. Caspar, for example, wants nothing but to work in the business he has inherited and to win the woman he loves. Gilbert's is a subtler kind of modernity. If the wants on which Caspar premisses his practical reasoning are the traditional ones of love and work, those on which Gilbert claims to conduct his life are the pleasures of good form, aesthetic and social. This can be read as signifying a loss of Americanness and an inability to assimilate the values of Europe in the way Ralph assimilates them — in which case Gilbert may be regarded as a socially marginalised and so humanly vacuous victim of a new cosmopolitanism. On the other hand it can be read as laying bare the hardness of his heart. Finally it can be seen as an intellectually defensible recognition (such as a sympathiser with Pater or Nietzsche might have made) of a terrible truth — that in a world without fixed points of reference, there is nothing to hold on to but the arbitrary, explicitly artificial and ultimately meaningless formalities of life — signifiers with nothing to signify but their own reflexively acknowledged emptiness.

By way of contrast with her lover and her husband, Isabel is unwilling, or at least uncertain, about developing a plan of life simply on the basis of her own wants, however impressive the wants of someone as finely constituted as herself might be. Her problem is that she has to work out the consequences in practical terms of such an intuition. In response to her declaration that she wishes to be treated with justice, Ralph warns her 'that justice to a lovely being is after all a florid sort of sentiment' (I 221). This is a characteristically difficult statement to interpret. Ralph as we have observed, speaks with some authority as a man who has won his spiritual independence, but perhaps in this case he is reacting with some embarrassment to Isabel's declaration because he knows that in the matter of her inheritance he has treated her with some disingeniousness. On the other hand (or perhaps at the same time) he may be gently directing her towards an awareness of the dangers of relying on such grand moral categories as justice in the conduct of everyday life.

In spite of this warning, however, Isabel persists in her search for a vision of justice and a plan for its application to her own circumstances. When the manipulative part played by Madame Merle in the making of her marriage becomes clear to her, for example, she prays, in the midst of her uncertainties. 'Whatever happens to me let me not be unjust . . . let me bear my burdens myself and not shift them upon others!' (II 159). As we have seen, she subseqeuntly makes undertakings to Pansy which take the form, apparently, of absolute obligations. Even more striking is the pressure this 'old passion for justice' (II 356) exercises on her when she recognises that Gilbert's claims on her are specious, yet feels that his apparent sincerity is 'a merit' towards which something is due. In the face of everyone else's scepticism, Isabel persists in this pursuit of objective values, even if with very doubtful success. The exact nature of her difficulty, however, remains obscure. Is her practical reasoning vitiated by pursuit of a chimerical goal (as Ralph's warning implies) or is it confused by fear of the demands justice will make on her, in which case hers would be a classic case of a Thomist conscience struggling to subdue its own wants so as to act according to an objectively valid logic of goodness?

9. In either case, Isabel has two very difficult problems. First, the world in which she lives is not one that reveals the ends of things in their essences, and consequently a self-disclosing system of values is not obviously available to those who live in it; and secondly, though her pursuit of justice is clearly based on the Godwinian intuition that 'justice is a rule of conduct originating in the connection of one percipient being with another', and therefore implies some kind of solidarity between persons, she seems entirely alone in her idealistic commitment to it. She needs, therefore, to belong to society (to avoid an individuality like Caspar's which refuses social adaptation), yet at the same time to resist mere social determination of her values and conduct.

Her relations with Madame Merle and Gilbert can be understood in the light of this dilemma. Isabel is initially drawn to Madame Merle because Madame Merle is wholly without 'tonic wildness' (I 274), 'too perfectly the social animal', who exists 'only in her relations, direct or indirect, with her fellow mortals', and yet who is also 'deep', 'her nature' speaking 'none the less in her behaviour because it spoke in a conventional tongue'. Madame Merle has thus apparently achieved the kind of synthesis of convention and individualism for which Isabel herself is seeking — except that she is also a wicked woman whose secret individuality is grounded in all but flawless willingness to defy the norms implicit in the social conventions which she observes so scrupulously in her outward actions.

Gilbert, on the other hand, presents himself as more overtly the individualist. If Madame Merle's individuality is implicit in her conventionality, Gilbert's respect for social form seems to be a consequence of his having chosen a plan of life for himself. This at any rate is the claim he makes when Isabel confesses to a chronic inability to stabilise her own plans. 'I make a new one every day', she says (I 380) and regards herself as frivolous in consequence: she thinks one should 'choose something very deliberately, and be faithful to that' (I 381). Thus prompted, Gilbert confesses his own chosen path. It is 'to be as quiet as possible . . . Not to worry — not to strive or struggle. To resign myself. To be content with little.' Gilbert is of course being manipulative in this scene, and he is no less so when he tells Isabel that her wandering about as if the world belonged to her is 'beautiful' (II 14), and that everyone ought to make life 'a work of art' (II 15) as she does. But this does not mean that he is also speaking insincerely or untruthfully. There is no reason to doubt that he had indeed made a 'studied . . . wilful renunciation' (I 381) of all that is positive in life except for 'Correggios and crucifixes'.

Moreover, in spite of Isabel's imagination supplying 'the human element which she was sure had not been wanting' (I 383) in this profession, and in spite also of Ralph's believing her 'deluded' (II 75) in inventing a theory about Gilbert, and then loving him 'for his very poverties dressed out as honours', there is a real possibility that she understands and chooses him and what he represents deliberately and clear-sightedly. Perhaps she is afraid of the demands justice might make upon her, and chooses his commitment to form as a way of avoiding them with a substitute ideal almost as good. In any case, even after their marriage has degenerated, she can still sympathise with his desire for its continuance as a matter of form, form not understood merely as social convention but as a quality akin to art, to Correggios and crucifixes — and to justice. Recognising the 'blasphemous sophistry' (II 356) of his arguments against her going to see the dying Ralph, she acknowledges none the less that he has spoken 'in the name of something sacred and precious — the observance of a magnificent form' — indeed it is the sincerity of this profession that, as we have seen, arouses in her once again 'her old passion for justice'. Their marriage thus seems to have been based on almost identical and certainly compatible wants and to break down when Isabel recognises that wants can no longer serve as the premisses of her practical reasoning, that she must act after all in the light of her old passion. If this is so, the last chapter represents her sacrificing everything to that value: like Godwin and Parfit, she accepts claims on her life that extinguish it.

10. In such a case, Isabel's quarrel with her husband is in effect a quarrel with Kenny, if only because Kenny's view of freedom is one which Gilbert would share. It would be possible, after all, to illustrate everything Kenny says about willing in terms of Gilbert's notions of the satisfactory: making Pansy obedient to my will is something I want; x is one way of doing it; y is another way of doing it; but if x not y; I can x; I can y, and I can refrain from either or both; I find that at present there is an opportunity for me to do either or to refrain from doing either or both; I can choose between x and y and inaction, or between choosing and bringing further wants into play, in relation perhaps to other aspects of x and y. I am therefore a free connoisseur of Corregios and crucifixes. To put it another way, freedom based on the defeasibility of practical reasoning about wants does not distinguish in principle between the freedom which Satan and the fallen angels exercise in concluding their great consult at the end of the second book of *Paradise Lost* and the freedom which Adam and Eve enjoy in deciding whether or not to work together in Eden. As Kenny (1975) notes,

> Strength of will . . . is not directly a moral phenomenon; it is a necessary, but not a sufficient condition for a good life: it can be exercised in the pursuit of evil ends or indifferent purposes, and can minister to vices or neutral traits of character as well as to virtues. (107)

This, however, is far from being the obvious and uncontentious observation it seems to be, for the problem with *Paradise Lost* is that Satan's strength of will (as Blake, Godwin, Shelley and Empson point out) invites admiration in itself. Yet so does the serene, intelligent fortitude of Jesus in *Paradise Regain'd*. Kenny might argue that these differences are simply the consequence of strength of will ministering to different traits of character, but this would be to suppose that willing one thing strongly is the same as willing another strongly, that good and bad personal qualities can be linked to willing without affecting either its strength or its nature.

Such a supposition is not obvious. Kenny's identification of spontaneity and indifference thus precludes important possible discriminations; in particular it precludes our considering in what ways freedom itself, and in particular strength of will, might be a value.

11. As we have seen, the Pope holds that willing most emphatically is such a value:

> surrender to the good in truth [he writes] forms in a way a new moral reality within the person. This new reality also has a normative factor and manifests itself in the formulation of norms and in their role in human actions. (156)

In other words, the principles by which we try to act are necessarily and essentially conditioned by our sense of how we act. This is why, in the Pope's words, 'the performance itself of the action by the person is a value' (322). Whether one accepts or rejects the Pope's highly specific account of acting, his arguments in this matter seem convincing. Thus even Kenny's treatment of wants as premises can never have anything but an intermediate status between impulse and norm. I may believe that I am free in all my practical reasoning and that to act intentionally as well as freely all I need is a logic of satisfactoriness because there is no logic of goodness based on the natural ends of things for me to act on; I may also perceive — the counter-example of Gilbert Osmund notwithstanding — that my love for others and my dependence on them and theirs on me, make esteem and joy reciprocal, and I may find myself wanting to take the wants of others into account; but as the Pope's argument and Isabel's example show, I cannot stop there: what I value must be consistent with the *way* I perceive myself and others operating as agents, irrespective of whether or not I *want* to be that kind of agent; and those perceptions, as well as my wants with respect to myself and to them, must be among the assumptions on which my practical reasoning is based.

The arguments of both Godwin and Kenny tend to confirm this conclusion. Both deny that mature human beings can *become* free, one because he thinks it impossible, the other because he thinks that as practical reasoners they are so already to the fullest extent possible. But if we accept either of these beliefs we must modify our wants in the light of it, in other words, we must predicate our practical reasoning on judgements about essences, and specifically about what is revealed of the essences of persons in their acting. But these are general notions about the nature of things; and if they condition the particular answers to questions about what wants are worth wanting, or ought to be pursued or resisted, they necessarily draw practical reasoning into the territory of norms. Even Gilbert would claim that his way of acting on the basis of *his* wants was truer to the nature of things, or rather to the nature of people, than acting such as Isabel apparently attempts in the name of justice. There are thus hypothetical imperatives which tend inexorably to the categorical. Godwin was right: when we act 'voluntarily' we necessarily do so on the basis of 'a rule of the utmost universality'.

12. This structurally integral relationship between action and norms is, however, one of mutual dependence. If beliefs about the nature of acting serve as premises alongside wants in my practical reasoning, my sense of the normative in its turn conditions my beliefs about my capacities as an acting person. The extreme claims of justice felt by Godwin and by Isabel, for example, enable each, reflexively, to form a judgement about how that they themselves might be able to act. Indeed the more absolute or universal the norms against which I so define myself, the more absolutely I am defined. Satan's self-disclosure in *Paradise Lost* is stronger than Gilbert's in *The Portrait of a Lady* because norms are so much clearer and grander in the one world than in the other. The same logic applies to good and worthy actions, however defined. Absolute norms make absolute demands, and a self formed in their light must be willing to surrender itself to them. Fénelon's butler must consign his body to the flames, Parfit must enter his Teletransporter, Samson must commit his life to providence, Jesus in *Paradise Regain'd* must accept the logic of his messianic vocation, and Isabel must offer up her future to the ideal of marriage and fidelity to her word. Irrespective of whether or not such actions are reasonable, wise or good, they constitute and proclaim those who perform them as persons who have seen themselves and the nature of things in a certain light and plan to act accordingly. Acting, however we judge it, may be a source of norms in its own right independently of our wants; but those norms can in turn confirm or disturb our sense of ourselves as agents.

This pattern is strikingly confirmed by Parfit's account of his own conversion to Reductionism. In celebrating his liberation from the self, he secures his selfhood at another level.

The truth [he argues] is very different from what we are inclined to believe. Even if we are not aware of this most of us . . . would be strongly inclined to believe that our continued existence is a deep further fact, distinct from physical and psychological continuity . . . This is not true.

Is this truth depressing? Some may find it so. But I find it liberating and consoling. When I believed that my existence was such a further fact, I seemed imprisoned in myself . . . I now live in the open air. There is still a difference between my life and the lives of other people. But the difference is less . . . I am less concerned about the rest of my life, and more concerned about the lives of others . . .

After Hume thought hard about his arguments, he was thrown into 'the most deplorable condition imaginable, environed in the deepest darkness' . . . The arguments for Reductionism have on me the opposite effect. Thinking hard about these arguments removes the glass between myself and others . . . I care less about my death. This is merely the fact that, after a certain time, none of the experiences that will occur will be related, in certain ways, to my present experiences. Can that matter all that much? . . .

Because it affects my emotions in these ways, I am glad that the Reductionist view is true. This is simply a report of psychological effects. The effects on others may be different. (281–2)

Indeed they may, and that very difference may be a kind of deep further fact about Parfit, which tells us nothing, admittedly, about his continued existence apart from his physical and psychological continuity, but which enables us to think of him, and him to think of himself, as one who has adopted Reductionism for his *own* reasons. He is thus, possibly, the kind of being who is related in a consistent way to what occurs in the world — a way for which his heart or *haecceity* is in some sense responsible. Parfit's Reductionism is Parfit's, just as Godwin's and Isabel's differing versions of Justice are theirs and theirs only. This would explain why persons embrace extreme points of view: the extremism confirms them as persons, and the confirmation of their personal status justifies the very norms which make extreme demands upon them.

13. The note of altruistic fanaticism in the thinking of philosophers such as Godwin and Parfit, and of fictional characters such as Isabel, can thus be explained as a possible

consequence on the one hand of the inevitable drift of practical reasoning towards the normative, and on the other of the mutually reinforcing relationship between norms and agency. With such a structure we could defend ourselves against the ultimately depersonalising logic of social determinism, though such a mutually reinforcing structure would necessarily be a logically frail one. Hence, perhaps, our sense of a defiant perversity in the way Godwin and Parfit present their points of view. Common sense tells us, after all, that there is little enough chance of human intercourse ever being organised according to the principles of Godwinian justice, or Parfitian rationality, yet neither Godwin nor Parfit allows himself to be much disturbed in consequence. Could this be because their reasons for being reasonable are ultimately self-defensive?

James, on the other hand, directly in the voice of the narrator, and indirectly through his characters, notably Ralph, continually focuses on the possibility that Isabel's idealism may indeed express irrational fears about her own existential status rather than effectively constitute her as a person, that the naive idealism of her moral attitudes may result from the vulnerability of her ego. In his important description of her in the sixth chapter, for example, he notes her clear-eyed sense of what it is to act wrongly — it is to inflict 'a sensible injury upon another person . . . to be mean, to be jealous, to be false, to be cruel' (I 68–9) — yet this, plausibly, is how some readers may think she acts towards Caspar in their final scene together, inflicting a sensible injury on him, in panic at the prospect of abandoning the starry-eyed conception of her duty out of which she has constructed an ultimately dishonest version of herself.

There is space in James's text for a more complex reading, however. After the description of Isabel's idealism in the sixth chapter, he adds a remarkable warning: 'Of course the danger of a high spirit was the danger of inconsistency — the danger of keeping up the flag after the place has surrendered; a sort of behaviour so crooked as to be almost a dishonour to the flag', (I 69). Perhaps this is what happens in the last chapter; perhaps we are meant to see Isabel as crookedly flying the flag of justice (to Pansy, to marriage as a magnificent form) even though she has really surrendered to her fear — her fear of passion, of being no one, of having been hopelessly in the wrong. James's carefully chosen expressions, however, have to be given proper weight. The flag is not wholly dishonoured; Isabel may behave crookedly in her last scene, but she may at least be acting. If we read the last chapter pessimistically in the light of the sixth, therefore, we may still think of her as an agent in the full sense, and not the determinant of extra-personal forces. But we may do so only if we also see her as a true backslider. This suggests that the ultimate test of the notions of the person and of norms is whether they can be separated in action by sin. Once again the crucial significance of the tenth book of *Paradise Lost* to the entire tradition of Western humanism becomes apparent: there are thus grounds for thinking that nothing in that tradition really makes sense, if Milton's account of the fall proves, after all, to be incoherent.

7

Evolution and Transcendence

1. I suggested at the end of the last chapter that our preoccupation with our status as moral agents and with extreme moral positions might be explained as no more than a defence against the existential insecurity of consciousness, but that such an explanation would fail if we were to prove ourselves capable of discovering high and serious moral truths and yet of acting on them only intermittently. Evidence of a human capacity to commit sin would thus be evidence also in favour of a mutually reinforcing structure of freedom in the fullest sense and real moral responsibility. But for such an argument to succeed it would have also to explain the experienced insecurity of our lives and to show that that insecurity was consistent with our claim to freedom and objective moral knowledge. In this chapter, therefore, I shall attempt to show that the vulnerability of our egos is inherent in the human condition, but that none the less we may claim to be acting persons and not merely products of impersonal social and biological contexts.

One possible reason for the insecurity of consciousness is suggested by Bakhtin's arguments about the sociality of all signs including that of the person. But it does not seem obvious that social determination of reflexive self-identification would be sufficient on its own to account for such widespread deep-seated insecurity. That insecurity is more easily explained in terms of 'nature', a category which Bakhtin relativises rather too conveniently. By 'nature' I do not mean the individuated nature which I hold to be the basis of personal *haecceity*; nor do I mean 'human nature', which is largely a socially determined concept, nor 'the biological specimen' the functioning of which could never be examined independently of social determinations; I mean only that part of us which in principle operates independently of history in its broadest sense — the genetic processes of human life.

We have to understand ourselves as located between what Elliot Sober (1984) calls 'the group above and the gene below' (26). The only connection (outside a few laboratories in recent years) between these two spheres is the individual organism, and the fact that relations between them appear to be inherently arbitrary accounts, I believe, for the insecurity in our sense of ourselves with which I am concerned. It is here that we discover the element of chance in the human condition which threatens our sense of self-control and of responsibility for what we do. In *The Art of Logic*, Milton quotes Aristotle's judgement that 'Things done through ignorance seem not to be voluntary' (228). Yet certainty of such ignorance seems to be a consequence of modern biological theory, with uncomfortable results for libertarians like Kenny and Davidson (not to mention the Pope), as well as for historical determinists like Bakhtin.

2. As we have already noted, philosophers frequently use the metaphor of levels to show that physiological determinism does not preclude freedom in consciousness. In his celebrated essay, *Chance and Necessity* (1970), Monod applies this metaphor to the relation between the organism and its genetic inheritance, and thereby seriously disturbs the compatibilist's reliance on it. He argues that we must distinguish between the genetic, biochemical level operating as a coded structure of molecules (DNA), and the decoded physiological level in the individual subject, and that the interactions between these levels are inherently arbitrary. The governing interactions by which instructions in the DNA molecule are translated into physiological process, he writes,

> contain several successive steps, bringing into play several components each of which recognizes exclusively its immediate functional partner. The components involved at the beginning of this chain of information-transfer enact their role in complete ignorance of what is 'going on' at the

other end of the chain. (106)

From this he concludes that the nucleic acid code, 'universal in the biosphere', is chemically arbitrary — a blind mechanism comparable with 'a milling machine which notch by notch moves a piece of work through to completion' (106–7), as in 'an assembly line in a machine factory'. Another analogy might be the punched card system in traditional textile-weaving machinery which was a precursor of part of modern computer technology. It is a feature of such systems that *the translation mechanism is strictly irreversible* (107). Information is always conveyed from the punched card or the nucleic acid to the cloth or the organism, and never vice versa. No living thing can 'instruct' its nucleic original about the need for modifications in future encodings; DNA cannot learn from the experiences of the organism.

The discovery that nucleic acid stores process-instructions explains the curious aberration at the end of *Personal Knowledge* and possibly Polanyi's relative lack of influence since its publication. Polanyi ends his essay by suggesting that the machine-like elements in evolution could not operate without a rational input into the biosphere which is independent of its machine-like elements — just as a machine can only operate through the intentions of an operator. The humblest organic process, he maintains, must somehow 'know' what it is about. This Bergsonian hypothesising has little to recommend it. Nucleic acid, on the other hand, solves Polanyi's problem very satisfactorily. DNA contains the 'knowledge' which Polanyi attributes even to germ plasm, but compared with the knowledge to which true intelligence has access, it is radically incomplete since it lacks the second capacity of mind, which seems to have evolved only very late in the thought experiment, and which enables the results effected by changes in coded in-put (the senses) to be evaluated *at the time of in-put* in terms of their effects on *an internally imagined world*. This seems to be the difference between computers (and most animals) and people. The 'intelligence' of nucleic acid may thus be compared to that of brain-damaged human beings who can 'instruct' their bodies how to act, but cannot 'see' and so assess the resulting actions. Unlike human beings, however, a successful evolutionary system only requires an instructing capacity; all it needs in addition to enhance organic fitness in the long term is a small element of instability in the instruction-giving, self-reproducing system, and a very large number of encodings and decodings to counteract the tendency of random changes, as Sober puts it, to 'diminish rather than enhance' (105) performance.

The arbitrariness in this process occurs between levels and not in any one of them: since there is no logical connection between a particular instance of genetic coding and its outcome in the structure of the resulting organism, each can operate without arbitrariness on its own level without excluding arbitrariness from the system. Sober points out that 'the randomness of mutation does not mean that mutations are inherently unpredictable' (104) — it means 'simply that mutations do not occur *because* they would be beneficial' (105). Suppose, for example, that nucleic acid were known to mutate systematically, so that over a given period every possible genetic mutation and combination of mutations would be effected a given number of times. The resulting changes in the related organisms, however, would still be arbitrary. There are two ways this is so. Firstly, there seems to be no natural connection between the molecular instruction and the resulting organic form, any more than there is a natural connection between three dots in morse code and the letter S: very different instruction systems in textile machinery can produce identically patterned cloth. Secondly, there can be no systematic matching of particular changes in the code and particular factors in the environment. At the very most, statistically probable results might be computed, granted a similar degree of predictability in the environment as we are assuming at the level of the code, but even then the 'blindness' of each individual mutation with respect to the organism and its circumstances would be unaffected.

3. Evolution, then, only takes place when changes in the coded instructions happen to enhance the organism's 'teleonomic' performance in life. The word 'teleonomic' is used by Monod to refer to what, like most biologists, he holds to be 'one of the fundamental characteristics common to all living beings without exception: that of being *objects endowed with a purpose or project*' (20). We have already come across this idea in Dennett's account of the thought experiment. It is this, Monod argues, which distinguishes living things 'from all other structures or systems present in the universe' — except, of course, those structures and systems made by living beings themselves, and these lack the two other fundamental properties of life, the power of reproducing and of doing so consistently. (Polanyi would argue that they also lack the capacity to inform their functioning with purposes of their own.) Monod, then, defines 'the essential teleonomic project as

146

consisting in the transmission from generation to generation of the invariance content characteristic of the species' (24). The project to which the biological specimen is thus committed is not contained in its own life, nor on the level at which that life is lived. It is a purpose which includes the transmission of the code. The purpose of the code is admittedly a new biological specimen, but the purpose of the new biological specimen is to transmit the code; neither is its own end.

It follows that if human beings have projects which in any sense are natural to them — purposes which derive from the potentialities inherent in the biological structure they inherit and the relationships they are born into, social relationships included — those projects must always relate to, and be consistent with, the infra-personal teleonomic project which all human beings have been organised to serve, but which they can never experience directly. Thus egoism, the living being's interest in its own present life, is really altruistic: its unfelt purpose is to secure the transmission of the code. Similarly the individual's instinctive or sympathetic involvement with others must ultimately serve selfish reproductive purposes, or at least be consistent with them.

We need to distinguish, therefore, between social and reproductive altruism. Some socially altruistic behaviour, for example, is not biologically altruistic at all. Families which co-operate instead of competing may enhance the reproductive powers of most of their members, and groups so co-operating may operate sanctions against 'anti-social' behaviour which makes the latter reproductively disadvantageous. It does not follow from this, however, that no individual is capable of behaviour which is truly altruistic in a biological sense, that is, which helps the reproductive performance of others not genetically related to the altruist at the expense of his or her own genes, but such altruism would only be possible if no special genetically based factors were necessary to its development. Any reproductively altruistic behaviour which was dependent in whole or in part on particular mutations of which such behaviour was the sole or principal effect would tend to diminish in a given group of gene transmitters, unless it were distributed evenly in the population. *A fortiori*, any such genetically dependent behaviour which resulted in none of the altruist's own genes being passed on at all (directly or through the agency of a close relative), could not survive the process of natural selection. It would seem, then, that while the life of the family, or herd, or group (and that includes the life of social classes) may introduce complex subordinate ends into the human condition, the only final test of the cross-generational viability of a way of life is its contribution to (or at any rate its consistency with) the fitness of the individuals who follow it in serving the teleonomic project of which they are a part.

4. This explains, perhaps, the feelings of alienation and irrelevance provoked by literary representations of extreme unselfishness, by the rationalist altruism of Godwin and Parfit, by acts of pure unselfishness such as Isabel may be engaging in at the end of *The Portrait of a Lady*, and by voluntary celibacy. But it also offers a possible explanation of how such 'anti-life' behaviours might have developed. They can be understood as products of an evolutionary logic which offsets lesser disadvantages with greater advantages. Among human beings the teleonomic project is dependant on self-consciousness (the ego) which operates most effectively when it perceives itself to be more or less in charge of the whole organism (though of course it may be only marginally so). Occasionally, however, this strategy is counter-productive, when, for example, the ego becomes anxious about its autonomy and status, and reacts in ways that conflict with the priorities it is designed to serve. This would be the psychological equivalent of the relative weakness of the human spine, which occasionally extinguishes an individual's chances of reproduction, but which generally ensures our advantageous upright posture and bipedal locomotion.

Mendelian genetics and the discovery of DNA have given these ideas a specificity they previously lacked, but they are precisely addressed in the poetry and fiction of Thomas Hardy and the novels of Joseph Conrad. For each of these writers, the end to which life is structurally committed is one which we cannot adequately identify, never mind identify with, yet not even the assimilation of this tragic truth frees us from our sense of self and moral allegiances. The power of Hardy's writing derives largely from his willingness to side with the ego and with values in this unequal contest. He assumes that once values have supervened upon the teleonomic project, they are not to be argued away, that there is, after all, a truth about good even if the discernible ends of things do not disclose it. Such, certainly, is the implication of the account in *Tess of the D'Urbervilles* of the dairy-maids falling in love with Angel Clare:

> The full recognition of the futility of their infatuation, from a social point of view; its purposeless beginning; its self-bounded outlook; its lack of everything to justify its existence in the eye of civilization (while lacking nothing in the eye of

Nature); the one fact that it did exist, ecstasizing them to a killing joy; all this imparted to them a resignation, a dignity, which a practical and sordid expectation of winning him as a husband would have extinguished. (190)

Tess and her friends are genetically programmed to seek Angel Clare as a mate, but this programming is inappropriate to the environment they have been born into. Instinctively they resort to a group-solidarity which enables them to endure frustration, but supervening on this adaptive response ('resignation') is a value ('dignity'). There is thus a partial transcendence of the teleonomic project in Hardy's world — values achieve a real autonomy — but people do not: those who discover values must become backsliders or martyrs or both, for it is an illusion to imagine that consciousness can make good the 'brain-damaged' character of the immanent will. Individuals may instruct their bodies how to act, and assess the effects of doing so, but consciousness can never instruct or judge the whole project. Dennett denies that this is a problem, but he ignores the intensity with which human beings react to the claims which values make on them. The appalled sense of self-estrangement with which they frequently regard their own behaviour, while acknowledging it to be their own, is witness to this.

5. A marxist might respond to these pessimistic conclusions by claiming that they rely too heavily on individualist categories. Hardy's tragic protagonists become both backsliders and martyrs because he can only envisage values being generated in individual consciousness. But the true nexus of values is the collective struggle to live, which survives individual failure and is therefore the only basis for subordinating the project of nature to that of humanity: transcendence in this view is the achievement, not of willing, but of history, not of the dairy-maids individually, but as a group.

In order to evaluate this argument, it will be necessary first to examine the relation between ideas in general and evolutionary theory. Monod argues that all ideas (like the altruistic behaviours we considered earlier) are themselves subject to evolutionary laws. Ideas, he maintains, 'have retained some of the properties of organisms . . . they too can evolve' (154), their social viability depending not just on their truthfulness, or practicality, but also on their 'performance value' and 'spreading power' (155). An idea's fitness, for example, could be based on its capacity to inculcate 'greater cohesiveness, greater ambition, and greater self-confidence' in a group — however 'wrong' or 'impracticable' it might be. Mormonism might be cited as one such idea. A marxist would not find this an unacceptable argument since it seems inconsistent with the theory of ideology. But Monod also suggests that the 'spreading power' of ideas may depend on 'pre-existing structures in the mind, among them ideas already implanted by culture, but also undoubtedly upon certain innate structures which are very difficult for us to identify'. If this is so, socio-historic 'transcendence' of the kind proposed by marxism may prove difficult to defend.

Distinctions need to be respected here if the implications of Monod's argument are to be grasped. In one sense, the application to ideas of words like 'survival', 'fitness' and 'selection' can only be metaphorical. Biologically, the only kind of evolution is that which involves complete sets of decoded genetic instructions transmitting further complete sets of encoded instructions. According to Sober, a useful measure of such evolution is 'change in gene frequencies' (30) in a given population, and in his view this rules out

> purely *cultural* evolution, at least in one sense . . . i.e. changes in the frequencies of cultural traits that are not reflected in any changes in gene frequencies. The rise of Islam in the Middle Ages and of capitalism in certain Italian city-states are cases in point. (30)

But Sober also holds that 'cultural characteristics . . . [can] have a "genetic basis" [and] thereby evolve in the proprietary sense of the term'. He thus accepts that some ideas may be dependent at least in part on biological factors. Monod argues that both islam and marxism ought to be so regarded, because they (and mormonism for that matter) belong to a family of 'animist' theories which dates from times when human survival depended more on the maintenance of tribal cohesiveness than on truth or even 'practice', and that this condition was sufficiently protracted to have 'influenced the genetic evolution of the innate categories of the human brain' (155). Animist beliefs, as Monod defines them, '*explain* man by assigning him his place in an immanent destiny, a safe harbour where his anxiety dissolves'. They include all religious systems, and post-religious systems such as marxism. 'The immense influence of Marxist ideology', Monod suggests, is . . . due . . . probably . . . to its ontogenic structure, the explanation which it provides, both sweeping and detailed, of past, present, and future history' (157). Marxism, he argues, meets an 'imperious need . . . inscribed somewhere in the genetic code' (156).

But, a marxist might reply, so does language, yet the languages we learn are not determined in advance by the genetic code, nor can a language thus learned by 'chance' determine the truth or otherwise of what we say in it. Thus even if marxism does appeal to innate tendencies in the mind, its capacity to discern and implement the goals of the class struggle remain unaffected. But language has other functions besides that of saying things; speech individuates us (every voice pattern is distinct) and unites us to a particular group; it facilitates inter-personal responses, including sexual interaction, play, aggression and various kinds of bonding, conscious and unconscious. Independently of local cultural elements, it facilitates a dynamic which is basically biological and common to all language-using groups. A comparable dynamic may reasonably be predicated of animist beliefs. Like language, they seem crossed and shaped by biologically determined priorities. In terms of the teleonomic project, therefore, it may matter as little whether one is a jew, a christian, a follower of islam, a mormon or a communist, as it does whether one speaks Hebrew, Italian, Arabic, English or Russian. But in that case one could only judge between one animist belief and another, in terms either of their inherent truthfulness or their teleonomic value, if one had already ceased not only to hold, but also to need, such beliefs, and thus achieved on one's own account the very transcendence which such creeds claim themselves to offer.

6. Monod claims to have found a way of making this leap: we can ensure that the blind priorities of the teleonomic project inscribed in our genes have been superseded, he asserts, only if we recognise and act on *the postulate of objectivity*. The postulate itself is simple: it states that 'in the realm of ideas, . . . those presenting objective knowledge [are] the *only* source of real truth' (158), but the implications and consequences of accepting it, according to Monod, are immense.

He supports these claims with a number of arguments. He suggests in the first place that the postulate produces such feelings of discomfort in minds genetically disposed to seek for animist explanations that acceptance of it must be different in kind from the acceptance given to animist creeds. 'Cold and austere, proposing no explanation but imposing an ascetic renunciation of all other spiritual fare', he writes, the postulate of objectivity is unable to 'allay anxiety' but rather intensifies it by bringing to an end 'the ancient animist covenant between man and nature, [and] leaving nothing in place of that precious bond but an anxious quest in a world of icy solitude'.

His second argument in favour of the special status of the postulate is based on 'its prodigious powers of performance', powers sufficient, he claims, to have transformed the economic and social order of mankind. He concedes that certain social conditions and a certain level of technological and economic advance were probably necessary for its production in a form which would have this transforming effect, but he insists that of all ideas, however produced, only the postulate has advanced scientific practice. It is therefore self-validating, whatever genetically based effect it might have on us. This is further shown, he claims, by the fact that it has exposed our moral isolation; it has left us without an external authority from which to derive our values; it has subverted

> every one of the mythical or philosophical ontogenies upon which the animist tradition, from the Australian aborigines to the dialectical materialists, has based morality: values, duties, rights, prohibitions . . .
> . . . All the traditional systems placed ethics and values beyond man's reach. Values did not belong to him . .
> Today he knows that they are his and his alone, but now he is master of them they seem to be dissolving in the uncaring emptiness of the universe. (160–1)

The Hardyean note is unmistakable.

7. But Monod turns sharply from the abyss above which Hardy broods so compulsively. He denies that 'objective truth and the theory of values are [as] eternally opposed' (161) as they might appear. Like Milton, Newman and Polanyi, he assumes a continuous interaction between willing and thinking: 'values and knowledge', he writes, 'are always and necessarily associated in action as in discourse', in the first place because action 'brings knowledge and values *simultaneously* into play, or into question', and in the second, because '*the very definition of "true" knowledge rests in the final analysis upon an ethical postulate*'. Thus even though the postulate of objectivity 'forbids any confusion of value judgements with judgements arrived at through knowledge' (162), these categories 'inevitably unite in the form of action, discourse

included' (162). Moreover,

> the positing of the principle of objectivity as the condition of true knowledge *constitutes an ethical choice and not a judgment reached from knowledge, since, according to the postulate's own terms, there cannot be any 'true' knowledge prior to this arbitral choice.* (163)

Thus the transcendence necessary to liberate humanity from biological necessity is established by the existence of the postulate and not by its consequences, however impressive; for logically it could not itself be an item of knowledge; it must rather stand in relation to knowledge as, according to Polanyi, the user's intention stands in relation to the design of a machine. It can therefore only come into existence through an act of self-transcendence by which the mind precipitates itself in a direction which in principle could not be wholly determined either by genetic programming or by social conditioning or by a combination of the two. In other words, the 'ethic of knowledge does not impose itself on man; *on the contrary, it is he who imposes it on himself*' (164), and as 'the only ethic compatible with' the modern world which it created, it is 'the only one capable, once understood and created, of guiding its evolution'. Yet this service of 'true knowledge' (165) chosen as 'a transcendent value' and 'for . . . use' involves no dehumanisation in those who accept it, for the ethic of knowledge must necessarily respect the human being 'as the creator and repository of that transcendence'. Indeed on such an attitude, Monod contends, 'real socialism might be built' (166). The only

> source of truth . . . and moral inspiration [he concludes] for a really *scientific* socialist humanism . . . [is] science itself . . . the ethic upon which knowledge is founded, and which by free choice makes knowledge the supreme value — the measure and guarantee of all other values . . . which bases responsibility upon the very freedom of that axiomatic choice.

8. Do these arguments succeed? Monod's claim that the postulate of objectivity is alien to some important genetically organised predispositions is obviously flawed, since this would not stop its being consistent with others. The discomfort which the postulate produces in minds predisposed to adopt animist world-

views, for example, could appeal to a functional instinct for asceticism: membership of a select band of savants devoted to an austere ideal might meet the needs of intellectuals struggling to survive in a world otherwise dominated by ruthlessly instinctive competitors. Nor is it an accident that the argument from asceticism has been offered in defence of both christianity and islam, while, as Monod's own rhetoric shows, puritan idealism has an obvious spreading power of its own. In any case, acceptance of the postulate need not imply transcendence. It might be entertained initially as a hypothesis, tested subsequently for its effectiveness, and finally accepted on account of its prodigious powers of performance out of calculated self-interest. For Monod's argument to succeed, he would have to show that animistic minds are incapable of entertaining conflicting wants and deciding between them.

But there is a deeper objection to Monod's argument. He makes much of the claim that the postulate has to be adopted as an ethical stance before it can be applied to the study of reality, but this does not make the postulate special, for as we have noted several times, no structure of thought, animist or non-animist, can logically justify itself. But that is not all. Peter Strawson (1974) has shown that the same is true of the great mass of day-to-day acts of mind. Of the 'attitude . . . of involvement or participation in a human relationship' (9) he makes two points. First, to adopt it, that is, to treat people as people and not things, 'the objective attitude' (9) — Monod's postulate — must be abandoned: the two stances, he claims, 'are profoundly, *opposed* to each other'. Secondly, the 'general structure or web of human attitudes' (23) can only be discussed if its autonomy is assumed. In it 'there is endless room for modification, redirection, criticism and justification', but all such adjustments are 'internal to the structure' which 'neither calls for, nor permits, an external "rational" justification'. In effect, to choose the postulate of objectivity we must rely on what Polanyi calls 'personal co-efficients' and Newman 'the Illative Sense'. But this means that what Monod takes to be an historically unique, soteriologically portentous event — acceptance of the postulate of objectivity — is rather an entirely normal, and therefore, on his premisses, a biologically determined event.

Monod, however, is at least right to this extent, that if we do adopt the postulate and by its means become familiar with nature as geneticists understand it, the claims of any biologically or socially determined attitudes can no longer be accepted at face value. The problem cannot be disposed of, as Strawson appears to believe it can, by our assuming that since we will continue spontaneously to live with our ordinary inter-personal attitudes, we can and will continue to regard them as all right. Certainly the evidence of fiction, of James and Hardy, suggests that intimations of alienation arising out of our knowledge of nature can penetrate and disturb our ordinary, inter-personal lives. In any case, the claims of objectivity are as logically impervious to criticism from the general structure or web of human attitudes as vice versa. A psychiatrist, for example, might *know* a patient's behaviour to be compulsive, the patient's wife could *know* it to be blame-worthy, and neither be in a position to challenge the conclusions arising from the other's premises.

9. The impasse, however, is less grave than it appears: psychiatrists and members of their patients' families often do communicate, because people have a capacity to move from one attitude to the other. This clearly derives from powers which operate independently of both attitudes, which can ajudicate between them, drawing doubtless on the Illative Sense or subsidiary awareness, and which are therefore finally able to unite them into a single, comprehensively human attitude. It is in this territory, I believe, that the structure of human freedom can at last be elucidated. I shall explore it by comparing the language of objectivity and the language of involvement or participation in order to show first in what ways they differ and then how those differences might be composed into a larger, entirely human whole.

Unfortunately, the most obvious examples of the language of participation, day-to-day speech, must be excluded from this analysis (at least in the first instance) because they are incalculably caught up in the stream of gesture and expressive exchange which we could only analyse linguistically in the light of a previous analysis of language. We are left then with examples of the language of participation which have been 'purified' of non-linguistic elements, with language preserved in memory or in writing and so detached from an originating non-linguistic context, in short with literature.

This is less limiting than it might seem because of the two levels on which all language acts signify. The most obvious, primary level of signification is that of the signified, what a speaker or writer is found to have expressed, but there is necessarily a secondary level of signfication in all utterance by which it signals the powers or stance required for its interpretation. And it is this secondary level of meaning that offers indirect but exact evidence of that level of mind at which judgement between objective and participatory attitudes must take place. By applying systematic, introspective procedures, such as those used in *The Acting Person*, to this secondary level of signification, we may also discover implicit but demonstrable evidence of human powers which are not accorded formal and explicit recognition at the primary level of signification but which point in the direction of true transcendence.

10. The choice of texts for this exercise is not particularly important. For convenience I have selected a passage from Kenny's *Freedom, Will and Power* to represent writing informed by the language of objectivity and a sonnet by Milton to represent the language of literature. The texts are these:

(i)

The doctrine of liberty of indifference was first propounded in detail in the course of theological debates about freedom and predestination in the sixteenth century. The foremost component of the concept was the Spanish Jesuit Luis Molina, who defined freedom (liberty of indifference) in the following terms:

An agent is free if, given all necessary conditions for ϕing, it can both ϕ and not ϕ. (1)

Here the necessary conditions constitute the opportunity for ϕing: the 'can' refers to a two-way power or ability. In the present chapter I propose to discuss the 'can's of ability and opportunity with a view to evaluating the doctrine of liberty of indifference and relating it to the earlier discussion of liberty of spontaneity.

1 *Id liberum dicimus quod positis requisitis ad agendum in potestate ipsius habet agere aut non agere (Concordia Liberi Arbitrii 14*, 13d2) (123).

(ii)

Lawrence of vertuous Father vertuous Son,
    Now that the Fields are dank, and ways are mire,
    Where shall we sometimes meet, and by the fire
    Help wast a sullen day; what can be won
From the hard Season gaining: time will run

On smoother, till *Favonius* re-inspire
The frozen earth; and cloth in fresh attire
The Lillie and Rose, that neither sow'd nor spun.
What neat repast shall feast us, light and choice
Of Attick tast, with Wine, whence we may rise
To hear the Lute will toucht, or artfull voice
Warble immortal Notes and *Tuskan* Ayre?
He who of those delights can judge, and spare
To interpose them oft, is not unwise.

11. If I were encountering either or both of these passages for the first time, I would presumably recognise and at once register that both are (mainly) in English, the one in prose, the other in verse. I would take in the italicised Latin footnote and the ϕ signs in Kenny's paragraph, and the *Lawrence*, *Favonius* and *Tuskan* in Milton, and make a quick judgement about my ability to interpret texts with such features in them, about what the experiences of doing so and of having done so might be like, and about the positive value for me of such possible experiences. Next I would either give them fuller attention or turn elsewhere, while registering at some level that this experience of preliminary inspection and evaluation had been mine, and that it was I who could, or could not, would or would not, enter on the work of reading either or both passages in full.

The first connection which a reader makes with a text is thus mainly on the secondary level of signification. The next stage, however, obviously requires a more specifically cognitive effort to register the primary meanings of each passage. Nevertheless that effort will also confirm, modify or disprove the preliminary judgements about the secondary or implicit significations which we have just analysed. I may discover, for example, that the first text is not as I surmised just about Molina, but is also a modest exercise in technical philosophising, and that the second has unanticipated religious implications. One way or another, I will come into fuller contact with the implicit meanings of each text, and a fuller sense of the specific input each requires from me for its interpretation.

12. Let us now consider this process more closely in relation to the Kenny passage. I will presumably realise quite quickly that my reactions to the fact that Molina was a Spanish Jesuit are irrelevant to the text's primary significations. In Monod's terms, the text invites me to operate within the constraints of the postulate

of objectivity. This applies particularly to my reactions to Kenny's translations of Molina's Latin into the language of modern logical discourse. Thus over and above what Kenny says explicitly, on the primary level of signification, about the liberty of indifference, his words speak implicitly of my capacity as a putative reader to react in a disciplined way to words on the page, to understand the author's definitions, to respect them at least for the purposes of following the line of thought being developed, to attend to logical connections, to prevent illogical associations from obstructing my attention, and so forth. The reflection of such cognitions in consciousness will presumably result in my once again experiencing these demands as demands made on me; I will judge them as such and decide whether and how far I will respect them. In short, a text which purports to be scientific, logical or philosophical predicates at the secondary level of signification quite specific responses which the reader must be able to recognise, to enact and so in a sense to become, if the text is to be understood at the primary, explicit level of signification.

13. Comparable but different demands arise from reading Milton's poem. This sonnet addressed to the young Edward Lawrence is related to those parts of *Christian Doctrine* where Milton explicitly sanctions 'the discriminating enjoyment of food, clothing and all the civilized refinements of life, purchased with our honest earnings' (732), and represents as qualities consonant with christian living the virtues of 'COURTEOUSNESS . . . [which] makes us affable and easily approachable' (769), and 'URBANITY [which] entails not only elegance and wit (of a decent kind) in conversation, but also the ability to discourse and to reply in an acute and apposite way' (769–70). It invites me in consequence to place myself in a different relationship to reactivity from the one required by the Kenny paragraph. For example, Milton evidently hopes for a favourable reaction to the fact that Lawrence's father was a courageously outspoken baptist. This is very different from the rigorous self-control which Kenny's reader must exercise in recalling Molina's membership of the Society of Jesus.

A more fundamental difference between the two passages is that they reverse the relationship between the primary and secondary levels of signification. In Kenny the secondary level simply establishes the conditions required for interpretation of the primary meaning; the primary level remains autonomous. It is unaffected, for example, by whether it is warm admiration for the

Jesuit order or icy antipathy which the disciplines of reading require me to suppress. Even the ideal of a mind dispassionately attending to the logical coherence of the argument is irrelevant to its possible validity. The reverse is the case with Milton. In order to assimilate the primary meanings in his sonnet, I must not only exercise precisely indicated interpretative powers and disciplines, but also let my cognitive and conscious awareness of those powers coming into play modify my reading of the poem at the primary level.

These interactions are susceptible to detailed analysis. The eighth line, for example, assumes a capacity in the reader to recognise the reference to Matt 6:28 and Luke 12:28, and also to find the intrusion of this evangelical reference after the classical *Favonius* unexpected and possibly inappropriate. No less striking is the mild evocation of an erotic as well as a mystical tradition by means of the addition of the Rose to the Lillie which markedly alters the impression made by the words of Jesus in the Gospels. So too the immediate return to pagan values in the reference to an *Attick* not a Eucharist feast, to the secular singing of a *Tuskan* air, and to immortality of a thoroughly this-worldly kind.

The poem also assumes my capacity to react to an unusual rhyme-scheme in this sestet. Irregular sestets are common in Milton: in four sonnets besides this one the return of a rhyme is delayed for four lines. In all these other cases, however, the lines so rhymed are the ninth and the thirteenth, and the effect of disconnection is offset by a more easily remembered rhyme returning in the final line. But in this sonnet the sense of connection established by the couplet rhyme in the twelfth and thirteenth lines is disrupted by the loosely connected rhyme at the end of the fourteenth, which seems lame and detached in consequence, an impression increased by the delayed caesura after 'judge', and the grammatically weak construction, 'And spare / To interpose them oft', which follows it.

These effects of disconnection and inappropriateness are, of course, meant to be overcome. The poem not only depends on my being able to discover consistency and integration in apparent inconsistency and disintegration, but also to allow the personal experience of this mental work to modify and enrich the primary meanings of the text. Considerable emphasis, for example, is given both rhythmically and syntactically to the word 'judge'. My capacity to appreciate the skill with which this is done is not only assumed by the text, but also precisely exemplifies what the word 'judge' as Milton uses it actually means. In order to understand Milton's sense of 'judgement', I must take cognisance of my own experience in interpreting the humanist and christian signs in the poem, and I must make reference to truth about value with respect both to the poem's primary meaning as modified by my experience of interpreting it, and to the latter experience of value precisely as my own. The poem engages me cognitively, consciously and reflexively: to assimilate Milton's use of the word 'judge', I must in effect *act* it.

14. The differences between interpreting scientific and literary language are now clearer. The former, while contingent upon the interpreter's being able to adopt an appropriately disciplined response to the secondary level of meaning, preserves the autonomy of the primary level. Literary language, on the other hand, exploits secondary meanings at the primary level. So of course does everyday speech, and we must therefore further define the language of literature by referring to the element of pleasure motivating it: the child's pleasure in nonsense-talk is a kind of ur-literature, the joke its most widespread form.

Scientific and literary language also have a specifiable relation to values. Thus some kind of judgement concerning truth about good is a condition of scientific reading. As we have already noted, objectivity can be motivated by mere curiosity or the pursuit of power. But it always requires the elimination of such motives from the work of interpretation: a degree of self-control, which borders on the ethical and may easily pass into it, is the *sine qua non* of scientific reading. Exactly the reverse is the case with literary reading. It begins in the value-free area of play between levels of signification, and moves, sometimes disruptively, into the area of morality. At a certain point it may incite the reader to make judgements about its own verbal strategies, like those of the young Lawrence is invited to make in Milton's sonnet. Thus the true poet (by which term I mean the teller of a good story as well as the maker of a great poem) may finally invite and require from the reader a reference to truth about good perceived as a problem involving an entire set of significations. Within the general structure or web of inter-personal activity, therefore, both science and literature create opportunities for what may be called responsible linguistic practice.

15. They do so however indirectly — through silence. The secondary level of signification is necessarily implicit. This is so even when a text alludes to its own procedures. Fielding's *Tom*

Jones, for example, leaves the reader with the extra task of grasping the implications as well as the meaning of its authorial interventions, and of making a judgement about their impact on his primary significations. In other words, literature obeys the general rule of being unable to supply the rules for its own interpretation. Even a flaunted rhetoric cannot explicitly invite critical responses to itself without ceasing to be itself. There is always a point at which readers are left to their own resources, and in some works this point is itself a secondary sign, as in the sonnet to Lawrence, which, out of respect for everything the word 'judge' has to convey, has to be silent about the intransitive and personal responsibilities a full appreciation of it requires.

We may distinguish, therefore, between a silence in literature about the activations which a text elicits, and a silence about the active and deliberate judgements which it may require but cannot explicitly define, still less compel. And that is not the end of the matter. I can read Milton's sonnet, cognise and subsequently experience both reflectively and reflexively its explicit and implicit meanings, and finally form a judgement about the urbane courtesy of his attitudes to his readers, what it means for him to remain silent about what he hopes from them, even though his successful communication of all that the word 'judge' can imply, when applied to civilised intercourse and entertainment, depends on their co-operation. The poem thus puts me into judicious contact with Milton's sense of my potentialities both as a guest and as a reader, and with his dependence on them. But my reaction to that reticence is by no means predictable. I may resent Milton's failure to direct my responses in a way that I feel is aesthetically or morally necessary, or I may admire the technical skill with which he has avoided just such explicitness. I may thus contain my judgement of the poem within the limits of propaganda or aestheticism. But I can also make Milton's sense of my unpredictability yet another aspect of the poem's meaning, part of what he silently yet precisely indicates he is allowing for. I can acknowledge a moral significance in his willingness to leave me to judge for myself even if I do so wrongly, and I can see this too as integral to what the poem signifies.

Encapsulated in the sonnet, therefore, is a principle of intimacy in separateness, a movingly exact, yet entirely open authorial voluntariness, which I can value as a good and make my own. This openness, it is worth repeating, is Milton's and not mine. His choice, that I should choose for myself, is specific and complete — it is in the poem — mine exists only as a possibility, but precisely as a possibility it is Milton's self-effacing gift to me. He invites me into the intimate, domestic world of his desires, hopes and affections, yet, like a good host, he leaves me to myself, and in this very self-effacement, he becomes in the poem fully and movingly himself, manifesting all those facts of his powerful mind and damaged body 'that are simultaneously his wealth and his specific limitation' in the integral reality of an acting person.

The sonnet to Lawrence thus contains necessarily implicit but none the less exact traces of what Strawson calls 'involvement or participation with others in interpersonal human relationships'. This conclusion stands even if we adopt the principle that Milton's poem may not be discussed as if the poet in the text and the man he is addressing were historical persons, whose intentions and choices are available for scrutiny. The validity of the instance is not lessened by its being deemed fictional. Fact or fiction, a precondition of the poem's being read is its capacity to signal a relevant set of inter-personal attitudes which, as the means by which we will be able to make sense of it, are logically independent of the sense it makes. Included in that set of attitudes is an ethical stance which in principle meets all the requirements of the *actus voluntarius* as the Pope describes it. Here, after all, we have the marks of a will — I am reluctant not to call it Milton's — with a clearly apprehended object in the intentional order (the reader's autonomy) which as an object cannot determine choice no matter how fully it is known. Indeed the more Milton's sensitivity and truthfulness unite to apprehend and value the reader's freedom as an end in itself, the more profoundly voluntary that sensitivity and truthfulness become. And this structure, it seems to me, has general application. There is one, and only one, truly discerned but non-coercive value which the mind can cognise and respond to with unqualified freedom, and that is the freedom of another person. It would seem then, on the evidence this poem contains about the potentialities of ordinary inter-personal attitudes, that a true transcendence in thought and action is possible.

16. The implications of this conclusion are philosophically significant. We have seen that Milton's is more or less a scholastic or Thomist version of the will. Now as O'Connor has pointed out

St Thomas' theory seems to entail a consequence that he can hardly accept, namely, that when the rational considerations in favour of a course of action are perfectly complete and decisive *and are seen to be so*, we really have no choice as to whether we accept the course of action which they support. (53)

This is exactly the point made by Godwin who, like St Thomas, was much concerned to represent choice as under the control of reason:

> to ascribe freedom to our voluntary actions [Godwin writes], is an express contradiction in terms. No motion is voluntary, any further than it is accompanied with intention and design, and has for its proper antecedent, the apprehension of an end to be accomplished. So far as it flows, in any degree, from another source, it is involuntary. The new-born infant foresees nothing, therefore all his motions are involuntary. A person arrived at maturity, takes an extensive survey of the consequences of his actions, therefore he is eminently a voluntary and rational being. (I 376–7)

And therefore also a determined one, determined, that is, by reasons. Godwin then goes on to describe the vicious regress which is apparently entailed in the notion of attributing freedom to internal acts, and which, as we saw earlier, O'Connor thinks St Thomas attempted and failed to resolve. Godwin cannot see how a free internal action can begin in the mind. I must have reasons for an action if it is to be voluntary; but if I have my reasons they will determine what I do, and if I claim my choice of reasons is voluntary, I must have reasons for making that choice, and so on.

> Trace back the chain as far as you please [he writes], every act at which you arrive is necessary. That act which gives the character of freedom to the whole, can never be discovered; and, if it could, in its own nature it includes a contradiction. (I 378)

But Milton has discovered such an act and no contradiction is apparent. In acknowledging the freedom of his reader and attuning his writing to it, he makes no attempt to survey the consequences of the restraint he thus imposes on himself, for the reader's 'voluntary and rational being', which that restraint has chosen to respect, is literally incalculable. Consequently there is no question of his considerations on the subject of this restraint being incomplete or indecisive as a child's might be: he *knows* that he must either choose the reader's freedom as an end in itself without regard to consequences, or not choose it at all. He has thus implicitly recognised that his own freedom consists not in a choice *between* objects, but in making freedom itself his principal object.

17. The language of literature is thus capable of disclosing freedom while that based on the postulate of objectivity is not. This does not mean however that mathematicians, logicians and scientists are unfree. They would be so only if science were the work of autonomous intellects engaging with problems of pure theory according to strict, self-justifying principles. But in science at least, this cannot be so. As Polanyi points out,

> the knowledge comprised by science is not known to any single person. Indeed nobody knows more than a tiny fragment of science well enough to judge its validity and value at first hand. For the rest he has to rely on views accepted at second hand on the authority of a community of people accredited as scientists. (163)

This entire enterprise, moreover, is located in the larger complex of social, educational and economic activity. The practice of publishing experimental procedures and results by which science advances is thus subject to modification by political, institutional and commercial priorities. Indeed, it is doubtful if any scientific enterprise is ever really 'pure'. While it may be obvious, for example, that research and development in nuclear energy will inevitably be contaminated by non-scientific priorities, subtler cultural and institutional factors almost certainly operate even on the most innocent theoretical inquiries. At this level, the only guides to action, the only norms of behaviour, must be based on an empirically based assessment of likely results.

But scientists are also interdependent at a deeper level, for example in the acts which becoming scientists require of them. As Polanyi puts it:

> the learner . . . must believe before he can know. But . . . the intimations followed by the learner are based predominantly on . . . confidence in others . . . The continued transmission of articulate systems, which lends public and

enduring quality to our intellectual gratifications, depends throughout on these acts of submission (208).

This is self-evidently true of philosophy and mathematics also. So is Polanyi's next point, that science involves private acts of 'heuristic conjecture . . . a passionate pouring of oneself into untried forms of existence' (208). It seems that all those who adopt the postulate of objectivity have to accept and respect each other's intellectual autonomy: 'even though intellectual standards are acquired by education while our appetitive tasks are predominantly innate, both may deviate from current custom; and even when they conform to it they must both be ultimately accredited by ourselves' (174).

In these delicate and complex relations of submission, mutual interdependence of equals, and intensely private speculation and understanding, the grant of freedom could clearly have a place. It would operate first at the level of personal, implicit in-put, as a commitment to trust and to being trusted, emancipating philosophers and scientists from the need to base decisions about communicating with their fellows on calculations about the probable effects of doing so. There is no reason to suppose, of course, that such unqualified trust has ever informed the purposes of all intellectuals operating throughout the system. On the other hand, there is every reason to suppose that numerous philosophers and scientists have in fact felt and articulated a deep sense of the inter-personal character of their work and of the moral duties arising from it — to respect the autonomy of their fellow-scientists and, in the last analysis, to tell them the truth, the whole truth and nothing but the truth about their own work. Respect for such principles could, of course, be pragmatically or ideologically determined; it could be conditional; but it could also be based on a recognition and acceptance of freedom as a possible nexus for all intellectual activity.

It should now be clear how the psychiatrist and the family of a patient can communicate. On the one hand both parties may be pragmatists, voluntary agents in Godwin's sense, but not free agents in mine, in which case the implicit but mutually recognised subsidiary input to their discussion will be based on a willingness on the part of the psychiatrist to limit the application of 'objective' criteria and of the family to allow 'objective' data to influence judgements based on ordinary inter-personal experience: ultimately, however, one side will have to concede in principle to the other, though both may collude in keeping the concession hidden. But if both sides are prepared to operate within the framework of the grant of freedom, neither need abandon their respective stances, objectivity on the one hand, and ordinary inter-personal attitudes on the other; for objectivity as a value informed by the grant of freedom can respond to any stance which is *capable* of being chosen freely: neither attitude, therefore, is exclusive of the other.

We can now finally return to the Kenny passage. I suggested earlier that like the Milton poem such texts can be informed by responsible silence. But in objective discourse the function of that silence is to preserve the absolute autonomy of the primary level of signification. In writing, therefore, the scientist and the logician must display the reserve not of a host but of a servant. This is why the language of objectivity can appear coercively impersonal without, necessarily, being so. The price the scientist and the logician pay for their commitment to the grant of freedom is effectively a *complete* self-effacement. But far from this being a less significant moral stance than that manifested by Milton in his sonnet, it approximates, as we shall see in a later chapter, to the will of Milton's God in *Paradise Lost*.

8

The Law of Freedom

1. To anyone wishing to defend the traditional concepts of free will, personal identity and objective moral values, the conclusions reached at the end of the last chapter must seem exhilarating. In this chapter I hope to strengthen that impression. But two difficulties must be faced before I do so. The first represents unfinished business from the last chapter. I need to show that the structure of transcendence for which I am arguing is consistent with the origins and development of human life as Monod describes them.

If Monod is in general correct, we must assume that a capacity in human beings to imagine their own and other people's freedom and responsibility is genetically or socially determined and is therefore contaminated by the principle of doubleness which the teleonomic project introduces into all life-processes at whatever level. It is a matter of common observation, however, that we are not programmed into complete and unqualified acceptance of each other's autonomy in all the circumstances of life. At the most there seems to be a widespread, probably genetically-based predisposition among some of us to regard other people as free agents and to welcome their being so. This could easily be explained in terms of teleonomic performance: it might be shown, for example, that a cultural predisposition towards non-coercive relationships can enhance the cohesiveness and adaptability of members of a group. From the biological point of view, therefore, the tendency to allow freedom to others would not be an end in itself, and of course to persist among human beings it would have to enhance the reproductive performance of individuals. Even so, such a grant of freedom could properly be described as a free act, or more precisely as the necessary stance making free actions possible, the point at which (without supernatural grace, or magic or occult powers necessarily intervening) the synthesis of synchronic and diachronic interaction between subjectivity and nervous tissue trancends the roots of chance and necessity from which it apparently springs.

The difficulty is to envisage how this could come about, since it seems to presuppose what it seeks to establish. But let us imagine a being born with a new, randomly developed adaptive mechanism which encourages the false working assumption that others can act freely, and a capacity to consent to their doing so. Let us also suppose that this tendency only comes into play in the course of day-to-day exchanges with other intelligences, primarily in considered words and gestures of encouragement and assent. Such behaviour might involve calculations about what other people so encouraged will do, in which case no consequent choice could be described as entirely free. But it might also derive from a genuine desire to behave in such a way as to allow the other full freedom of action. No choices made in the light of such a desire could be determined by reasons in advance. Informed with such an intention, practical reasoning would be truly defeasible. Such a development would be in the ultimate adaptive mechanism, the point at which, in pursuit of survival, the project of reproduction ceased to rely exclusively on the supremely sophisticated but essentially prudential computations of a highly reactive cerebral system, and launched itself into genuinely creative inter-personal activity; the thought experiment would have achieved authentic transcendence, and the facts of personal identity and responsibility would have supervened upon a universe which until that moment had been rigorously determined.

2. My second difficulty arises from my having apparently attributed to Milton a conception of willing which he nowhere explicitly espouses. In later chapters I shall show that he *almost* espouses it, and thereby considerably enriches the concept of freedom which I am proposing. But that may not be though sufficient to justify my presenting him as witness-in-chief for that

concept. Besides, in one important respect, he seems to oppose my
view of willing, in so far as his doctrine of God is inconsistent with
an interpersonal conception of freedom.

I referred in the first chapter to Milton's assertion in *Christian
Doctrine* that 'God could certainly have refrained from the act of
generation and yet remained true to his own essence, for he stands
in no need of propagation' (209). But if freedom is an inherently
interpersonal stance, this means that God could not have been free
independently of the General Decree 'by which HE DECREED
FROM ETERNITY . . . ALL THOSE THINGS WHICH HE
PROPOSED OR WHICH HE WAS GOING TO PERFORM
. . . singly and by himself' (153). The General Decree itself would
have been a free act, since to will the generation of another acting
person is to act freely in my sense. But Milton insists that that very
act was not of God's essence, and on my argument this would mean
that freedom was not of God's essence either.

No such problems arise, of course, in a trinitarian theology
which permits us to think of the Father willing the freedom of his
consubstantial Son from all eternity; of the Son freely deferring to
the will of the Father; and of the Holy Spirit (and not mere negation) proceeding from this mutually self-effacing union as the
unimpeded expression of the Father's will. Traditional trinitarianism thus implicitly contradicts Kant's argument (1783), also
mentioned in the first chapter, that we cannot 'find a concept of
freedom appropriate to pure beings of the understanding, e.g.
God, in so far as his action is immanent' (109n). If freedom is
interpersonal, the freedom of a trinitarian God would also be
immanent: *pace* Kant, it would not have 'to begin through an act'.
For Milton, however, as for Kant, freedom consists precisely in
the capacity to initiate actions in time — hence, as we have seen,
his belief that the generation of the Son would not have been free
had it not taken place in time. The freedom of Milton's God is
thus a private property, like his wisdom and holiness.

3. This is a less serious objection to my view of Milton,
however, than it might seem. Indeed in a certain light the fact that
he contradicts what I maintain he believes might be construed as
evidence in favour of the position I am defending. As my analysis
of the sonnet to Lawrence suggests, the grant of freedom belongs
to the territory of responsible silence. It is part of that input, or
'ethical stance' or 'subsidiary awareness' which is a condition of
any systematic consideration of issues. To adopt the distinction
developed by Bakhtin, it must first be thought of as an inner sign

that engulfs or washes over those outer ideological signs which constitute the shared moral vocabulary of a community, 'a dim unprocessed thought' (33) quietly awaiting embodiment within a 'unified ideological system'. Thus if neighbours, acquaintances or even enemies recognise or anticipate the reciprocal giving and taking of freedom, they cannot do so merely on the basis of explicit declarations ('I desire your freedom') since such declarations would any way require a prior ethical stance to be true, and evidence for the influence of such a stance could only be supplied by readings of the implicit meanings in their verbal and non-verbal signalling.

This applies especially to the reading of narrative. In the Second of Book of Samuel, for example, it would be easy to give reasons, such as Hume or Fielding might deem adequate, for the actions of Saul, David and Jonathan, but it would be far more difficult to decide how far those reasons and actions were silently and responsibly informed by an acceptance of the autonomy of others. The uncertainty is greatest in David's case. The best evidence of his freedom in a far from obviously honourable early career is his refusal to kill Saul in the cave and his lament on the deaths of the king and his son. As readers of the narrative, however, we are on our own when we make a judgement on this question, just as we are on our own when we judge the inter-personal implications of Milton's lines to Lawrence and their bearing on the arguments advanced in *Christian Doctrine*. But if David's actions may belie what is in his heart, so may Milton's theological logic. Granted the preverbal character of the stance which all language requires, it is entirely possible for a person to be informed by intuitions which if verbalised would be inconsistent with that person's explicitly expressed opinions. No inner sign can guarantee a logically consistent relationship with associated outer signs, not even the inner signs of freedom.

4. This has important implications. The first relates to equality. There is a tendency among philosophers to attach a special value to minds of a philosophical bent. Hume, for example, praises Academic or Sceptical philosophers who 'talk of doubt and suspense of judgement, of danger in hasty determinations' (41) which he contrasts with 'the supine indolence . . . rash arrogance, lofty pretensions and . . . superstitious credulity' of ordinary minds. His Academics accordingly enjoy a less confined spontaneity than other people. Godwin reveals a similar bias in favour of intelligences like Fénelon's over those like that of Fénelon's butler; Monod writes of the importance of his postulate to 'those

who bear or will bear responsibility for the way society and culture will evolve' (160), and Parfit believes that specialists in 'Non-Religious Ethics' (454) ought to have considerable social influence in a nuclear age. Even Polanyi defends liberal societies on the grounds that they alone establish the right relationship between the ideals of our culture which are 'anchored in the works and lives of our masters' (377) and the experience of ordinary people. All indulge in the élitist fantasies of the articulate. The grant of freedom, on the other hand, operates independently of the agent's capacity to articulate it. It can inform the verbal vacancy of the world of Wordsworth's 'The Idiot Boy' and be entirely absent from a sophisticated rationalist text like *Political Justice*. I can think of few clearer illustrations of its apparent working, for example, than the tenderness shown to Tess by her fellow dairy-maids when they discover her engagement to Angel Clare in *Tess of the d'Urbervilles*, and her decision consequent upon that tenderness to tell Angel of her earlier relationship with Alec.

5. The priority which the grant of freedom enjoys over articulate or articulatable reasons also enables us to restate compatibilism on a sounder basis than that provided by the arguments either of Kant or of Kenny. As we have seen, Kant (1783) holds that

> all acts of rational beings, in that they are appearances . . . stand under natural necessity; the same acts, however merely with respect to the rational subject and to its faculty of acting according to mere reason, are free. For what is demanded for natural necessity? Nothing further than the determinability of every event in the world of the senses according to constant laws . . . while the thing in itself that lies at the ground and its causality remain unknown. But . . . *the law of nature stands*, whether the rational being is the cause, by reason and through freedom, of the effects in the world of the senses, or whether it does not determine these effects out of grounds or reasons. For in the first case the act happens according to maxims the effect of which in appearance will always be in conformity with constant laws; in the second case, . . . it is subject to the empirical laws of sensibility, and in both cases the effects are connected according to constant laws. (111)

Seductive as this argument may seem, it depends on its location of freedom in the unknowable territory of 'the thing in itself . . . and its causality'. Hence the attractiveness of Kenny's transposition of the level metaphor to the distinct languages of physiology and consciousness. But this argument assumes that any laws predictive of bodily movement would be 'physical' in the sense of operating independently of subjective experience; and no such laws have ever been stated, nor ever could be. Moreover, Kenny's argument trivialises freedom by destroying the distinction between spontaneous and free actions and so between the freedom with which I open an egg at the big or little end, and the freedom with which I stand by a friend in trouble.

The grant of freedom has none of these disadvantages. It resolves the problem of freedom and necessity by distinguishing between the level of explicit meanings (or maxims) and the level of implicit meanings which enable us to believe and interpret them. These correspond to focal and subsidiary awareness, and so belong together as intimately as consciousness and brain-states do; yet just as in Kant's scheme maxim-governed acts of freedom are manifested at the level of appearances as if governed by the deterministic laws of nature, so everything I do in the light of a subsidiary grant of freedom can also be performed for stateable reasons based on what I know, or guess, or conclude. Consequently the same actions done for the same focally specific reasons may be free or unfree depending on whether or not they are informed by a supervenient subsidiary willingness to operate in a free inter-personal context. Again in line with the Kantian scheme, new causal chains can come into being through the grant of freedom without disturbing the coherence of focally perceivable reasons and causes, and they can do so both in individual minds and between persons, as heart speaks to heart. However, in opposition to the Kantian model, freedom is not confined to beginnings: it is possible to live in an unchanging state of habitually free relationships.

The grant of freedom also resolves other problems with which we have been concerned. Thus even if Kenny were right in maintaining that the defeasibility of practical reasoning makes the freedom of indifference identical with that of spontaneity, we could still distinguish between practical reasoning based on the grant of freedom and that based merely on wants. On the other hand, if we conclude with Dennett (as I think we should) that practical reasoning requires a decider-switch to bring it to conclusions, we could still distinguish between these occasions when the decider-switch operated on a consciousness debating with itself in the light of the grant of freedom and those when it was merely trying to decide between conflicting wants. In short, if the grant of freedom conditions our behaviour in any significant way it must do so at the level of the heart, as a disposition of the whole person.

6. So understood, it enables us finally to clarify our ideas about backsliding and rationality. Davidson, it will be remembered, represents backsliding as a form of madness; the grant of freedom, on the other hand, enables us to see it as an inappropriate lapsing into sanity. I become incontinent in this new sense if I make the all-out unconditional decision to act merely on the basis of reasons or possible outcomes when my all-things-considered plan of life suggests that I ought to respect the freedom of others. Willing the freedom of others is inconsistent with a weighing of consequences in terms of happiness, theirs, mine or the world's in general. That is why, Parfit's arguments notwithstanding, those close to me in space and time have claims on me that those remote from me never can have: I can act towards them with a prompt and unconditional openness made specific by the shared circumstances which enable heart to speak to heart. There is thus a real sense in which I must choose between being a rational and free agent.

And that is why it is so easy to be a backslider. As later analysis of divine and angelic willing in Milton's works will make clear, cases of perfect obedience, of perfect love, of the perfect enactment of a plan of life predicated on the grant of freedom, are quite plausible; but so is an instability between a free and a manipulative or utilitarian stance, an instability we may not always notice as it occurs, since what is affected in the first instance is our subsidiary awareness. We are all of us 'fallen'; we may know ourselves and others to be capable of freedom, but we may find ourselves trapped in reasons or decision-making processes, at the mercy, in O'Connor's words, 'of considerations in favour of a course of action [which] are perfectly complete and decisive' (53), or subject to the control of Dennett's decider-switch, or Davidson's maverick causal chains. Alternatively we may splash around spontaneously in the defeasible shallows of reasoning premissed on wants. In one way or another, we may find ourselves unable to make respect for the freedom of others a consistent guide to our actions. The message of scripture, of the jewish and christian traditions, of literature generally, of Milton in particular, and of day-to-day experience is that inter-personal freedom is a difficult goal to perceive, never mind to choose and uphold.

Once lost, moreover, there seems to be no certain way of repossessing it. The mind that accepts the priorities of reason, appetite and motive not informed by the choice of freedom has no reason to restore itself to an awareness of its possibilities, still less to an acceptance of them. Such states are not necessarily signs of turpitude. Sorrow, anxiety, cold, hunger, loneliness and pain, or, alternatively, just indignation, urgent and energetic commitment to a cause, devotion to another person, or to groups of persons (family, the sick, comrades at work or in war), a strong sense of obligation under the law or sheer hard work — all these calls upon our attentions and energies can extinguish our subsidiary awareness of interpersonal freedom and so our openness to its demands: 'Martha, Martha, thou art anxious and troubled about many things, but one thing is needful' (Luke 10: 41).

7. It would be a mistake, however, to conclude from the apparent naturalness of backsliding that moral truth is inherently uncertain. On the contrary, in spite of its grounding in the implicit level of meaning, the grant of freedom gives us access to something very close to what Newman, in one of the *Tracts for the Times* (1835), calls Objective Truth, that is, a

> Religious System considered as existing in itself, external to this or that particular mind: by Subjective, is meant that which each mind receives in particular, and considers to be such. To believe in Objective Truth is to throw ourselves forward upon that which we have but partially mastered or made subjective; to embrace, maintain, and use general propositions which are larger than our capacity, of which we cannot see the bottom, which we cannot follow out into the multiform details; to come before and bow before the import of such propositions, as if we were contemplating what is real and independent of human judgment. Such a belief, implicit, and symbolized as it is in the use of creeds, seems to the Rationalist superstitious and unmeaning. (34–5)

Understood in the light of the grant of freedom, however, even scientific culture reveals how such truth might be known with absolute certainty.

I pointed out in the last chapter that it is entirely possible for the grant of freedom to inform intellectual activity based on the postulate of objectivity, and that it has probably often done so. Science is inter-personal: it depends on trust and disclosure. Such trust and disclosure could be conditional and pragmatic; on the other hand there is no reason why the exchanges between scientists should not be as unconditional and open as those between Milton and Lawrence. But to maintain such a level of trust, certain norms would have to be accepted unconditionally, among them a commitment not to falsify or conceal data, in effect to be completely truthful, not just for the sake of the truth but for the sake also of the freedom of other truth-seekers. But the formulation of such a principle or maxim would constitute a 'truth' different in kind from the data, empirical and theoretical, of science as such or the norms of scientific behaviour as an activity justified in terms of results. In Newman's terms, the latter would be Subjective Truths — that which the individual scientist 'receives in particular and considers to be such' — and would be inherently corrigible and provisional. But scientists who intuited and assented to the full intellectual freedom of other scientists would find themselves embracing, maintaining and using a general proposition about truthfulness which was larger than their capacity, of which they could not see the bottom, and which they could not follow out in detail, yet which they could only accept unconditionally as the incontestable corollary of the inter-personal trust which scientific freedom assumes and requires.

8. Science, however, is not the only inter-personal activity, and strictly comparable certainties and maxims must arise from the grant of freedom in other areas of life as well. It would be entirely possible, for example, to conduct one's sexual life on decent principles of prudence and concern for the happiness of oneself and others — in which case, any rules of conduct which one adopted would be provisional, and subject to modification in the light of circumstances — but sexual relations based on the grant of freedom would logically require the unconditional acceptance of unchanging norms of conduct. A lie to a sexual partner, for example, about one's thoughts or feelings or acts, even one that took the form of a cautious silence, would be an offence against that partner's freedom and a negation of one's own: it would result from fear of how he or she might think or feel or act in consequence of learning the truth; it would express a will to control, not to liberate, and would entail submitting oneself to the exigencies of exercising that control. Equally lovers who entered a clandestine relationship would limit their joint freedom and impose specific limitations on each other, presumably out of fear of the reactions of other people. The maxims of sexual freedom,

therefore, would prohibit all relationships based on deceit or secrecy, and they would do so absolutely since the grant of freedom is negated if it is made conditionally. (These conclusions have obvious relevance to *The Portrait of a Lady*.) In principle, we may anticipate comparable maxims arising out of the application of the grant of freedom to the entire range of our social, economic and personal relationships.

9. But if the commandments of freedom are thus exact and absolute, their application to the circumstances of living must remain complex. The scientific maxim requiring full disclosure of results and conclusions, for example, does not entail an obligation on all scientists to communicate with each other without restraint in all circumstances. It could only do so if science, in the largest sense, were the only collaborative inter-personal activity in which the obligations of freedom might arise. But even within science itself, no less specific and indefeasible obligations must come into play as a consequence of particular collaborations with immediate colleagues, or from social and political allegiances, or possibly religious beliefs. It is also true that we live in time and in particular situations; that too is a condition the grant of freedom must accept in order to be itself. Its absolutism, therefore, can never be absolute. As St Paul repeatedly argues, a purely legalistic framework effectively negatives freedom. But freedom remains the territory in which norms of action are necessarily absolute. The grant of freedom thus presents us with an acute problem. It requires us to submit our actions unconditionally to judgement according to its norms but leaves us with the immensely difficult and possibly unsolvable problems of judging between any incompatible claims those norms may make on us and of applying them to situations which are in any case irreducibly particular. Does this mean that the maxims of freedom are finally useless, and the grant of freedom itself a mirage?

Some arguments of Newman (1870) suggest not. As I noted in the Introduction, Newman describes certitude as 'proper to the individual' (82), and so as thwarting rather than promoting 'the intercourse of man and man' (82–3). He also describes it as 'directed to this or that particular proposition; it is not a faculty or gift, but a disposition of mind relative to a definite case' (183). He thus regards the incidence of certitude as radically unsystematic: it cannot be accounted for in terms either of generalisable relations between minds or of stateable relations between propositions. It follows that no two certitudes can be compared with one another. My certitude concerning the roundness of the earth is not weakened by my knowing that in the past there were people who seem to have been certain the earth was flat because one certitude cannot be 'equal to' or 'the same as' another, not even two certitudes entertained by the same intelligence. I am no more or less 'certain', for example, that the earth is round than I am that my children have distinctive and knowable personalities. It follows that reflexively each certitude is a unique and incommunicable discovery about myself: only I can judge the indefectibility of my certitudes because only I have incommunicable access to how I know them.

Ferreira, however, quotes Newman as questioning whether he ought 'to be as open to listen to objections brought . . . against the honour, fidelity, love . . . of a friend, as against the received belief that the earth is 95 million miles from the Sun' (124), which suggests that matters of fact are somehow less certain than some matters of inter-personal knowledge, and that certitudes can, therefore, be compared. This apparent difficulty can be overcome, however, if we locate the difference in the proposition rather that the certitude. What Newman is certain of with respect to the distance of the earth from the sun is (a) that the evidence in favour of the received opinion is overwhelming and (b) that this is the kind of fact which in principle if not in practice is corrigible in the light of new data. Whether he is right to assert that this element of corrigibility can be excluded from what one knows of other human beings, and therefore from the certitudes which one entertains with respect to them, is beside the point. What is clear is that it can be precluded from one's certitude with respect to the maxims arising from the grant of freedom: I can *know* with indefectable certitude, for example, that adultery would be an offence against the freedom of my marriage.

But what of subtler and more complex situations? The maxims of freedom may conflict with one another (as they possibly did in the minds of some scientists working on the first atom bomb), or 'common sense' may suggest that in a particular situation another person might not be able to cope with freedom: it is not obvious, for example, that complete frankness about one's passing sexual impulses ought to be communicated to an harrassed or anxious partner. Here a second principle in Newman's thinking comes into play, his conviction that some certitudes involve willing as well as perceiving. Hence his denial (1870) as we have seen of legitimacy to certain kinds of of inquiry as being 'inconsistent with assent' (125), and his apparently illiberal conclusion that 'a

Catholic is not allowed to inquire into the truth of his Creed . . .
if he would retain the name of believer'. Whether Newman's
argument is sound with respect to catholicism is again not to the
point: it is certainly sound with respect to the maxims of freedom,
particularly when they seem to be in conflict, or when there
appears to be no obvious way of applying them in a particular
situation. Clearly such dilemmas may incite inquiry. I may *choose*
to question whether I am *really* bound to strict accuracy in report-
ing my experimental results, or to marital fidelity in circumstances
of stress and loneliness, but if I do so I cannot without absurdity
claim to be a believer in those maxims, or even a free agent. On
the other hand, I may accept the contradictions of freedom and
struggle in good faith to live with them. Thus even if the maxims
of freedom do not tell me what, in a given case, I should do, they
can remain in my mind as principles which I know to be true
because I have committed myself to them, and not merely as principles to which I am committed as long as I think them to be true.
In this sense, I am free to constitute cognition and consciousness
as conscience in the full sense, as certitudes concerning bare truth
about good which I have chosen to know for myself.

10. All this finds surprisingly detailed confirmation in Milton's
account in *Paradise Lost* of the fall of Eve, whose conversation with
the Serpent can be exactly represented as a movement from
fidelity to truth about good to an unlawful inquiry, in consequence
of which she sinfully abandons the inter-personal nexus of
freedom. We need to remember that before her fall Eve makes her
own assents. She may have had to learn about things from God,
Raphael and Adam, but their words are testimony only and *The
Art of Logic* tells us 'that in an investigation of the exact truth and
nature of things very meager probative force is commonly attributed to testimony . . . divine or human' (319). Thus the 'Faith,
Love, Vertue unassaid' (IX 335) of which Eve speaks before leaving Adam are truly hers and give her the *right* to work alone.
Adam bears witness to her moral self-sufficiency at this point in
the last words he speaks to her before her fall: 'For God towards
thee hath done his part, do thine' (IX 375).

Eve's decision to leave Adam is thus at root an act of significant
religious devotion and moral earnestness. Accordingly when she
meets the Serpent her reactions are wholly appropriate.
Confronted with its remarkable transformation, she properly
decides to develop her ideas about the potentialities of animals,
particularly as she has already speculated about their sensible

behaviour:

> for in thir looks
> Much reason, and in thir actions oft appears
>
> (IX 558–9)

This is a topic on which a change of mind following investigation is entirely legitimate in Newman's terms, since it does not involve any Objective Truths. Eve herself, therefore, remains intellectually and morally alert as her reply to the Serpent's next speech makes clear:

> Serpent, thy overpraising leaves in doubt
> The vertue of that Fruit, in thee first prov'd
>
> (IX 615–16)

Quite properly she follows the Serpent to the Tree and so discovers the alleged source of its newly developed powers. Her next speech is proof of an as yet unflawed integrity:

> Serpent, we might have spar'd our coming hither,
> Fruitless to mee, though Fruit be here to excess,
> The credit of whose vertue rest with thee,
> Wondrous indeed, if cause of such effects.
> But of this Tree we may not taste or touch;
> God so commanded, and left that Command
> Sole Daughter of his voice; the rest we live
> Law to our selves, our Reason in our Law
>
> (IX 647–54)

Thus the moment Eve realises what tree the Serpent has been talking about she brings her investigation to an end. To proceed further would be to move, in Newman's terms, from investigation to inquiry, which would involve her withdrawing her assent from propositions about Objective Truths to which as a creature of God and the wife of Adam she is irrevocably committed. Her next speech, therefore, the last she speaks 'yet sinless' (IX 659), is dogmatic in exactly Newman's sense: in other words she resorts to a 'use of creeds [which] seems to the Rationalist superstitious and unmeaning'. Her words are:

> Of the Fruit
> Of each Tree in the Garden we may eate,
> But of the Fruit of this fair Tree amidst
> The Garden, God hath said, Ye shall not eate
> Thereof, nor shall ye touch it, lest ye die
>
> (IX 659–63)

By the end of Satan's next speech, however, her thinking has degenerated into that of an inquirer, in the sense deplored by Newman, and in consequence of this she assents to the false proposition that

> Here grows the Cure of all, this Fruit Divine,
> Fair to the Eye, inviting to the Taste,
> Of vertue to make wise
>
> (IX 776–8)

11. But, we may ask (following Empson), how can an assent as such, or a false inference, be sinful? Why may we not regard it as a tragic mistake, arising possibly out of intellectual weakness, but not something for which anyone can justly be blamed? There is no doubt, after all, of the Serpent's urging interesting and serious arguments, as when it puts the question

> will God incense his ire
> For such a petty Trespass, and not praise
> Rather your dauntless vertue, whom the pain
> Of Death denounc't, whatever thing Death be,
> Deterrd not from atchieving what might leade
> To happier life, knowledge of Good and Evil
>
> (IX 692–7)

At one level the answer is simple. It is sinful for Eve to become an inquirer in this case, because of the certitude with which she enunciates her creed in lines 659–63 — that is, because those lines specify Objective Truths and Eve *knows* that they do so beyond any possibility of error. The problem with such an explanation is that we are not, and could never be, in a position to accept or reject it. Like any other person, Eve is enclosed in her own reasons when she makes an assent, and consequently when she achieves certitude. God excepted, she alone is judge of the powers of her own cognitive and conscious life in such matters. On similar grounds, she alone can know why she decides to abandon the dogmatic principle and become an inquirer. But this does not mean that we are unable to scrutinise the evidence, and at least make judgements about probabilities and possibilities. If we were not able to do so, Milton's entire project in narrating the fall would be redundant. It makes sense, therefore, to scrutinise her speeches for evidence, and in particular to identify differences between the kinds of things she says in her sinless state, and the kinds of things she says after her fall to see if any relatively persuasive explanations present themselves.

Eve's sinless, 'dogmatic' speeches may be characterised as radically inter-personal: she locates herself, her essence within the triad God on the one hand and the plural 'Ye' — Adam and herself — on the other. This personalistic vocabulary gives a significant character to our sense of her sense of her duty. 'Duty', the Pope writes, 'may be viewed as . . . the consequence of a ready-made and preexistent moral or legal principle' (163). An unexplained prohibition on the eating of a particular food might be an example of such a principle.

> In this approach [he continues] duty may appear to be
> something derived from without the subject-person . . .
> [But] *duties* with regard to other people present themselves
> differently; they occur in virtue of an interpersonal *nexus* of
> 'participation'.

It is only on account of this inter-personal nexus that mere law can be understood as belonging to the person. Thus in one sense, Eve's duty is obedience to an externally imposed law, but in another it is obedience to God and trust in him, and fidelity to Adam. This the dogmatic, maxim-informed content of her first speech acknowledges. She knows that God has a plan, a future for Adam and herself, a scenario, in which their obedience or disobedience to the injunction about the forbidden fruit is a part. But she does not know God's reasons, though she does know that her not knowing is itself part of his scenario, the specific demand which accepting his sovereign will for Adam and herself makes upon her. She thus knows herself to be subject by nature to the limitations of inter-personal dependence; she is defined essentially by the limitless yet specific opportunities afforded by 'participation' in a providentially constituted set of relationships. Her own nature is thus the stage on which the drama of her obedience is enacted.

Newman (1870) sees this as a condition general to human beings.

> My first elementary lesson of duty [he writes] is that of resignation to the laws of my nature, whatever they are; my first disobedience is to be impatient at what I am, and to indulge an ambitious aspiration after what I cannot be, to cherish a distrust of my powers, and to desire to change laws which are identical with myself (273).

From this standpoint, the laws of Eve's being under obedience are the laws of inter-personal relationships. She can determine her life in the light of reasons and wants certainly, but also and more fundamentally in the light of the specific, incontrovertible obligations revealed by the logic of obedience and love, both of which require from her an acceptance of God's freedom, and Adam's, not just in principle but in the situation she finds herself in that morning in Eden.

Her first disobedience is not an action in defiance of those laws but a rejection of the consciousness or conscience that makes them such. This she achieves by indulging an ambitious aspiration after what she cannot be — a consciousness with no other way of thinking or feeling but that suggested by the seductively open and easy laws of reason and process. This is evident in the emergence of a deterministic vocabulary in the speech which precedes her fall beginning 'Great are thy vertues, doubtless, best of Fruits' (IX 745–79), which is full of abstract subjects and passive verbs and past participles — 'kept from Man, and worthy to be admir'd, / Whose taste . . . / Gave elocution to the mute . . . / his forbidding / . . . inferrs the good / By thee communicated, and our want: / For good unknown, sure is not had.' The fruit is speciously personified, but the whole speech expresses a repudiation of the personal. Eve's sin is thus to depersonalise life; it is a surrender (as the second love-making scene confirms) of will to appetite, of man and woman *acting* as erotic partners, to *what happens* sexually in and between them. It is a withdrawal from 'participation' in the mutuality of free and acting persons.

12. Exactly the reverse of this deformation of the life of Eve seems to be depicted in *The Portrait of a Lady*. Again this is not formally demonstrable. We can no more know the truth about Isabel than we can the truth about Eve, and in any case our own deepest convictions on the subject, if Newman is correct, must

remain private to ourselves. Nevertheless there is a body of evidence to suggest that Isabel Archer exemplifies a supreme altruism, a transcendence of calculation which is grounded in the grant of freedom and the absolute moral injunctions to which it calls her.

Isabel's role as the giver of freedom in the novel comes most sharply into focus in her relations with her husband and Madame Merle, both of whom, and especially Gilbert, are consistently represented as taking exactly the opposite attitude, and as then finding that as coercers they are themselves coerced. Ralph is the first to notice this —

> that under the guise of caring only for intrinsic values Osmond lived exclusively for the world. Far from being its master as he pretended to be, he was its very humble servant, and the degree of its attention was his only measure of success. (II 144)

The contrast between Gilbert and Isabel in this respect is subsequently given authorial endorsement:

> Her notion of the aristocratic life [we are told] was simply the union of great knowledge with great liberty; the knowledge would give one a sense of duty and the liberty a sense of enjoyment. But for Osmond it was altogether a thing of forms, a conscious, calculated attitude . . . He had an immense esteem for tradition; he told her once . . . that if one was so unfortunate as not to have it one must immediately proceed to make it . . . [From] what source he had derived his traditions she never learned. He had a very large collection of them, however . . . and . . . [the] great thing was to act in accordance with them; the great thing not only for him but for her. (II 198–9)

As Isabel herself comes to realise, for him the 'real offence . . . was her having a mind of her own at all' (II 200). It is this which makes Gilbert and Ralph enemies, the latter being as Gilbert recognises, 'an apostle of freedom' (II 245), and therefore a threat to the project on which Gilbert has set his heart, to deny Isabel 'freedom of mind'.

Such projects, however, extinguish Gilbert's own freedom and Madame Merle's as well — notably in their pursuit of Lord Warburton as a husband for Pansy. 'How much you must want to make sure of him!' (II 264), Isabel exclaims at one point, an insight reinforced in a later conversation with Madame Merle who is convinced that for her own reasons Isabel is putting pressure on Lord Warburton to abandon his pursuit of Pansy. 'Let him off — let us have him!' (II 326), she cries. The 'us' alarms Isabel. 'Who are you — what are you', she asks, 'What have you to do with my husband? . . . What have you to do with me?' (II 326-7). 'Everything!' Madame Merle answers, and Isabel realises at last that Madame Merle has 'married her'. Two important developments in Isabel's thinking occur almost at once — she sees Madame Merle as *wicked*, and she realises that Gilbert must have made her pay cruelly for involving him in a marriage which has become unutterably distasteful to him; at which thought, characteristically, she exclaims 'Poor, Madame Merle!' (II 331).

13. Isabel, then, is defined as someone who leaves other people in their own willing. (So, incidentally, does her aunt, Mrs Touchett.) The response of those others to the freedom thus bestowed upon them is an exact, and in some ways painful, measure of their goodness. Thus it is no exaggeration to say that, in the face of Isabel's unqualified toleration of their wickedness, Gilbert and Madame Merle cast themselves into an internalised hell.

In her last scene with Gilbert, Isabel interrupts him as he is working meticulously in water colours copying an antique coin. The telegram has just arrived, summoning her to Ralph's deathbed. She tells Gilbert of her wish to go; he forbids her to do so, and says any decision on her part contrary to his wishes would be 'the most deliberate, the most calculated, opposition' (II 354). She protests at the injustice of this, and declares that it is his opposition to her that is 'calculated' and even 'malignant'. In reply he speaks quietly but eloquently of their union, and almost persuades her that it is 'like the sign of the cross or flag of one's country . . . something sacred and precious — the observance of a magnificent form' (II 356), thus reviving an image which the authorial commentary has made a symbol of Isabel's good faith. But she persists and the following exchange takes place between them:

'I suppose, that if I go you'll not expect me to come back', said Isabel.

He turned quickly round, and she could see this movement at least was not designed. He looked at her a little, and then, 'Are you out of your mind?' he inquired.

'How can it be anything but a rupture?' she went on; 'especially if all you say is true?' She was unable to see how it could be anything but a rupture; she sincerely wished to know what else it might be.

He sat down before his table. 'I really can't argue with you on the hypotheses of your defying me', he said. And he took up one of his little brushes again. (II 357–8)

The loss of control is slight, but it matches exactly Gilbert's inability to confront the possibilities opened up by Isabel's power to choose. Her freedom is an undiscussable chaos. As he takes up his little brush again, he shrinks from it into his own impotence like a touched sea-anenome. In its affected, unheroic way, the gesture is comparable with Satan's plunging from the pinnacle of the Temple in *Paradise Regain'd*, 'smitten with amazement' at the unself-regarding continence of the Son of God.

Madame Merle's moment of damnation follows quickly. It is perhaps less decisive (the prospect of repentance is held out) but more explicit than Gilbert's. Having decided to return to England, Isabel goes to see Pansy in her convent; she has been told the full story of the girl's parentage by Gilbert's sister and at the convent she meets Madame Merle, who realises that Isabel now knows the whole truth, and that her 'only safety' (II 378) is 'in her not betraying herself'. But she is not so well-defended as Gilbert, and Isabel senses her insecurity at once.

That Madame Merle had lost her pluck and saw before her the phantasm of exposure — this in itself was a revenge, this in itself was almost the promise of a brighter day. And for a moment . . . Isabel enjoyed that knowledge . . . [If] she had turned and spoken she would have said something that would hiss like a lash. But she closed her eyes, and then the hideous vision dropped. What remained was the cleverest woman in the world standing there within a few feet of her and knowing as little what to think as the meanest. Isabel's only revenge was to be silent still — to leave Madame Merle in this unprecedented situation. (II 379)

Isabel's freedom is to be silent, *not* to inflict pain — it is a reticence again comparable with that of Milton's Jesus — Madame Merle's punishment being precisely Isabel's refusal to inflict punishment and so leaving her *unable to think*, unable to use the freedom permitted her.

14. The contrast between the paralysis which the grant of freedom thus induces in Gilbert and Madame Merle, and the vital play of feeling, thought and action between Isabel and Ralph, could not be greater. A passage describing these complexities must be quoted at length.

> Ah yes, if Gilbert were jealous of her there was perhaps some reason . . . It was not that they talked of him — it was not that she complained. His name was never uttered between them. It was simply that Ralph was generous and that her husband was not. There was something in Ralph's talk, in his smile, in the mere fact of his being in Rome, that made the blasted circle round which she walked more spacious. He made her feel the good of the world; he made her feel what might have been. He was after all as intelligent as Osmond — quite apart from his being better. And thus it seemed to her an act of devotion to conceal her misery from him . . . It lived before her again . . . that morning in the garden at Florence when he had warned her against Osmond . . . She had told him then that from her at least he should never know if he was right; and this was what she was taking care of now. It gave her plenty to do; there was passion, exaltation, religion in it . . . [In] playing a part before her cousin, [she] had an idea that she was doing him a kindness . . . [The] kindness consisted mainly in trying to make him believe that he had once wounded her greatly and that the event had put him to shame, but that, as she was very generous and he was so ill, she bore him no grudge, and even considerably forebore to flaunt her happiness in his face. Ralph smiled to himself, as he lay on the sofa, at this extraordinary form of consideration; but he forgave her for having forgiven him. (II 203-4)

Clearly, at this stage, the relation between Isabel and Ralph is flawed because there is a withholding of truth on both sides, but its foundation, originating in Ralph, and indirectly reflected back on him from Isabel, is an exchange of freedom which goes far beyond his being the ultimate source of her mere wealth.

It is this which makes possible the unbearable beauty of the final unqualified openness between them when Ralph is dying. He confesses to having enriched her and so to having probably 'ruined' (II 414) her; she admits to having 'always tried to keep [him] from understanding; but that's all over' (II 415). 'I always understood', Ralph says. 'I thought you did', Isabel replies, 'and I didn't like it. But now I like it.' 'You don't hurt me. You make me happy', Ralph tells her, and there is 'an extraordinary gladness in his voice'. They have moved into a perfected mutuality which is identical with the autonomy each grants to the other. Isabel is thus free to make a remark that is puzzling and possibly troublesome to Ralph — but that is the price both must pay for freedom. He asks her if it is all over between Gilbert and herself. 'Oh no', she answers; 'I don't think anything's over.'

15. This is a troublesome remark because it seems to contradict the implications of her decision to defy Gilbert and come to see her cousin. Her last recorded words to Gilbert quoted above, indicate her sense at the time that to leave Rome would be to end her marriage. Overwhelmingly her friends — Ralph above all — see her decision to do so as as act of self-liberation. 'I don't believe', Ralph tells her, 'that such a generous mistake as yours can hurt you for more than a little' (II 417). For his part, Caspar feels personally liberated by Isabel's action since until her defiance of Gilbert he felt obliged to accept her presentation herself as a loyal and faithful partner in a settled and successful marriage. When he meets her in the garden, however, he can say to her:

'. . . today I know on good authority. Everything's clear to me today. It was a good thing when you made me come away [from Rome] with your cousin. He was a good man, a fine man, one of the best; he told me how the case stands for you. He explained everything; he guessed my sentiments. He was a member of your family and he left you — so long as you should be in England — to my care . . . Do you know what he said to me the last time I saw him — as he lay there where he died? He said: "Do everything you can for her; do everything she'll let you" ' (588)

Even in death, Ralph respects Isabel's freedom, and in repeating the words, 'everything she'll let you' Caspar shows that he does so too. They accept that shared longing to liberate Isabel from Gilbert does not license their attempting to control her, even though Isabel's desire to be free of him too is hardly to be doubted. But unlike them, she cannot see that anything is 'over'. Why not? What flag is she continuing to fly, and with what justification?

Having listened to Gilbert's objections to her going to see Ralph, Isabel thinks at length about the significance of doing so: 'going when Osmond wished her to remain' (II 361), she decides, would be an act of 'violence'.

> What he thought of her she knew, what he was capable of saying to her that she felt; yet they were married, for all that, and marriage meant that a woman should cleave to the man with whom, uttering tremendous vows, she had stood at the altar.

Her faithfulness is thus to a principle rather than a person, to an ideal or maxim which she has thought out and accepted for herself. But she then acts in defiance of the norm of wifely obedience which she has imposed on herself: she defies Gilbert and goes to the dying Ralph. This decision cannot, however, be described as backsliding, no matter how serious her commitment to the vows of marriage, because in leaving Rome she is evidently acting in the light of other obligations equally entailed in the free inter-personal exchanges of her life. The point that she makes in her final exchange with Ralph, however — it was the point, too, of her last question to Gilbert — is that even if one does from time to time have to act in defiance of a deep conviction, one does not stop being bound by it subsequently; that is the sense in which nothing is ever 'over'. She has over-ridden the demands of one obligation in deference to the demands of another, but the first obligation remains in place — the generosity motivating a mistaken promise cannot of itself justify setting it aside. In any case she has given fresh undertakings to Pansy. The issue therefore is not whether she has escaped from Gilbert, but whether she may set aside the unconditional obligations which arise inexorably from the logic of her decision to live as a free being. She decides not to do so. She has entered, it seems, the drama of participation from which Eve fell.

For many readers a conscience as demanding as this would be better described as a sado-masochistic super-ego, and as my earlier remarks about James's procedures as a writer make clear, it is possible that he may have thought so too. But even that would not be inconsistent with the kinds of insight into the workings of freedom which I believe the novel may make available to us. The whole concept of freedom for which I am contending, after all, is necesarily elusive and fragile; it can easily be concealed behind explicit meanings which seem to prohibit it; it is a principle of knowledge in ignorance, of intimacy in isolation, of vision in blindness. Its certainties are those of the wise heart, its confidence faith. It cannot be directly represented in logical or scientific language. It is violated to the extent that arguments are adduced which purport to determine assent to it. Nevertheless, *The Portrait of a Lady* seems to me to illustrate with terrible clarity three major principles: that freedom consists solely in willing the freedom of others; that willing the freedom of others imposes on those who undertake it obligations which are absolute, specific, open-ended and irreversible; and that a conscience informed by such a logic can indeed act, as the Pope puts it, in the name of bare truth about good. Such a conscience, in Newman's celebrated words (1875) 'is the aboriginal Vicar of Christ, a prophet in its informations, a monarch in its peremptoriness, a priest in its blessings and anathemas' (250). The possibility of acting according to conscience is the one hope that Isabel Osmond finally holds out to us — and it leaves the young Caspar Goodwood desolate.

9

The Spirit of *Différance*

1. Up to this point my project has been to define the circumstances in which the full freedom of indifference may be properly attributed to rational beings. However, as I indicated in the Introduction, this could only be done by suspending consideration of the insights into the operations of language known broadly as deconstructionism. This will not have surprised anyone familiar with these ideas, since mine has been a persistently theological topic and in the words of Roland Barthes (1968), the deconstructionist notion of writing 'liberates what may be called an anti-theological activity, an activity that is truly revolutionary since to refuse to fix meaning is, in the end, to refuse God and his hypostases — reason, science, law' (147). Derrida (1967(b)) similary argues that writing reveals a stage or set on which 'the punctual simplicity of the classical subject is not to be found' (227). Deconstructionism thus threatens to obliterate the stage or set on which I have tried to dramatise my main argument, since if there was ever a territory in which the classical subject might be deemed to flourish it is surely the works of Milton. The deconstructionist challenge cannot, therefore, be ignored, and it will therefore be necessary to examine briefly, but I hope not inaccurately, some of the less recondite arguments advanced by

deconstructionist criticism in recent years.

2. Deconstructionism derives from post-Saussurean analysis of signs, a topic already touched on in my discussion of Bakhtin's objections to phenomenology. A rudimentary account of signs would distinguish between the sign itself — the signifier — and that for which it stands — the signified, the latter being always an idea and never an object in reality (the referent). If I say the word 'dog', for example, only my 'meaning' enters the minds of those I am addressing, not a living animal, nor even in most cases anything so definite as a picture. The weakness of such a description of sign-making activity, however, is that, in Derrida's words, it is grounded in 'the principle of non-contradiction' (217) which he regards as 'the cornerstone of all metaphysics or presence'. This requires that the meaning of a sign should be fixed in a larger system of meaning which is finally coherent and unambiguous, so that when I speak in the company of others we all of us know what is meant, we are present to each other, and the thing meant is present to us all. But words do not have fixed meanings. The word 'dog', for example, does not stand consistently, uniquely and exclusively for one of a species of four-legged animals. It can also be used of a person, as a verb, or (in the case of Winston Church-ill) of a mood. We work out what it means in each case from the other signs among which it is placed: 'The dog gnaws a bone'; 'I will dog his footsteps'; 'The black dog is upon me'. This is simply to illustrate Bakhtin's observation that a 'sign can be illuminated only by another sign' (36).

In the traditional view, however, such slippage of meaning is limited. There is supposed to be a core meaning to which the word 'dog' is tethered which limits the play of sense facilitated by other signifiers. A word's meaning is supposed to be determined by its 'root', for example, or by a strong idea to which it has become attached in the course of linguistic history. Again, there is the commonly felt conviction that if the sense of a word is not tied to its own meaning, it is tied to what I mean when I use it, and that it can be made to perform the tricks I wish it to perform in the semiotic circus-ring. One way or another, we traditionally assume that the contexts which make it possible for a word to signify something are under control. Accordingly in our assumptions about language, Derrida suggests, we 'conceive of structure on the basis of a full presence which is beyond play' (279), and it is this conception which deconstructionism challenges.

3. Briefly deconstructionism denies that meaning is ever fixed

or fixable, and that any attempt to constrain the play of signifiers expresses anxiety or betrays a will to violence. Deconstructionists point out how the openness of language to multiple and contradictory interpretation is particularly obvious in the case of writing because writing is extended in space, its signifiers visibly in waiting, concretely registering the independence of the signifier from the signified. Writing is language with meaning absent, without the presence of an intending mind or a living context to keep it under control. Hence the compulsion to exercise such control by further writing. Scripture provokes the commentator, literature the critic. As Michel Foucault remarks, 'Commentary averts the unpredictable in discourse by giving it its due: it allows us to say something other than the text itself, but on condition that it is the text itself that is spoken and, in a sense, fulfilled' (quoted in Sheridan, 1980, 125). The commentator or critic, Derrida (1979) argues, thus opposes the illogicality of language which he suggests Nietzsche discovered in metaphor. Metaphor, Nietzsche wrote, 'brings about an identification of the nonidentical; it is thus an operation of the imagination'. Derrida's citation of this remark (83) is followed by an admission that philosophers have always known about the illogicality of language, and have therefore insisted on 'the secondary nature of the sign in relation to the idea' (84). But Nietzsche, Derrida argues, has shown metaphor to be 'the very structure or condition of possibility of all language and concepts'.

It follows that signifieds are really only the shadows cast by signifiers, not substantial things to which signifiers are attached as so many labels: meanings do not control language but rather language is both constitutive of meanings and indifferent to them. This is because the signifier is ineradicably *different* from what it signifies. It does not even inhabit the same moment, because there is an inevitable delay between the moment a word is heard and the moment when its function is recognised. This effect is less obvious when language is spoken because speakers and listeners work in the illusion of synchronic interaction: experientially speech generates spontaneous and intimate presence. But writing turns the apparently trivial delays of speech into measurable linear space. It confirms the distance from one end of a sentence to the other, and the time between utterance and understanding. Writing thus puts on record the fact that the sign is never what we like to think it is, that signifier and signified are *different* and that the connections between signifiers by which the signifieds are produced are always subject to delay. Hence Derrida's coinage *différance* — a sign which implies delay and which elides with the orthodox *différance* to suggest the structurelessness of language in logic, time and space.

Différance, however, does not endow the signifier with simple chronological priority over the signified. Derrida (1967(a)) attacks the prejudice of 'an Idea or "interior design" as simply anterior to a work' (11), but he also attacks the obverse of this prejudice which subordinates the work to whatever design is discerned in the limitless play of signifiers. This, he suggests, would turn the users of language into Creator-Gods: it would ignore their 'finitude' and 'solitude'. The Old Testament prophet was right, therefore, to be terrified putting pen to paper and getting things wrong — for writing is always secondary — it reveals what is already there. Hence Derrida's necessarily awkward formulation (1967(a)) to which I alluded in the Introduction:

> Meaning must await being written or said in order to inhabit itself . . .
> . . . Writing is *inaugural* . . . It does not know where it is going, no knowledge can keep it from the essential precipitation toward the meaning that it constitutes, and that is, primarily, its future. (11)

Meaning, therefore, already is what it has yet to become. Deconstructionism insists on the limitations of language while affirming its limitless freedom; it privileges the signifier but denies it the status of source or origin. It acknowledges no boundaries, no controlling intelligence and will, neither God nor subject nor object. It offers perpetual anxiety — 'we must *decide* whether we will engrave what we hear', Derrida writes, '. . . whether engraving preserves or betrays speech' (9) — but also affirmation —

> the joyous information of the play of the world and of the innocence of becoming, the affirmation of a world of signs without fault, without truth, and without origin which . . . determines *the noncenter otherwise than as loss of the center.* (292)

4. If these arguments have merit, much of what I have been arguing for seems doomed. My analysis of reading the sonnet to Lawrence, out of which I developed the notion of the grant of freedom, for example, apparently relies on assumptions about text

and reader which deconstructionism shows to be misconceived. Thus, for Derrida, texts do not exist. He argues that metaphysicians have traditionally assumed that the complete and perfect text of a work was to be found somewhere — in an unpublished manuscript, in the mind of the author, in the mind of God, or perhaps just in principle, and that consciousness could get hold of such a text and learn it completely and definitively. But, he insists, there 'is no text written or present elsewhere which would then be subjected, without being changed in the process, to an operation and a temporalization . . . which would be external to it' (211). This applies to all texts, actual and conceivable, from his own books to the Book of the Universe, i.e. the comprehensive description of the world hypothesised in possible-world arguments. There is an affinity between this view and Kenny's argument (1979) that in 'advance of the decision to create . . . God cannot know which of the relevant counterfactuals are true' (70) and that therefore the moral consequences of a particular act of creation of free agents cannot be anticipated. 'Texts' and 'worlds' cannot exist knowably prior to their being read or actualised. They arise out of a forgettable past and precipitate themselves into a future which alone can constitute even what they currently are. Texts, therefore, can tell us nothing definitive about their readers, and consequently my entire argument about primary and secondary signification seems unviable. We really are completely without a centre, even the reader-subject discovering noncentre as something other than loss of the centre.

5. The attentive reader of Milton, however, might question whether this is really so. Thus there is abundant evidence that Milton himself was aware of *différance* (without, of course, knowing the word) and that he understood presence and so the classical subject in its light. In *Paradise Lost*, for example, Raphael is quite explicit about the impossibility of relating

> To human sense th' invisible exploits
> Of warring Spirits

$$(V\ 565\text{--}6)$$

'God, as he really is', Milton writes in *Christian Doctrine* 'is far beyond man's imagination, let alone his understanding' (133); the best we can do is 'to form an image . . . in our minds which corresponds to his representation and descriptions of himself in the sacred writings'. What he chooses to give us concerning himself, therefore, are privileged signifiers only. We may 'believe that it is not beneath God to feel what grief he does feel, to be refreshed by what refreshes him, and to fear what he does fear' (135), but that does nothing to bridge the great gulf fixed between all signification and the Divine Referent. God can only appear in discourse as Nietzschean metaphor, as a series of signs with no claim to 'truth', but invested none the less with a legitimate effectiveness in the human imagination sufficient to generate a sense of real and specific obligations in our minds.

This is the view adopted in the poem by Raphael when he undertakes to delineate

> what surmounts the reach
> Of human sense . . .
> By lik'ning spiritual to corporal forms,
> As may express them best
>
> (V 571-4)

Like the author of *Christian Doctrine*, Raphael is an optimist about language, but only after he has taken careful account of the independence of the signifier from the signified. Hence the ambiguity of 'express them best' which may mean that Raphael will make the best of a bad job or that his choice of metaphors will be effective in spite of everything. The latter view is strengthened by Raphael's next words:

> though what if Earth
> Be but the shaddow of Heav'n, and things therin
> Each to other like, more than on Earth is thought?
>
> (V 574-6)

The difficulties of narration, may after all, be less than they seem. Thus the one set of significations that we thought we had clearly grasped, namely that 'difference' means difference, can itself be undermined. It can mean astonishing sameness. This does not, of course, reinstate any definite connections between signifier and signified in discourse about God, but it does open up optimistic possibilities within the play of signifiers.

6. Milton's sense of linguistic play, however, is not confined to his writing about the celestial order. The reckless cosmology of *Paradise Lost* as suggested by the dance of the angels in the Book V extends the freedom of signs from heaven to earth:

Mystical dance, which yonder starrie Spheare
Of Planets, and of fixt in all her Wheeles
Resembles nearest, mazes intricate,
Eccentric, intervolv'd, yet regular
Then most, when most irregular they seem,
And in thir motions harmonie Divine
So smooths her charming tones, that Gods own eare
Listens delighted

(V 620–7)

The dance is 'mystical' — it signifies a secret — and the sign of this sign is the intricately schematised motion of the planets and fixed stars around the earth: the ingenious equations of the final stages of Ptolemaic astronomy are probably in Milton's mind, but this is a Ptolemaic text in a putatively Copernican age: in reality the stars may not be fixed and the sun may not be a planet. At this point, however, we are so absorbed in the graceful freedom of the signifiers that the transition from doubtful science to pure rhetoric in the personification of Harmony (who is both feminine and divine and therefore a pagan figure) is effected without any sense of strain. So is the transformation of God from the thunderer of his Son's epiphany ten lines earlier to a princely connoisseur of music and choreography in a renaissance court.

But that is not all. This cluster of images has appeared before. In Book I when the great mass of fallen angels are reduced to the size of smallest Dwarfs, they are said to be

like that Pigmean Race
Beyond the *Indian* Mount, or Faerie Elves,
Whose midnight Revels, by a Forrest side
Or Fountain some belated Peasant sees,
Or dreams he sees, while over-head the Moon
Sits Arbitress, and neerer to the Earth
Wheels her pale course, they on thir mirth and dance
Intent, with jocund Music charm his ear

(I 780–7)

Here the revels are balefully subject to the inconstant moon, the dancers are not angels but 'elves — explicitly fictional creatures — and the charmed ear is not God's but that of a drunken rustic. Nevertheless, Hell is here perversely signifying Heaven, though this would hardly be matter of comment if such cross-signification were always as apparently casual and intermittent as this example appears to be. But it is not: it is quite systematic, and we have therefore to accustom ourselves to a text which allows signs even of God himself to slip and slide into theological and moral anarchy.

The most confusing example of this anarchy is probably the intrusion of the two overtly allegorical figures, Sin and Death, into the action of the poem. Their fictionality is flaunted, notably in the allusion to Greek myth in the story of the conception of Sin. It is indicated also in the casual reference to Death as a 'Goblin' (II 688), which places him in a fantastic frame exactly comparable with that of the 'elves' who entertain the peasant in Book I. Yet Sin and Death do more than intrude upon the story; as nearly every commentator has pointed out, they become types, not only of Adam and Eve, but, with Satan, of the Trinity also. Like the Son and Eve, Sin comes forth from her progenitor and is embosomed with him. In Book II, in words redolent of Heaven and of Eden alike, she reminds Satan how she had at first seemed 'Sign Portentous' to the rebel angels,

> but familar grown,
> I pleas'd, and with attractive graces won
> The most averse, thee chiefly, who full oft
> Thy self in me thy perfect image viewing
> Becam'st enamour'd
>
> (II 760–5)

Here an overt fiction masquerades both as a fact and as a type or sign of other fact, a signifier, which is explicitly a signifier only, acting the part of a signified, and in such a way as to suggest the fictionality of every other person and thing in the poem, up to and including the Father viewing his own perfect Image in the Son.

7. Milton, then perceives and exploits the centrelessness of language in his treatment of both God and the cosmos, but we have still to examine whether he does so with the kind of anxiety which a disciple of Barthes would expect him to exhibit. This will require our analysing his treatment of the divine attributes, specifically God's omnipresence, immutability and omniscience as they relate to his conceptions of the divine and the human.

We know from *Christian Doctrine* that Milton thought that matter was part of the divine substance from which God's will had been withdrawn. We have therefore to think of space and matter as existing within Milton's God, however peripherally, as well as of his God pervading them. For Milton, then, God is presence and centre. Does this mean that the idea of God underwrites the illusion of presence and centre in his writing? The poem apparently says as much. Raphael assures Adam that

> As God in Heav'n
> Is Center, yet extends to all, so thou
> Centring receiv'st from all those Orbs; in thee,
> Not in themselves, all thir known vertue appeers
>
> (IX 107–10)

On analysis, however, these words are more complicated than they seem. The orbs Raphael refers to are the heavenly bodies, and, as we saw in considering the angelic dance, the reader is expected to know that the earth may not be the centre of the universe after all. Consequently the 'vertue' discovered in those orbs must be a consequence of Adam's conscious assumption of the role of the centre; in his perception of them, and not in their physical relation to the earth, 'all thir *known* vertue appeers'. Thus Adam's centredness is affirmed, and yet — since the earth is not the true centre after all — he is decentred as well. But so by implication is God, to the extent, at least, that 'As' in the first line quoted means 'In the same way as'. Thus the centre is apparently not tethered to the centre either in Adam's case or in God's.

This notion is developed further when Adam is decentred and faces expulsion from Eden and apparently exile from God's presence. Michael, however, explores the situation more deeply:

> *Adam*, thou knowst Heav'n his, and all the Earth.
> Not this Rock onely; his Omnipresence fills
> Land, Sea, and Aire, and every kinde that lives,
> Fomented by his virtual power and warmd:
> All th' Earth he gave thee to possess and rule.
> No despicable gift; surmise not then
> His presence to these narrow bounds confin'd
> Of Paradise or *Eden*: this had been
> Perhaps thy Capital Seat, from whence had spred
> All generations, and had hither come
> From all the ends of th' Earth, to celebrate
> And reverence thee thir great Progenitor.
> But this præeminence thou has lost, brought down

To dwell on eeven ground now with thy Sons:
Yet doubt not but in Vallie and in plaine
God is as here, and will be found alike
Present, and of his presence many a signe
Still following thee, still compassing thee round
With goodness and paternal Love, his Face
Express, and of his steps the Track Divine

(XI 335–54)

The centre is thus provisional and unstable. Unfallen Adam would have been patriarchial ruler and Eden the centre of the human world, but with the fall it has lost that pre-eminence, and Adam has lost his own centrality: he must now dwell on 'eeven ground' with his sons. (Milton is making a strongly republican point here.) In reality, of course, the notion of Eden as centre was an illusion any way, since God's omnipresence has always filled the universe, and even now foments and warms all living things. Consequently in losing his centrality Adam loses nothing since God, who is the real centre, is not himself centred but spread out everywhere. At the same time Adam becomes, or remains, central, because he is surrounded by signs or traces of God's fomenting and warming power. The divine centre is thus orbital like the stars, even though — or rather precisely because — the stars are not really but only symbolically in orbit around the earth. In insisting on God's omnipresence, therefore, Milton makes all centredness, divine and human, a signifier only, and so subject to the endless displacements of that condition.

8. But, a deconstructionist might argue, do not Michael's words plainly imply the full presence of God since not even the Fall can erase his Track or trace in creation? 'An unerasable trace', Derrida (1969(a)) argues, '. . . is a full presence, . . . a son of God, a sign of parousia' (230). This is a fundamental objection and it can only be addressed through a consideration of Milton's treatment of God's relation to time and to creation.

We have seen that Milton believed that only tensed actions could be free, yet it is impossible to fix any moment in the poem when God acts *in propria persona*. Even the supreme act which he performs singly and by himself — the generation of the Son — is never present in the narrative, but is referred to through a series of subsequent and symbolic epiphanies. The first of these is particularly mysterious:

As yet this World was not, and *Chaos* wilde
Reignd where these Heav'ns now rowl, where Earth now
    rests
Upon her Center pois'd, when on a day
(For time, though in Eternitie, appli'd
To motion, measures all things durable
By present, past, and future) on such day
As Heav'ns great Year brings forth, th' Empyreal Host
Of Angels by Imperial summons call'd,
Innumerable before th' Almighties Throne
Forthwith from all the ends of Heav'n appear'd
Under thir Hierarchs in orders bright

(V 577–87)

This fascinating sentence begins in uncentred space, or if centred
only by anticipation in the fictional sign of a centred earth; it then
introduces the notion of a 'day' in chaos, but only to decentre and
supplement it, to decentre it by locating it in Eternity, to supplement it, by enclosing it in Time (so as to 'protect' it from Eternity)
and by enlarging it structurally with references to present, past
and future, and 'Heav'ns great Year' — an astrological signifier
antedating the creation of the heavenly bodies and their mystical,
36,000-year dance. The moment of the begetting is thus concealed
by being specified. So is the action itself. The subject of the most
important though technically not the main clause of the sentence
emerges late — meaning here has emphatically to wait in order to
inhabit itself. Nor when it finally appears is that subject God, but
only 'Th' Empyreal Host'. We are told that the angels are 'calld'
but not by whom and when they obey they approach not God
himself but 'th' Almighties Throne'. Finally in the lines following
those quoted another main clause appears as from nowhere.

We are then given a mysterious picture, of the Father,

By whom in bliss embosm'd sat the Son,
Amidst as from a flaming Mount, whose top
Brightness had made invisible

(V 597–9)

The throne has thus become a mountain top so bright as to render
the Father invisible and Son's position uncertain, for either he is
sitting *beside* (by) the Father, or he has been embosomed *by* him

in bliss and is sitting *amidst* the brightness. And when at last God speaks he announces an action which has already been effected:

This day I have begot whom I declare
My onely Son

(V 603–4)

Actor and action are programmatically displaced: 'this day', for example, appears to be a period subsequent to the creation of the angels, but Satan and Abdiel will be arguing before the dawning of the next 'day' about whether the newly-begotten Son was instrumental in their own creation, and as Carey and Fowler point out in their note on line 601, the titles with which the Father addresses the heavenly host echo the account in Col: 1 16 of the Son's agency in creating the angels. Thus in his most momentous act, neither the acting God, nor the moment of his efficacy is textually present in Milton's account.

The creation of the world is equally mysterious. Adam sees the problem clearly: 'what cause', he asks Raphael,

Mov'd the Creator in his holy Rest
Through all Eternitie so late to build
In *Chaos*

(VII 90–3)

(The words 'so late' highlight the problem of locating movements of time in eternity: 'so early' would be just as appropriate.) In the account of the creation, which this question prompts, we are told that the world was made through the agency of the Son 'in a moment' (V 154), but that its making can only be unfolded to human ears in time. God's acts, therefore, 'Immediate . . . more swift / Then time or motion' (VII 176–7), cannot be expressed through the deferrals of signification, and consequently God cannot be used to underwrite presence in the poem any more than he can be relied upon to constitute its centre. In the poem, in discourse, he can never be *there*.

9. The implications of this are deeply paradoxical. God is logically absent from a story in which he is palpably a character with a tendentious speaking part. The paradox can be resolved, however, if we take account of God's immutability and omniscience. The God of *Paradise Lost* is explicitly described as 'Immutable' (III 373) even though his acts take place in time, while in *The Art of Logic* Milton argues that 'opinion . . . does not

belong to God, since He knows all things equally through their causes' (328). As we have seen, Kenny disputes both claims, maintaining (1979) that 'an immutable being cannot know what we know by means of tensed propositions' (53) and that even divine knowledge could not extend to the future actions of truly free creatures. Kenny's arguments, however, fail to take account of the ways in which the doctrines of divine omniscience and divine immutability make sense of each other.

In claiming that God knows all things through their causes, Milton attributes to him a perfect knowledge of what I have called the 'hearts' of his creatures, a unique relation, in other words, to alterity, as that concept is developed by Husserl. Husserl regards consciousness as the site and source of all phenomena whatsoever: consciousness and its experiences constitute for him the only unitary whole of which it is possible to speak. Consciousness, however, is always aware that it does not and cannot have a complete knowledge of the objects which it constitutes: 'the strictly seen front of a physical thing', writes Husserl (1950), 'always and necessarily appresents a rear aspect' (109); but he goes on to distinguish between those hidden aspects of physical objects which could be presented to consciousness were it able to locate itself 'elsewhere' and the *necessarily* appresented content of other consciousnesses. 'Appresentation . . . [which] involves the possibility of verification by a corresponding fulfilling presentation . . . must be excluded a priori', he writes (109) when 'someone else' is in question. In recognising other people as persons, I accept that they can only be known to me by what Husserl calls 'assimilative apperception' (111) and Milton 'opinion' — my necessarily incomplete interpretation or reading of their appearance and actions. Derrida (1967(b)), who agrees with Husserl on this point, puts it this way:

> the other as alter ego signifies the other as other, irreducible to *my* ego . . . The egoity of the other permits him to say 'ego' as I do; and this is why he is Other, and not a stone, or a being without speech *in my real economy*. This is why, if you will, he is face, can speak to me, understand me, and eventually command me. (125–6)

This argument appears to contradict my earlier contention that we can know each other's hearts, that, like Newman, we can have certitude with respect to our friend. What is at issue, however, is not the what but the how of inter-personal knowledge. According to Husserl, the Other is known as a system of harmonious appresentations, which 'can never show themselves *as* themselves' (114) but which point 'to further experiences that would fulfil and verify the appresented horizons', provided they are also appropriately related to the *presentations* I associate with them (i.e. my immediate perception of the Other's body). The process is one of *reading* the presented aspects of other people as signs or traces of the wholeness within them. I can read my way into their alterity, as David could read his way into the heart of Jonathan, and such readings can be successful without being complete: they stand in relation to the Other as Newman believes Dogma stands in relation to religious or Objective Truth: 'every successful understanding of what occurs in others', Husserl writes, 'has the effect of opening up new associations and new possibilities of understanding' (120). As we shall see in subsequent discussion, all the characters in Milton's later poems are represented as reading each other, more or less successfully, in this way — with one exception: God knows the hearts of his creatures immediately and not through signs, and it is in consequence of this that he can both live in time and enjoy immutability.

Milton's God is the one who knows without reading, who knows as he acts — 'in a moment'. He has always known, knows now, and always will know, both objectively (that is, in terms of physical causes none of which is even partially appresented to him because he is everywhere) and from within (that is, from the point of view of each created subject whose will, or heart, is a cause) all the sequenced experiences of every creature in the universe. He has always known, knows now, and always will know each and every moment of creation, both as an objective state of affairs and as every other being has separately experienced it, is experiencing it, and will experience it. He has always known, knows now, and always will know the parts, the whole, and the parts and whole together, which constitute his providence perceived in its totality. And that is why he is immutable: his knowledge of all possible or actual tensed propositions has been, is and always will be complete. Consequently time's movement through him brings nothing and take nothing from him. He has nothing to learn. He is sustained in the ecstasy of total knowledge. We have therefore to understand his attributes — his omnipresence, immutability and eternity of being — in a very strong sense indeed. Milton's God is not just present everywhere as the supremely knowing objective observer or reader of the Book of the Universe. He

203

is additionally the knower and experiencer of every event and every circumstance in every moment of every life that has been, is, or ever will be, and yet he is not himself implicated either in what happens in his creatures or in the actions they perform.

10. I argued earlier that certitude about the future actions of others is not incompatible with those actions being free, but my argument was illustrated with certitudes arising from readings of presented data as signs of the appresented heart. According to Derrida, however, such appresentation is a condition of the other's remaining other. This suggests that omniscience such as Milton's God enjoys would destroy the ontological independence of the creature from the Creator. There are two reasons why it does not do so. The first can be stated simply. A God who is transcendent in relation to alterity would be a threat to other beings only if he were able to participate in the drama of inter-subjectivity, and this Milton's God cannot do. He is *logically* inaccessible to them — 'invisible / Amidst . . . glorious brightness . . . / Thron'd inaccessible' (III 375–7). Nothing of him can be *presented*. Therefore, *we have no access to the appresented horizons of his Egoity*. Milton perceives his God as the beginning and the end of all things, their centre and their site, but he also perceives him as a necessarily non-functioning presence, a non-functioning centre, a non-functioning author. Indeed his purpose in *Paradise Lost* is to deconstruct any such functioning (or interfering) God which his readers may have in their minds.

He has therefore finally to convince us that 'the Father' in his own poem is a cipher merely, one signifier among many, of the inexpressible reality. Other signifiers of the same reality include the Son, Adam and Satan. Blake was right to see the chief figures in the poem as interchangeable. But it is the Son who is uniquely the sign, the figure of speech, the rhetorical trope of the Father. In him 'all his Father . . . / [is] substantially express'd' (III 139–40); he is the

> Divine Similitude
> In whose conspicuous count'nance, without cloud
> Made visible, th' Almighty Father shines
> Whom else no Creature can behold
>
> (III 384–7)

In the words attributed to the Father, the Son alone is 'My word, my wisdom, and effectual might' (III 170). One has to say 'attributed to the Father', for if the Son himself is the only finally valid sign of the Father in the entire universe, then the words and actions of the figure who is given the name of the Father in the poem can only have the function of illuminating and confirming the signifying function of the figure who is given the name of the Son. They can tell us nothing directly about the Father. Thus while Milton's Father, as God, is superior to the Son as not-God, the *sign* of the Father, both in *Paradise Lost* and in the text of creation, is subordinate to the *sign* of the Son. It follows that the character who so distresses Blake, Godwin, Shelley, Empson, Carey and Hill has least importance on those occasions and in those speeches when he seems most discouragingly to be present.

11. The Father, then, is not to be found in *Paradise Lost* or the Book of the Universe, not even, at least in his fulness, in the sign of the Son, for while the Son may be a complete realisation of the Father's nature, he appresents only aspects of it — the Father's 'effectual might', for example, and not his latent omnipotence. Even when the Father's 'unclouded Deity' (X 65) blazes forth upon him, he still only expresses 'all his Father manifest' (X 66), and not the Father's unmanifested depths. But the Son, too, is invisible. As the transparent expression of the Father he conceals *himself* from all scrutiny except the Father's. What he is in himself can only be understood indirectly through the system of signs in which he locates himself, specifically in the light of those other bearers of his title, Son of God. These, in the first instance, are the angels (including the fallen angels) but subsequently, since he becomes a man, human beings also. To illuminate the sign of the Son, therefore, and so at one remove, the sign of the Father, we have to turn to the signs of humanity, and in particular to Adam and Eve and the Jesus of *Paradise Regain'd*, each of whom is a reader and re-reader of the self and others. To grasp the sign of humanity, therefore, and through it the sign of the Son in which can be glimpsed the self-revelation of the Father, it is necessary to re-examine the act of *reading* in Milton's poems, by which his characters make sense of themselves, the appresented Other, and the contextually presented world.

On the day of her creation, Eve wakes up 'much wondring where / And what' (IV 451–2) she is. From the beginning she is in a world of signs — she can ask questions, even if she lacks sufficient words to make complete sense of her context. Hence the periphrastic awkwardness of her narrative, which represents her gazing at the sky and then recognising in the lake's 'liquid Plain' (IV 455) the sign of 'another Skie' (IV 459). But this new sign contains an image as the former does not and so signifies other than at first appears. The image in the lake, however, is not the sign of someone else that it seems at first, but a sign of herself. Moreover, it reflects her incompletely, just as the lake is incomplete as a sign or image of the sky. To find a fuller image of herself (though at the same time one which is disturbingly different) she must meet Adam. Thus for Eve every sign reveals its own incompleteness, and thereby facilitates further significa- tion, further appresented horizons.

Adam enters the world of signs more assuredly. He speaks as lord of sublunary signification, though he is not the source of his own words since they were in use when the world was being made by the Word. (Signifiers are thus prior to their referents if not to what they signify.) Yet each word that Adam discovers leads him beyond himself to the question of his own origins, and even when his surmise about those origins is confirmed in a dream, together with his authority as constituter of signs, his mind moves unerr- ingly towards the terrain of uncertainty, where what is expressed cannot be named:

> O by what Name [he asks], for thou above all these,
> Above mankinde, or aught then mankinde higher,
> Surpassest farr my naming, how may I
> Adore thee . . .?
>
> (VIII 357–60)

Thus Adam and Eve in their reading of the universe do not discover fixed and defining meanings, but absences and traces. But are they unerasable traces, as Michael's references to 'the track Divine' seem to suggest, and so finally based on a meta- physic of presence? To clarify this problem we need to consider the 'readings' of Jesus in *Paradise Regain'd*.

Like Adam and Eve, Jesus is a reader and a sign of reading, a text subject to interpretation and self-interpretation in time. He develops in and through his readings of Scripture, of the world, of the signs of the times, and of himself. Moreover, like that of Adam and Eve, his reading involves him in a continual reinter- pretation of what he has already read. He describes for example, how he first read himself against other children and found himself more 'Serious to learn and know' (I 203). So he turned to learning, to the Law, and as his knowledge of the latter increased and found confirmation in the Temple, he re-examined himself and found in himself a spirit to perform 'victorious deeds . . . heroic acts' (I 215–6) first for the liberation of Israel, then for that of the world, though his preference was always for persuasion rather than force. However, alerted by his mother to the fact that he was 'no Son of mortal man' (I 234) but of 'the Eternal King' (I 236), he read the Scriptures yet again and discovered there the existence of his own messiahship. In consequence he had once more to rethink the future, substituting 'a hard assay even to the death' (I 264) for the victorious and heroic deeds which had earlier attracted him. But he still remained in waiting, a private man, until his baptism confirmed his Sonship of God, and indicated that the time had come for him to proclaim the Authority which he derived from Heaven. Now for the first time his self-reading is to be tested, and in his conduct during that temptation we can at last decipher the reality of which all such reading is the sign.

12. We know from *Christian Doctrine* that Milton perceived Jesus as a man uniquely capable of thinking and acting for himself. This is because as the Only-begotten Son his generation antedates the creation of the Holy Spirit, of whom he has no need. But the Spirit has to be communicated to Jesus's followers before they can imitate him in right thinking. Speaking first of himself and then of the Spirit, Jesus in *Paradise Regain'd* tells Satan:

> God now hath sent his living Oracle
> Into the World, to teach his final will,
> And sends his Spirit of Truth henceforth to dwell
> In pious Hearts, an inward Oracle
> To all truth requisite for men to know
>
> (I 460–4)

The same point is made in *Paradise Lost*. The Spirit is sent to human beings to help them read the Scriptures —

> written Records pure,
> Though not but by the Spirit understood
>
> (XII 513–14)

To understand the sign of humanness, therefore, it is necessary to examine the sign of the Spirit; but the Spirit is a notoriously fugitive element in Milton's theology. The chapter on him in

Christian Doctrine is negative and anti-trinitarian: as a person he is said to be inferior to the Father and the Son and in spite of the magnificent opening of *Paradise Lost* in which he is invited to act as Milton's inspiration, he is strikingly absent from the scenes in Heaven, and his contribution to the creation is attenuated and subordinate. Even Sin and Death, who are not persons, figure personally in the action as he does not. But as Milton points out in *Christian Doctrine*, that is how the Spirit is treated in Scripture also.

He comes into his own, however, in those parts of *Christian Doctrine* which treat of Christian liberty — essentially the liberty to read the Scriptures. Here the Spirit figures as a signifier of considerable power:

CHRISTIAN LIBERTY [Milton writes] means that CHRIST OUR LIBERATOR FREES US FROM THE SLAVERY OF SIN . . . SO THAT, BEING MADE SONS INSTEAD OF SERVANTS AND GROWN MEN INSTEAD OF BOYS, WE MAY SERVE GOD IN CHARITY THROUGH THE GUIDANCE OF THE SPIRIT OF TRUTH. (537)

in controversies . . . each man is his own arbitrator, so long as he follows scripture and the Spirit of God. (585)

There is the external scripture of the written word and the internal scripture of the Holy Spirit . . .
Nowadays the external authority for our faith, in other words the scriptures, is of very considerable importance . . . The pre-eminent and supreme authority, however, is the authority of the Spirit, which is the internal, and the individual possession of each man. (587)

So if any one imposes any kind of sanction or dogma upon believers against their will . . . he is placing a yoke . . . upon the Holy Spirit itself. (590)

This repeated emphasis makes clear why Milton is reluctant to focus on the Holy Spirit *in propria persona*. First, the Spirit is created by a free act of the Father's, an event which, for reasons we have already considered, is impossible to represent directly. Secondly, his presence in human beings confirms Christian and therefore human individuality. Nothing can be known of the Spirit between these two poles, at both of which he is wholly absorbed into the sign of another person, the Father (and so the Son) on the one hand, the Christian on the other.

The Spirit, then, is signified in the innermost reality of the human person. But the most human of human beings is Jesus; and even though his Truth is his and not the Spirit's, the operations of his human will are for us the supreme signifier of the Spirit as well as of the Father. But as followers of Jesus we can only read the Jesus-text by the power of the Spirit; to understand the mind and heart of Jesus we must attend reflexively, therefore, to the operations of our own minds and hearts as we read about Jesus in the Spirit of Truth. Thus the least regarded of the signs and persons in *Paradise Lost, Paradise Regain'd* and *Christian Doctrine* takes us to the heart of the matter. Finally the Spirit of Truth in ourselves, our *own* mental powers, informed but not determined by the Spirit, tell us all we can know about Jesus and so about the Father.

13. But what does a mind possess when it is possessed of the Spirit? Not, certainly, unimpeded access to the facts: the Spirit does not by-pass textuality. Even the Jesus of *Paradise Regain'd* has no privileges over Satan in this respect. Both are competent readers of the Jesus-text. At the end of the poem, for example, Satan tells Jesus:

> soon thou shalt have cause
> To wish thou never hadst rejected thus
> Nicely or cautiously my offer'd aid,
> Which would have set thee in short time with ease
> On *David's* Throne; or Throne of all the World,
> Now at full age, fulness of time, thy season,
> When Prophesies of thee are best fulfill'd.
> Now contrary, if I read aught in Heaven,
> Or Heaven write aught of Fate, by what the Stars
> Voluminous, or single characters,
> In thir conjunction met, give me to spell,
> Sorrows, and labours, opposition, hate,
> Attends thee, scorns, reproaches, injuries,
> Violence and stripes, and lastly cruel death,
> A Kingdom they portend thee, but what Kingdom,
> Real or Allegoric, I discern not,
> Nor when, eternal sure, as without end,

Without beginning; for no date prefixt
Directs me in the Starry Rubric set

(IV 375-93)

Not a word of this is 'untrue': because the allegoric is also real, and the real, especially the politically real, is simultaneously a deceit, Satan can even make good his promises, while in other respects his views are consistent with and confirmed by the opening speech of Jesus in Book I.

The two speeches, however, also diverge no less clearly, and a comparison of some remarks of Satan the morning after he delivers the speech just quoted and the end of Jesus's opening meditation reveals the nature of this divergence and therefore what it is in Jesus that the Spirit of Truth communicates to his followers. Having tormented the sleeping Jesus with horrific dreams and a storm-tossed night, Satan declares:

Did I not tell thee, if thou didst reject
The perfect season offer'd with my aid
To win thy destin'd seat, but wilt prolong
All to the push of Fate, pursue thy way
Of gaining *David's* Throne no man knows when,
For both the when and how is no where told

(IV 467-72)

Satan regards not knowing the when and how as intolerable. Accordingly (as we have already noted) his entire project in *Paradise Regain'd* is to fix the precise 'degree of meaning' attaching to the title Son of God when applied to Jesus. For him, to quote Barthes (1971), 'plural is the Evil' (160); he rebels against the freedom of a shifting title, how it is possible to become what you already are, to be found, as the Father himself expresses it in *Paradise Lost*. 'By Merit more than Birthright Son of God' (III 309). But Jesus in *Paradise Regain'd* waits for illumination. His speech concludes:

And now by some strong motion I am led
Into this Wilderness, to what intent
I learn not yet, perhaps I need not know;
For what concerns my knowledge God reveals

(I 290-3)

Aware of his own history as related by his mother, of the promises of Scripture, and of the title conferred on him by the voice from Heaven, Jesus can accept, in Barthes' words, that the 'plural of the Text depends . . . not on the ambiguity of its contents but on . . . the stereographic *plurality* of its weave of signifiers' (159). To fix a meaning, as Satan wishes to, is to consume the sign: instead Jesus accepts his self-reading as 'play, activity, production, practice' (162). Thus the difference between Satan and Jesus is in their responses to *différance*, upon which Satan seeks to impose totalitarian closure, but in which Jesus discerns by faith his Father's will. It would seem then, that in the Christian, the Spirit of Truth is precisely that openness to *différance* manifested by Jesus in *Paradise Regain'd*.

14. But what does such openness involve? In the first place a responsible awareness of oneself as the site of the problem and the challenge. This is made clear in Milton's account of the reading of Scripture. In *Of Civil Power* he writes,

> we of these ages, having no other divine rule or autoritie from without us warrantable to one another as a common ground but the holy scripture, and no other within us but the illumination of the Holy Spirit so interpreting that scripture as unwarrantable only to our selves and to such whose consciences we can so perswade, can have no ground in matters of religion but only the scriptures. And these being not possible to be understood without divine illumination, which no man can know at all times to be in himself, much less to be at any time for certain in any other, it follows cleerly, that no man or body of men . . . can be the infallible judges or determiners in matters of religion to any other mens consciences but thir own. (242–3)

Here we have a notably powerful affirmation of a world of signs in which the noncentre is determined otherwise than as loss of centre. Truth is Scripture only; the light required to read it by is both uncertain and deeply personal; we can only grasp what is said contingently and for ourselves alone. The act of doing so, however, is no desperate expedient, but a profoundly self-constituting human act.

Nevertheless, openness to *différance* also involves a deconstruction of the self, amounting to *total* self-effacement. At the beginning of *Paradise Regain'd*, Jesus accepts the prospect of 'many a hard assay even to the death' (I 264); he subsequently foregoes every opportunity for epiphany offered in the course of the poem; and by its end he has still not specified his own nature to himself — Scripture, his mother's narrative and the title given to him by the voice from heaven remain an irreducibly plural text requiring unlimited collaboration. He accepts, in effect, that he can never be fully in the presence of himself, that he continues to await supplementation. He thus collaborates in his own decomposition. But he is not effacing himself before nothing, as a modern deconstructionist critic like Vincent Leitch effaces himself before *différance*. For Leitch (1983), the 'qualities of play and detour characteristic of difference keep it from appearing as origin, as being-present . . . as master-concept or word. Neither process nor product, difference is nothing' (43). But for Jesus *différance* is everything. He is after all the sign of the Father. Consequently his self-effacement, his identification of himself with *différance*, not only reveals the hidden essence which the glory of Messiahship concealed in *Paradise Lost*, but also the will of the Father expressed by, and therefore concealed within, the sign of the Son. *Différance* in *Paradise Regain'd* is thus the glass in which Jesus sees that of which he is the image. In identifying himself with his own plurality as a text, he encounters not a mere reflection of himself such as Eve found in the waters of the Lake, but an image which is truer for being, as Adam later was for Eve, another person. He effaces himself before a reality greater than himself — his Father; but the Father, as the one of whom Jesus is the sign, must therefore be himself in a state of free and unconditional self-effacement before his Son. The ultimate reality in Milton's final poems, the most available sign of which is the Spirit of Truth working in the mind and heart of the Christian reader, is God's grant of freedom to the Son, and thence to all other acting persons in creation, his primordial and unconditional commitment, proclaimed in *Paradise Lost*, to

> the high Decree
> Unchangeable, Eternal, which ordain'd
> Thir freedom
>
> (III 126–8)

Milton's God, therefore, is not absent from creation merely as an expedient for making matter, nor even by virtue of there being no logical point of entry for a transcendental signifier into the cosmic text, but by choice, in the mystery of a total self-abnegation which effects total self-realisation. The text of creation is such as to preserve the complete autonomy of its primary significations; it is a supreme exercise in 'objectivity'. This is why Derrida's argument that the other is Other only through appresentation does not apply in God's case. Milton's God does not encounter the alterity of his creatures phenomenologically; rather, he separates himself from them and endows them with a sovereignty exactly comparable with his own self-expressing and self-effacing heart.

15. It follows that the justification of God's ways to man in Milton's works has nothing to do with the problem which has so exercised philosophers of whether the world God has actually created is or could be the best of all possible worlds. Such questions would only make sense of worlds which God could inspect like so many mechanical toys in the shop-window of possibility. That such an inspection would require God to buy the goods first (as Kenny argues) is not to the point because the measure and value of the act is not to be found in the goods purchased but in the motives and achievement of the purchaser. The good which is effected when God sets his creatures free is to be found not in them but in God, and consequently no inspection of what his creatures do with their freedom, nor what others might have done in their place, can tell us what God realises in himself in doing what he does.

Milton, however, declares that what the Father thus achieves in himself is known in the fullest possible measure to the Son, and that it will be made known to us through the Son. All the Son has freely done, is freely doing, and will freely do, will constitute a perfect revelation of the Father's own acting. Consequently God's ways will not only be just, but will be justified to his creatures; for if God is supremely good, a work of his which issues in a perfect expression of that goodness must in principle be the best of all possible works. But this justification is necessarily deferred: only when the Son's work is completely accomplished, and consequently only when the work of the Spirit in his followers is accomplished also, will his plenitude as a signifier be manifest, and the value of what has been done by and in the Father be accessible in a full and final form to creation as a whole. Justification of God's ways is thus ineradicably eschatological.

Nevertheless, men and women can even now assimilate the Spirit of Truth, which is the Spirit of the *Différance*, that is, they can choose like Jesus to live in the *complete* absence of God from the universe (how complete we will see in the next chapter) knowing in Jesus that that absence is *not* a subterfuge for metaphysical presence, and *yet* that it means that God is present everywhere, for God is *Différance*. They can thereby fulfil themselves as acting persons, uniting themselves through the Spirit to God's primary decree by willing freedom at large, and in particular by submitting to the sovereign freedom of God, not as slaves but as obedient sons and daughters. In doing so they can discover, in the image of themselves and of the Son thus formed in their consciences, a reflection of the self-fulfilling freedom of the Father. Thus faith, for Milton, is not just a logically necessary response to the fact that the revelation and beatitude have to be deferred; it is also an image and a realisation of them both. The blind man who looks into himself and there discovers that 'They also serve who only stand and waite' is one with Jesus on the Temple in *Paradise Regain'd* —

> To whom thus Jesus: also it is written,
> Tempt not the Lord thy God, he said and stood
> But Satan smitten with amazement fell
>
> (IV 560–2)

and both are already effectively in the condition of the angels before God's throne in *Paradise Lost*. 'My self', Raphael tells Adam,

> and all th' Angelic Host that stand
> In sight of God enthron'd, our happie state
> Hold, as you yours, while our obedience holds;
> On other surety none; freely we serve,
> Because wee freely love, as in our will
> To love or not; in this we stand or fall:
> And some are fall'n
>
> (V 535–41)

Faith is the habit of freedom, for freedom is not limited to moments of efficacy; its completion and perfection is unconstrained stasis. Consequently even the moment of ultimate epiphany, in which the self-realisation of the Father in the work of the Son and the rest of creation is united with his complete justification, the moment when God shall be All in All, and his Presence confirmed in all, will not extinguish *différance*. It will not

214

be a moment of closure. On the contrary, openness is eternally confirmed when the attempted and provisional closures of Sin and Death are finally eliminated, and all righteous beings affirm themselves for ever in unconstrained self-effacement before the inexhaustible horizons of the hidden life of God.

10

Freedom and History

1. The assimilation in the last chapter of deconstructionist insights into a traditional conception of voluntary behaviour and christian eschatology has one obvious weakness — that of seeming a-historical. In a way that Marx saw as being entailed in christianity, it apparently ignores the space between the experience of faith and its indefinitely deferred fulfilment and vindication. Milton, it seems, has achieved a dramatisation of the *actus humanus* and, quite literally, its apotheosis, at the price of its removal from the living world.

Interestingly, this is also a tendency of deconstructionist discourse, in so far, at least, as the play of signifiers between writer and reader, neither of whom is knowable, is deemed to emancipate texts from specifically historical constraints. For some deconstructionists (those replete with the pleasures of textuality) this is not a matter of serious concern, but for humanists committed to traditional notions of responsibility it matters a great deal. They need to perceive the world as an arena for serious and practical moral involvement. It is important, therefore, to recognise that Milton's stance assimilates deconstructionist insights but only to affirm a traditional concept of the person. Milton opposes the scepticism, hedonism, relativism and *angst* implicit in the textuality of *scripture* with the assurance and power of human

beings who think accurately and act reasonably — in the Spirit.
He has therefore to write *for* thinking and acting persons, not just
about them, and it is this which enables him — at least at the end
of his career — to engage directly and uncompromisingly with
historical circumstance precisely when thematically he is wholly
preoccupied with personal faith on the one hand and the last
things on the other.

As a result, Miltonic discourse on freedom ceases to be just a
text about the acting person and becomes (though only late in his
life and with great difficulty) a drama also, acted out on a stage
or set which is indisputably historical. Milton begins as a director
who is the authorised and authoritative interpreter of the script of
history; but his cast abandons him and he is expelled from theatre
and film-set; so he resorts to street-mime, improvisation and
soliloquy in order to make himself the sign, or more accurately the
trace of all that he wishes to say. By these means he more than
amply fills that historical space between personal faith and the
consummation of all things. His performance in this role thus
constitutes the concluding movement of my argument.

2. We begin with the pre-Restoration prose. From the first
Milton's is a deconstructionist script, even though he is also
convinced that in and through the Scriptures he has come into
possession of the truth. In *Of Reformation Touching Church-Discipline*
(1641), for example, he writes: 'The very essence of Truth is
plainnesse and brightnes . . . The *Wisdome of God* created
understanding, fit and proportionable to Truth the object, and end
of it, as the eye to the thing visible' (566). In *The Doctrine and
Discipline of Divorce* (1643), he writes: 'The hidden wayes of
[God's] providence we adore & search not: but the law is his
reveled will, his complete, his evident, and certain will' (292). And
in *Areopagitica* (1644), he declares the body of Truth to be
'*homogeneal* and proportionall' (551). 'Let her and Falsehood
grapple; who ever knew Truth put to the wors, in a free and open
encounter' (561). The epistemological optimism of these assertions, however, is rooted in clearly articulated recognitions that
the play of signification can never be closed. The truth whose
essence is plainness and brightness, for example, is defined in *Of
Reformation Touching Church-Discipline* as the pouring of God's
Spirit 'upon every age, and sexe, attributing to all men, and
requiring from them the ability of searching, trying and examining all things, and by the Spirit discerning which is good' (566).
The repetition of present participles here is as important as

217

the democratic attribution of capacity and reponsibility to young and old, male and female: the searching is a continuing enlargement of perspective. The passage from *Areopagitica* about truth being 'homogeneal' and 'proportionall' makes the same point even more strongly: 'To be still searching what we know not, by what we know, still closing up truth to truth as we find it . . . this is the golden rule in *Theology* as well as in Arithmetick, and makes up the best harmony in a Church' (551).

Even more striking is the context of Milton's argument in *The Doctrine and Discipline of Divorce* that the Law is God's evident and certain will. The Law does more than make prescriptions concerning human behaviour. In it, God

> appears to us as it were in human shape, enters into cov'nant with us, swears to keep it, binds himself like a just lawgiver to his own prescriptions, gives himself to be understood by men, judges and is judg'd, measures and is commensurat to right reason. (292)

Thus the Law's plainness ceases to be about behaviour only and becomes also a sign of its divine source, enabling us to see God as 'a just lawgiver' in 'human shape'. In promulgating the Law, Milton argues, God submits *himself* (and not just the Law as a text requiring interpretation) to the scrutiny of those to whom he promulgates it. This assumes something very important about all communicaticn: every utterance is a surrender not just of one's meaning but of oneself to the judgement of others. In promulgating the Law, God risks being personally misunderstood by all who fail to recognise that his holiness and his consistency are inseparable, that he could not have condoned divorce in the Pentateuch if it were truly contrary to a more general and holier moral law, applicable in principle to the whole human race:

> If he once will'd adultery should be sinfull, and to be punisht by death, all his omnipotence will not allow him to will the allowance that his holiest people might as it were by his own *Antinomy* or counter-statute live unreprov'd in the same fact as he himself esteem'd it.

Thus Milton is able to draw a positive and binding conclusion concerning the legitimacy of divorce by reading into the Law what it seems to imply about God and by then re-reading the Law in the light of that discernment. He insists that the text of the Law is open; we must cease to be 'superstitious through customary faintnes of heart, not venturing to piece with our free thoughts into the full latitude of nature and religion, [and so] abandon our selvs to serv under the tyranny of usurpt opinions' (343). Hence the daring of his own tendentious readings of Old and New Testament texts on the subject of divorce. But such freedom is still anchored to Truth. The textual openness of the Law does not entail the absence but the presence of its Author, and in the light of that presence the Law can be read and known.

3. For Milton, then, consciousness determines the meaning of a sign and not vice versa. This had pressing political significance in a society in which control of discourse was exercised by the bishops of the Church of England on behalf of the state: it involved Milton in an unremitting campaign against what Foucault (1971) calls 'the rancorous will to knowledge' (163). Foucault's main ideas will repay brief scrutiny.

Knowledge, Foucault suggests — ideas fixed in form and expressed so as to degrade other ideas to the condition of falsehood — 'rests upon injustice'. An assured dismissal of Milton's reading of scriptual texts in the divorce pamphlets, for example, on the grounds that they conflict with what is *known* about those texts, would only be possible in circumstances of actual social oppression. It does not follow that in circumstances of unqualified social justice Milton's readings of Scripture could be properly described as true for that would constitute them in their turn as a field of knowledge, and in Foucault's words (1975), 'There is no power relation without the correlative constitution of a field of knowledge, nor any knowledge that does not presuppose and constitute at the same time power relations' (27). Power for Foucault does not belong to people nor to institutions but to a complex of strategic situations in which discourse is deployed to achieve dominance, the dominance in question being precisely over the territory of interacting texts. This becomes obvious historically when societies begin attributing writing to authors, a development which has nothing to do with whether or not the identity of the writer is known: naming the writer is unimportant, for example, in seventeenth-century song-books and miscellanies, but in other texts, which challenge the current power-relations expressed and enforced as knowledge, the attribution of authorship becomes very important, for it is the function of 'the author' to be the one who is accountable for the meaning of a text, or whose meaning is authoritative with regard to it. The author, Foucault writes (1979), is thus a 'functional principle by which . . . one limits, excludes, and chooses . . . by which one impedes the free circulation, the free manipulation, the free composition, decomposition and recomposition of fiction' (159).

It is clear that Milton saw the ecclesiastical censor and ecclesiastical discipline as exercising this function in seventeenth-century England. The main text in dispute was, of course, the Scriptures, which had God as their author, and which could be scrutinised by the authorities for a body of knowledge which presupposed, constituted and justified specific power-relations. In combating these claims Milton had to avoid making counter-claims which implied an alternative body of knowledge and alter-native power-relations. The tensions this produced in his writing are in Foucault's terms identical with the stresses which constitute the English Revolution. Milton's deconstruction of the author function in spite of these difficulties can be illustrated by referring to two short passages, one from *The Reason of Church-government* (1641), written at the beginning of the revolutionary period, and the other from the *Second Defence of the English People* (1654), written at its height.

4. At a crucial point of *The Reason of Church-government* Milton asks, with undisguised irony,

> whether the Prelats in their function doe work according to the Gospel practizing to subdue the mighty things of this world by being weak . . . or whether in more likelihood they band themselves with the prevalent things of this world to overrun the weak things which Christ hath made chois to work by. (830)

He professes to find this a question almost impossible to answer, and he develops a little allegory to show how difficult it is to establish the truth about anything at all. In this allegory, Truth has to pass 'through the many little wards and limits of the severall Affections and Desires', and is presented by them to the Understanding only in 'such colours and attire' as please them. Sometimes she is allowed to appear in her own shape and visage but even then she can be confused with Falsehood whom the Affections and Desires can dress up to look like her if they wish. The situation being thus apparently hopeless for Truth, Milton affects an inclination to abandon the discussion. However, he pretends to pull himself together, out of concern for those who, 'either weakly or falsly principl'd, what through ignorance, and what through custom of licence, both in discours and writing, by what hath bin of late written in vulgar' (831), are unable to make up their minds about the powers of the episcopy. So Milton solemnly announces that he intends to give the Affections and Desires one more chance to conduct Truth truthfully to the Understanding. Recent controversy, he notes, has been concerned exclusively with the *administration* of ecclesiastical jurisdiction rather than 'to learn what it is, for had the pains bin taken to search out that', he declares, 'it had bin long agoe enroul'd . . . that jurisdictive power in the Church there ought to be none at all'.

That Milton refers in this allegory to 'Affections and Desires' rather than to signs cannot disguise the deconstructive humour of his tactics: he has enforced a dogmatic assertion about dogmatic assertions — 'that jurisdictive power in the Church there ought to be none at all' — by subverting all dogmatic assertions whatsoever. His perception of the field of discourse, of political controversy, therefore, has prevented a power relation being established upon it. This is entirely consistent with his prescription for Cromwellian government in the *Second Defence*. Here he urges Cromwell to honour himself,

> so that having achieved that liberty in pursuit of which you endured so many hardships and encountered so many perils, you may not permit it to be violated by yourself or in any degree diminished by others. Certainly you yourself cannot be free without us, for it has been so arranged by nature that he who attacks the liberty of others is himself the first to lose his own liberty and learns that he is the first of all to become a slave. (673)

It is not irrelevant to the general argument I have been advancing in this essay that Milton should insist that any one who denies liberty to others does not *become* a slave in consequence of doing so, but because self-enslavement is a *prior* condition of any such attempt to deprive others of their freedom. More particularly, the fact that Milton then warns Cromwell in the frankest terms of the consequences to his reputation of anti-libertarian policies illustrates the point I am currently developing, that a recognition of the relation between discourse and power is fundamental to

221

Milton's performance at this period; in this instance Milton demonstrates that Cromwell's authority in the state is not such as to deny Milton the right to complete discursive freedom.

5. The same text, however, the *Second Defence of the English People*, also reveals a weakness in Milton's thought prior to 1660, and therefore in the Revolution of which his writings are the expression. His own contribution to the Revolution, he points out, has not been in battle but in discourse:

> I concluded that if God wished those men to achieve such noble deeds, He also wished that there be other men by whom those deeds, once done, might be worthily praised and extolled, and that the truth defended by arms be also defended by reason — the only defence truly appropriate to man. (533)

The last point is consistent with his deconstruction of power relations: to defend the truth by arms is less than fully human. But Milton goes on to present himself precisely as *author* addressing 'the entire assembly and council of all the most influential men, cities and nations everywhere' (554). This would perhaps be no more than a pardonable expression of personal pride if it were not underwritten by the interventionist God of Milton's pre-1660 historiography. Like most of his contemporaries, he believed that political success was a *sign* of God's approval.

This structuring of history as knowledge took a specifically eschatological form. In *Of Reformation Touching Church-Discipline*, Milton saw himself participating in a scripturally anticipated drama which had begun when 'the bright and blissfull *Reformation* (by Divine Power) strook through the black and settled Night of *Ignorance* and *Antichristian Tyranny*' (524) and was reaching its final stages as insurgent English revolutionaries began paving the way for the establishment of the eschatological kindgom of the millenium. Whether the form of Christ's reign was to be real or allegoric was not clear, and some of Milton's opponents argued that it had already begun (in allegoric form) with the establishment of christian kingdoms following the conversion of Constantine. But for Milton in 1641, the text of the future was as he read it, and he could therefore address God at the end of this first contribution to the Cause with the assurance of one who knows that his prayer is already answered:

O thou that . . . having first welnigh freed us from *Antichris-*
tian thraldome, didst build up this *Brittanic Empire* to a
glorious and enviable heighth, with all her Daughter Ilands
about her, stay us in this felicity . . .

    . . . Hitherto thou has but freed us, and that not fully,
from the unjust and Tyrannous Claime of thy Foes, now
unite us intirely, and appropriate us to thy selfe . . .

    Then . . . this great and Warlike Nation . . . may presse
on hard to that *high* and *happy* emulation to be found the
soberest, wisest, and *most Christian People,* at that day when
thou the Eternall and shortly-expected King shalt open the
Clouds to judge the severall Kingdomes of the World, and
. . . shalt put an end to al Earthly *Tyrannies,* proclaiming thy
universal and milde *Monarchy* through Heaven and Earth
. . .

    But they . . . that by the impairing and dimunition of the
true *Faith* . . . aspire to high *Dignity, Rule* and *Promotion* here,
after a shamefull end in this *Life* (which *God* grant them)
shall be throwne down eternally into the *darkest* and *deepest*
Gulfe of Hell, where under the *despightfull controule,* the tram-
ple and spurne of all the other *Damned,* that in the anguish
of their *Torture* shall have no other ease than to exercise a
Raving and Bestiall Tyranny over them as their *Slaves* and
Negro's, they shall remaine in that plight for ever, the *basest,*
the *lowermost,* the *most dejected,* most *underfoot* and *downe-*
trodden Vassals of *Perdition.* (614–17)

Such prospects were hard to abandon. Even as the Revolution
crumbled about him nineteen years later, and he desperately
proposed a new constitution to the English nation in *The Ready and*
Easy Way to Establish a Free Commonwealth (1660), he could still
represent Britain as a participant in an unaltered eschatological
drama:

The Grand Councel being thus firmly constituted to
perpetuitie, ther can be no cause alleag'd why peace, justice,
plentifull trade and all prosperitie should not thereupon
ensue throughout the whole land; with as much assurance as
can be of human things, that they shall so continue (if God
favour us, and our wilfull sins provoke him not) even to the
coming of our true and rightfull and only to be expected
King. (444–5)

Concealed within the generous assertion of liberty which informs the political arena constituted in Milton's revolutionary prose, there is thus an ultimate power play: he can clear the decks of discourse, and renounce the power relations which discourse situates and effects only because he sees the hand of God in the events of the age, and is therefore confident that Christ's reign will vindicate his own reading of history. *Christian Doctrine* makes clear Milton's sense of the parousia as a political process by which true knowledge will at last be determined:

> This *judgment* . . . [he writes] will not last for one day only but for a considerable length of time, and will be a reign, rather than a judicial session. The same sense of the word *judgment* is applicable in the case of Gideon, Jephthah and the other *judges* who are said to have *judged* Israel for many years. (625)

6. As a consequence, Milton's writings illustrate what Derrida (1967(b)) calls 'the system of logocentric repression . . . organised in order to exclude . . . the body of the written trace' (197). By exciting in us (and himself) a vivid image of his own presence as orator to the nations, Milton's rhetoric suppresses important facts — that on the page his words have become mere traces of printer's ink, a random trail recording not his thought but its passage; that such traces and tracks can be erased, consigned absolutely to oblivion; and that such erasure is expressive of the essence of all signs and meanings. Milton's clinging to the hope of the Second Coming is a desperate refusal to recognise that the script of the English revolution could be extinguished, that is, to accept, in Derrida's words, 'the erasure of selfhood . . . constituted by the threat' (230) of the complete erasure of the trace. To the end, Milton the revolutionary clings to the prospect of a second coming for his revolutionary text, to the conviction that his words on the page are capable of resurrection.

Such a repression of awareness, Derrida argues, is ultimately socio-historical. It 'permits an understanding of how an original and individual repression became possible within the horizons of a culture and a historical structure of belonging'. In making orthodoxy a condition of community, human beings accept restraints modelled on logocentric repression and facilitated by it. It is thus to be expected that in 1641 Milton should have pictured the damnation of his ideological components — his enemies on the field of knowledge — in terms of the ultimate forms of social exclusion and oppression. In 1660, however, with the extinction of his hopes for the imminent 'return' of Christ, he had to face the implications of a complete erasure from the text of history of the signs of the English Revolution and the Second Coming of the Son of God.

7. There was a sense, however, in which he was prepared for this crisis. As a mortalist, he believed in the death of the soul with that of the body and in their joint resurrection. This was the fate even of Jesus: 'Christ', he writes in *Christian Doctrine*, 'the sacrificial lamb, was totally killed . . . God . . . raised not only Christ as man, but the whole Christ' (440). Thus *death* for Milton signifies certain and complete erasure. His position is a difficult one to maintain from a deconstructionist point of view, however, not because he believes none the less in a parousia or second coming which overcomes death, but because he claims to know the referent of the sign *death*. But Leitch makes a similar claim when he insists, against the grain of his own argument, that 'differance is nothing' (43). Milton, however, has the advantage of being consistent since he does not privilege the sign of erasure from being itself erased as Leitch privileges the sign of differance. In declaring that an unqualified acceptance of erasure is self-making as well as self-obliterating, he simply puts death on the same footing as every other sign he uses. Moreover outside the field of signification where such self-effacement necessarily is effected he may know experientially that his claims are true.

The supreme human exemplar of such self-constituting self-obliteration is, of course, Jesus, in whose death is signified the Father's utter self-effacement before his creation. The erasure of the trace is thus for Milton the eternal bedrock of identity and action, and this is what his mortalism signifies. But as long as he could play with the sign of imminent and active intervention by God in history in order to vindicate his own reading of it, his capacity to give a political significance to the paradox that erasure is itself erasable without being any the less complete was both limited and contaminated by a hidden totalitarian agenda. In 1660, however, he had to enlarge his mortalist convictions to cover the political arena.

This is why substantial portions of *Paradise Regain'd* and *Samson Agonistes* (when it was published and irrespective of when it was drafted) announce the death of politics. We are clearly meant to see Andrew and Simon in *Paradise Regain'd* as mistaken in their belief that liberation is imminent. Jesus places the age of republican virtue firmly in the past along with '*Gideon* and *Jeptha* . . . *Quintius, Fabricius, Curius, Regulus*' (II 439, 446). The Emperor (Tiberius — but the reference is to Charles II) is left to his own devices — 'Let his tormentor Conscience find him out' (IV 130) — while Jesus, though anticipating the ultimate restoration of the House of David, refuses to enforce his own claims. Liberty in the political sphere is now a temptation — it is Satan who proposes that Jesus liberate the ten lost tribes of Israel and Jesus (with humbling implications for God's now captive Englishmen) who replies

> As for those captive Tribes, themselves were they
> Who wrought thir own captivity, fell off
> From God to worship calves . . .
> Nor in the land of thir captivity
> Humbled themselves, or penitent besought
> The God of their fore-fathers; but so dy'd
> Impenitent, and left a race behind
> Like to themselves, distinguishable scarce
> From Gentils, but by Circumcision vain,
> And God with Idols in their worship joyn'd
>   (III 414–16, 420–6)

This is not only a coded reference to those Protestants who conformed with the romish idolatrie of the Anglican Church in the Settlement of 1660 and later, it also implies the more or less indefinite continuance of that Settlement. The message of *Paradise Regain'd* is that while the ultimate outcome is not in doubt — when Christ's

>   season comes to sit
> On *Davids* Throne, it shall be like a tree
> Spreading and over-shadowing all the Earth,
> Or as a stone that shall to pieces dash
> All Monarchies besides throughout the world
>   (IV 146–50)

— the realisation of that dream is indefinitely delayed.

In some respects *Samson Agonistes* is even darker. Israel is self-enslaved under the Philistines. More terribly, God's withdrawal of his providential support reduces the signs of the times to moral nonsense. His dealings with his elect are 'contrarious' (669); those whom he has 'solemnly elected' (678) are randomly cast down. Moreover, even when the Chorus entertain the prospect of a miraculous restoration of Israel's liberty through the agency of a newly revived Samson, Manoa's caution has an evidently exemplary force:

> *Chor.* . . . What if his eysight (for to *Israels* God
> Nothing is hard) by miracle restor'd,
> He now be dealing dole among his foes,
> And over heaps of slaughter'd walk his way?
> *Man.* That were a joy presumptuous to be thought.
> *Chor.* Yet God hath wrought things as incredible
> For his people of old; what hinders now?
> *Man.* He can I know, but doubt to think he will,
> Yet Hope wou'd fain subscribe, and tempts belief
> (1527–35)

In spite of the Chorus's being at least partially correct, the moral of this exchange points to patience rather than the optimism with which Milton felt able to express himself in 1641, when he wrote with such wonderful impatience in *The Reason of Church-government* 'Let us not therefore make things an incumbrance, or an excuse of our delay in reforming, which God sends us an incitement to proceed with more honour and alacrity' (795). In Milton's last works, politics are dead. Fleetingly, in 1672, he was deceived into thinking Charles II's Declaration of Indulgence might be an 'occasion' for political action, but there is no sign of political activism in any of his other writings after 1660. But this does not mean that they are a-political. It means rather that they have been emancipated from the logocentrism inherent in a millenarian text, that a space has been made in them across which may be traced, or in which may be enacted, the only sign of humanity with lasting or significant political content.

8. The exploration of this sign has been greatly facilitated by some modern readings of Milton, notably by Earl Miner (1974), two quotations from whom will serve to establish my general point. Of Adam's decision to sin with Eve, Miner writes:

> When Adam in distress gives first consideration to his 'Bond of Nature' (IX, 956) with Eve, the reader knows that the hero bound by nature is wrong not to prefer nature's

227

Creator, but he also feels the reality of Adam's tie to Eve.
So Adam sins, and so readers participate in the completion
of the mortal sin original by giving their sympathy to Adam
rather than to God . . . If we did not feel much of what
Adam feels, we would not think that a real choice was
involved, and the poem would lose its point. (264–5)

Similarly of Jesus's repudiation of classical culture in *Paradise
Regain'd* he asks:

> Can we trust ourselves and Milton in this? Trusting
> ourselves means acknowledging, or rather hazarding,
> ourselves in the literary experience. Trusting Milton means
> believing that he knew what he was doing, and that
> something right is going on when we find ourselves wishing
> what we obviously should not wish. At this juncture in the
> poem, in this temptation to take up pagan classicism and
> give up our religion, Milton catches us in our humanity . . .
>   That episode is one of Milton's greatest literary triumphs.
> We *know* we should respond as Jesus does, and we *know* to
> our depths that we do not. (285)

In the context of an argument concerned with deconstructionism
words such as 'know' and 'obviously' require quotation marks,
since what Blake and Empson knew as they read the poems was
certainly not what Miner knows, nor would agreement between
them be likely about what they were supposed to wish. Nevertheless Miner's relevance to what I have been suggesting is clear.
In the moral chaos consequent upon a fall such as Adam's, the
play of signifiers is likely to be hazardous as well as free.

This is especially so in the case of Adam's speech to Eve on the
occasion of his own sin, a speech quoted earlier up to the moment
of Adam's acting. The lines that follow are among the most
powerful love poems in the language:

> How can I live without thee, how forgoe
> Thy sweet Converse and Love so dearly joyn'd,
> To live again in these wilde Woods forlorn?
> Should God create another *Eve*, and I
> Another Rib afford, yet loss of thee
> Would never from my heart; no no, I feel
> The link of Nature draw me: Flesh of Flesh,

Bone of my Bone thou art, and from thy State
Mine never shall be parted, bliss or woe
(IX 908–16)

These are the words of a man who has just deliberately committed himself and his offspring to radical corruption, but one can read and re-read them over a period of twenty years or more without perceiving the evil they contain, Adam's total lack of concern for his frightened, lonely, malicious and endangered wife. But as Miner implies, there is a meaning in Milton's leaving this unstated — the same meaning which attaches to his shocking location of Athenian and renaissance culture among the fallen angels in Hell. That meaning is precisely that a writer can only prompt his readers to read according to the Spirit of Truth, since only the Father of Lies could think of their being *made* to do so. Milton constitutes the play of signifiers as a field in which the free acceptance of another's freedom — God's, the reader's, the author's — fills it, not with pleasure, but with value. Only by such means could he moralise his song.

9. An invitation and response of this kind, however, remains on the level of personal regeneration awaiting eschatological vindication. But a more specific pattern of trust in *Paradise Lost*, *Paradise Regain'd* and *Samson Agonistes* locates all three poems as political texts in a particular world. To recognise this, it is necessary to qualify the extreme deconstructionist claim that the play of signifiers is unconditionally free. In the great choric speech in *Samson Agonistes* beginning 'Many are the sayings of the wise' (652), for example, a general consideration of the mystery of God's apparently random providence focuses finally on the particular problem of his dealings with those whom he calls to prominence in public affairs and then dismisses from his service:

Nor only dost degrade them, or remit
To life obscur'd, which were a fair dismission,
But throw'st them lower than thou didst exalt them high,
Unseemly falls in human eie,
Too grievous for the trespass or omission;
Oft leav'st them to the hostile sword
Of Heathen and prophane, thir carkasses
To dogs and fowls a prey, or else captiv'd;
Or to the unjust tribunals, under change of times,
And condemnation of the ungrateful multitude.

If these they scape, perhaps in poverty
With sickness and disease thou bow'st them down,
Painful diseases and deform'd,
In crude old age;
Though not disordinate, yet causless suffring
The punishment of dissolute days, in fine,
Just or unjust, alike seem miserable,
For oft alike, both come to evil end

(687–704)

Admittedly, like the Book of Job, and with comparably universal implications, this deconstructs — that is, it subverts the structure of symbolic coherence — by which even biblical providentialism is constituted: in the Second Book of Kings, it is the wicked Jezebel whose carcass becomes a prey to dogs and fowls; here that fate befalls the elect. But the passage also invites comparison with another set of signs, more local and specific than those in the Old Testament. Ten of those involved in the execution of Charles I were hanged, drawn and quartered in 1660; there were two further executions in Scotland, including the entirely unwarranted one of the Marquess of Argyll; Sir Henry Vane was executed also, after showing great courage and loyalty to principle at his trial. (The Act of Indemnity from which those so tried and sentenced were excluded by name might also have excluded Milton but for the intervention of General Monck's brother-in-law and others.) In addition the bodies of Cromwell and three associates were exhumed and gibbetted, while those of twenty-three others were taken from Westminster Abbey and buried in a pit. All these were symbolic acts, but the meanings which emerge from them can only grimly be described as play. And it is into this specifically restoration 'text' that the lines just quoted were inserted when they were published in 1671. The carcasses to which they allude include that of Cromwell's mother (whose grandchildren were still alive), as well as that of Jezebel. We do not have to advance the complex 'archeological' arguments of Foucault, therefore, to attach Milton's text to its age: it is already tethered to it like a dog to its kennel. And it is this which gives Milton's trust of the readers for whom he published his poem its exact political edge.

10. Of course Milton had to be careful. His republican principles and prejudices are lightly scattered over all his later verse, but so allusively as often to be barely detectable. It is possible, for example, that the mildly anti-climactic phrase, 'or else captiv'd',

in the lines just quoted from *Samson Agonistes*, is a covert reference to the imprisoned John Lambert about whom there was much speculation among anti-stuart plotters until his death in 1683. It is also possible that Satan's declaration in *Paradise Lost* that he rules over the rebel hosts not only by 'just right, and the fixt Laws of Heav'n' (II 18), but also in consequence of the angels'

> free choice,
> With what besides in Counsel or in Flight,
> Hath bin achievd of merit
>
> (II 19–20)

is a jibe at royalist arguments that Charles II's hereditary title had been reinforced by contractual election in 1660. Clearer is the indictment of the Church and the Court in the celebrated lines on Belial in Book I of *Paradise Losi* particularly as it was normal royalist practice to sneer at dissenters as the Sons of Belial. Other covert sallies have been noted in passing in the course of this essay.

Milton gives freest expression to his political views in his account of the post-lapsarian world, and in *Paradise Regain'd* and *Samson Agonistes*. The victors and the vanquished among his contemporaries, for example, are alike attacked in the account of the years of peace preceding Noah's Flood. Michael tells Adam:

> Those whom last thou sawst
> In Triumph and luxurious wealth, are they
> First seen in acts of prowess eminent
> And great exploits, but of true vertu void;
> Who having split much blood, and don much waste
> Subduing Nations, and achievd thereby
> Fame in the World, high titles and rich prey,
> Shall change thir course to pleasure, ease, and sloth,
> Surfet, and lust, till wantonness and pride
> Raise out of friendship hostil deeds in Peace.
> The conquerd also, and enslav'd by Warr
> Shall with thir freedom lost all vertu loose
> And fear of God, from whom thir pietie feign'd
> In sharp contest of Battel found no aide
> Against invaders; therefore coold in zeale
> Thenceforth shall practice how to live secure,
> Worldlie or dissolute, on what thir Lords
> Shall leave them to enjoy
>
> (XI 787–804)

Equally anti-royalist is the identification at the beginning of Book XII of *Paradise Lost* of patriarchal with republican government, directly contradicting royalist arguments which identified paternal and royal authority as aspects of divine law. In *Paradise Regain'd* the office of kingship is defined in terms which preclude Charles II's ever exercising it, yet which open it in principle to everyone else:

> For therein stands the office of a King,
> His Honour, Vertue, Merit, and chief Praise,
> That for the Publick all this weight he bears.
> Yet he who reigns within himself, and rules
> Passions, Desires, and Fears, is more a King:
> Which every wise and vertuous man attains:
> And who attains not, ill aspires to rule
>
> (II 463–9)

Subsequently Jesus expresses his unreserved contempt for honour and glory to which royalist ideology attached such importance in the later seventeenth century. In *Samson Agonistes*, the Philistinian Lords are almost undisguisedly Milton's political enemies and oppressors.

11. Political implications of a very different tendency, however, can also be found in Milton's later poems, and they achieve far greater prominence than do those passages in which he gives vent to his republican principles. Gabriel's rebuke to Satan in Book I of *Paradise Lost* is a case in point:

> Was this your discipline and faith ingag'd,
> Your military obedience, to dissolve
> Allegeance to th' acknowledg'd Pow'r supream?
> And thou sly hypocrite, who now wouldst seem
> Patron of liberty, who more than thou
> Once fawn'd, and cring'd, and servilly ador'd
> Heav'ns awful Monarch? wherefore but in hope
> To dispossess him, and thy self to reigne?
>
> (IV 954–61)

These are royalist reproaches: they invite an identification of God with Charles I, while not, of course, prohibiting a comparable identification with Oliver Cromwell. Elsewhere Satan's role is

almost explicitly that of an anti-monarchical revolutionary. Like
the opponents of Charles I, he objects on constitutional grounds
to the imposition of 'New laws from him who reigns' (V 680); in
his speech to the Angels at the Mountain of Congregation, he
argues explicitly that submission to a 'King anointed' (V 777)
eclipses the dignity of the angelic host; and in his dispute with
Abdiel, he argues against a willing submission to royal authority,
echoing Milton's own protests in *The Readie and Easie Way* against
that 'greater number' (455) of his fellow countrymen who, 'for the
pleasure of thir baseness, compell a less most injuriously to be thir
fellow slaves':

> At first I thought that Libertie and Heav'n
> To heav'nly Soules had bin all one; but now
> I see that most through sloth had rather serve,
> Ministring Spirits, traind up in Feast and Song
>
> (VI 164–7)

I am not, of course, suggesting that Milton could not have
disproved all these associations had he been publicly confronted
with them (just as — perhaps — he could have pointed to *Samson
Agonistes'* date of composition to 'prove' its innocence of political
intent). Nevertheless, he clearly leaves himself open to the sneers
of opponents who might easily suppose that he failed to perceive
the likeness between Satan's and the Good Old Cause, and
between the latter's persistence in rebellion after defeat and his
own. Blake after all — no enemy of liberty or of Milton — made
such a supposition. And Blake's deconstruction can be reversed.
It makes as much sense to see Milton as an unconscious monarch-
ist as an unconscious diabolist, an adherent without knowing it,
not of the Devil's, but of the king's party. There are certainly
passages in *Paradise Lost* which invite a royalist interpretation. At
the very least the tension between its covert republicanism and its
potentially royalist narrative tends to establish a sense of the
futility of all ideological projects. This is reinforced by the poem's
apparent retreat into pessimistic and moralistic political determinism. In the words of Michael to Adam:

> Reason in man obscur'd, or not obeyd,
> Immediately inordinate desires
> And upstart Passions catch the Government

From Reason, and to servitude reduce
Man till then free. Therefore since hee permits
Within himself unworthie Powers to reign
Over free Reason, God in Judgement just
Subjects him from without to violent Lords . . .
Thus will this latter, as the former World,
Still tend from bad to worse, till God at last
Wearied from thir iniquities, withdraw
His presence from among them, and avert
His holy Eyes

(XII 86–93, 105–9)

This is an anti-royalist passage, but it is also deeply pessimistic. It is almost as if the sceptical cynicism of later Whig discourse (Rochester's, for example) is seeping into the text of *Paradise Lost*, enervating its puritan intensity rather as the totalitarian millenarianism of the Commonwealth poisoned the libertarian openness of the pre-Restoration prose.

12. The passage from Michael's speech just quoted, however, is preceded by an assertion that

true Libertie
. . . alwayes with right Reason dwells
Twinnd, and from her hath no dividual being

(XII 83–5)

It is followed by an account of God's choice of Israel as his people. There is thus an irreducible core of political optimism in Milton's work, and it is inseparable from his optimism about the human person. He does not say that the only kind of government which matters to the christian is introverted self-government. He simply insists that such rational self-government is a necessary but not sufficient cause of political freedom, and that all political behaviour must be subordinate to it. He therefore offers his poems to his Restoration audience, trusting to find among them readers capable of enough self-government in their reading (for reading also is choice) to sustain political hope. He keeps his text open, in circumstances often paralleled in our own century, of bitter social and political oppression, but his reticence is not mere prudence in the face of censorship and arbitrary power; on the contrary, there is a lack of caution, a real recklessness in the way he puts the dignity of the good Old Cause at risk by not spelling out his deepest meanings more clearly. He accepts the possibility of his most serious convictions being subverted by a dishonest reader or misunderstood by an intelligent one, because to encode rather than inscribe his protestant humanism would be to abrogate it; it would be to deploy language as if the Spirit of Truth had finally been erased from human consciousness; it would be to abandon his own freedom as a writer and a christian man, and to enter a world of discourse based on knowledge as a constituent of power.

It follows that the only kind of political action open to Milton even in the direst emergency is persuasion: truth should be 'defended by reason — the only defence truly appropriate to man'. Hence the tragic courage of *The Readie and Easie Way*, and why its sheer impracticality is such a powerful signifier. The essence of Milton's political vision is expressed in his peroration:

> What I have spoken, is in the language of that which is not call'd amiss *the good Old Cause*: if it seem strange to any, it will not seem more strange, I hope, then convincing to backsliders. Thus much I should perhaps have said though I were sure I should have spoken only to trees and stones; and had none to cry to, but with the Prophet, O earth, earth, earth! to tell the very soil it self, what her preverse inhabitants are deaf to. Nay though what I have spoke, should happ'n (which Thou suffer not, who didst create mankinde free; nor Thou next, who didst redeem us from being servants of men!) to be the last words of our expiring libertie. But I trust I shall have spoken perswasion to abundance of sensible and ingenuous men: to som perhaps whom God may raise of these stones to become children of reviving libertie; and may reclaim . . . to bethink themselves a little and consider whether they are rushing . . . and . . . to stay these ruinous proceedings; justly and timely fearing to what a precipice of destruction the deluge of this epidemic madness would hurrie us through the general defection of a misguided and abused multitude. (462–3)

There is no attempt here to disguise either the difficulty of winning the agreement of others except by abusing their reason, or the torrential power of the forces which usually determine great political events. But Milton still makes no concession to pragmatism. He trusts to have spoken persuasion; he asks no more and no less than that his readers bethink themselves a little and consider; and he knows only that God may raise stones to become children of reviving liberty, not that he will.

And this is exactly the stance he adopts in *Samson Agonistes*, and specifically in the movement from the Job-like despair of the choric speech, 'Many are the sayings of the wise', which we considered earlier, to the openness of

> Oh how comely it is and how reviving
> To the Spirits of just men long opprest!
> When God into the hands of thir deliverer
> Puts invincible might
> To quell the mighty of the Earth, th' oppressour . . .
> With plain Heroic magnitude of mind
> And celestial vigour arm'd . . .
> But patience is more oft the exercise
> Of Saints, the trial of thir fortitude,
> Making them each his own Deliverer,
> And Victor over all
> That tyrannie or fortune can inflict,
> Either of these is in thy lot
> *Samson*

(1288–72, 1279–80, 1287–93)

The entire speech articulates a high state of indeterminateness out of which emerge possibilities for choice of the most seriously human kind. Even the arrival of the Philistinian messenger with which it concludes introduces a sign awaiting interpretation, a command awaiting a response. Should Samson participate in the Idolatrous Rites of the Philistinian Lords with a display of strength not unlike the display of poetic power and embittered restraint of political utterance (so easily interpretable as submission) with which Milton entertained his post-1660 English public? And even when that question is answered, and having entrusted himself to providence Samson has performed his last great act, another question emerges in Manoa's closing speech:

> *Samson* hath quit himself
> Like *Samson* and heroicly hath finish'd
> A life Heroic . . .
>
> To *Israel*
> Honour hath left, and freedom, let but them

Find courage to lay hold on this occasion
                                        (1709–11, 1414–16)

For Milton, the profoundest truth about the Philistinian world of
Restoration England was that it remained an arena of choice, in
which it was possible to see the truth, to publish it and to act on
it — both as an individual and in solidarity with one's neighbours
— according to the Spirit of Truth: the obliteration of the Revolution could not extinguish the kind of participatory self-obliteration
on which republican and divine enterprises depended.

13. The word solidarity was introduced at the end of the last
paragraph to recall briefly *The Acting Person*. For it is an irony
(though not really a surprising one) that the twentieth-century
writer whose thinking is closest to Milton's in these matters is not
Empson, or Kenny, or Hill, or Althusser, or Derrida, but a Polish
Pope, and the sign, SOLIDARITY, which is one of the key
themes in the closing section of the Pope's book, and also one of
the most powerful of contemporary political signs, best expresses
that affinity.

The Acting Person, after all, is a Polish expression of christian
humanism, inserted into discourse determined by Polish history;
the later works of Milton are an English expression of christian
humanism, inserted into discourse determined by English history;
and the bonds between them are not just theoretical but historical.
The values proclaimed if not invariably respected by the *Szlachta*
(nobility) of the United Republic of Poland-Lithuania in the
seventeenth century have structural affinities with the values
proclaimed in Milton's defence of Cromwell's Commonwealth.
Milton's last act as a writer, after all, was to translate and publish
in 1674 the *Diploma Electionis S.R.M. Poloniae*, formally announcing Jan Sobieski's election to the throne of the Republic (or
Commonwealth, as Milton translates *Respublica*). The first of the
electors issuing this declaration is 'Andrew Trezebicki, Bishop of
Cracovia' (445) and thus one of the Pope's predecessors in his
former See. The Declaration proclaims Jan Sobieksi's valour
against the Turk; it expiates on the dignified unanimity with
which his election was effected; it promises 'Faith, Subjection,
Obedience and Loyalty' (451) to the new King 'according to our
Rights and Liberties', and, while announcing the imminent
coronation of the King at Kraków according to the rites of the
Roman Catholic Church, it declares that the King will continue
to respect the constitutional right of his subjects to religious

toleration: 'We will annoint and inaugurate him; Yet so as he shall hold fast and observe first of all the Rights Immunities, both Ecclesiastical and Secular, granted and given to us by his Ancestor of Blessed memory.'

Yet just as the Commonwealth extinguished itself with catastrophic suddenness, so the Republic of Poland-Lithuania was doomed to slow self-extinction in the century that followed. Both experimental constitutions were traces destined to complete erasure: 'Poland', wrote Edmund Burke, 'must be regarded as situate on the Moon.' For 123 years, from 1795 to 1918, and again from 1939 to 1945, Poland existed only in discourses, but it was discourse into which Milton would have fitted far more profoundly than the English Romantics (notably Byron) who in fact influenced Polish writing in the nineteenth century. Unfortunately Milton's Polish translator, Franciszek Ksawery Dmochowski, was also the translator of Boileau, and, according to the historian of Polish literature, Czesław Miłosz (1969), the polonizer of French notions of literary correctness. With Hugo Kołłątaj, Dmochowski was associated in the 1780s with desperate attempts to save the dying *Respublica* but his stance was conservative. He enclosed literary meaning and practice, and therefore Milton, in the unproblematical anti-prophetic world-view of the Enlightenment. The Milton of Blake and Shelley, therefore, and more importantly the baroque, protestant, revolutionary and defeated Milton of whom I have been writing, was largely unknown to Polish writers after the extinction of the *Respublica*. But if there was and is a cultural situation to which Milton speaks with urgent relevance it seems to be that of Poland.

It is against the background of this same cultural situation, of course, that *The Acting Person* is most illuminatingly read. It was inserted in the first instance into Polish discourse, into the strategic situation of the Polish People's Republic, and, like Milton's last three poems, it made restraint — in the form of a relentless abstractness of expression — into a form of self-disclosing silence. Its very abstractness, however, serves to clarify its 'Miltonic' priorities. Thus in mainstream phenomenology, the biggest problem requiring solution is that of inter-subjectivity, but in *The Acting Person* the biggest problem is participation, 'acting together with others' (323): how does such action 'retain that fundamental cohesion with the person' which is made manifest in the transcendence and integration of the *actus humanus*? *The Acting Person* uses the term *participation* to signify an acting together with others which is the equivalent of acting freely on one's own. Participation is a property of the person (and not of social relations) — what Milton calls 'free Reason' — and it 'determines that the person, existing and acting together with others, still exists and acts as a person' (326). The person who 'chooses what is chosen by others, or even *because* it is chosen by others . . . identifies the object of . . . choice with a value' (327) — a value 'homogenous' with, and belonging to, the person as an individual capable of self-governance and self-possession. Participation is thus the morally positive alternative to that deliberate conspiracy of falsification which we saw in an earlier chapter to be characteristic of the ideological community represented in Milton's Hell, and which makes his representation of that community so markedly at odds with marxist explanations of ideological formations as collective and unconscious.

No less opposed to participation as that concept is developed in *The Acting Person* are the two principles of 'individualism' which 'isolates the person who is then conceived of solely as an individual' (330), absorbed in the private self and private good, and 'totalism' which 'assumes that . . . the "common good" can only be attained by limiting the individual' (331). Both principles, it is argued, have 'at their origin the same intellecual conception' — namely, that 'in the individual there is only the striving for the individual good'. This is precisely the logic of Satan's position following his refusal to participate in the society of Heaven after the Son's exaltation has been proclaimed. Such withdrawal from participation is called 'avoidance' in *The Acting Person* (347), and it leads Satan first into individualism — as free and equal persons, he declares, angels are not subject to law, they are 'ordain'd to govern, not to serve' (V 802), and in any case are products of their own self-generation — then into the totalism of the infernal Nuremberg rally which precedes the building of Pandemonium in Hell. The speciousness of the totalistic unity of Hell becomes immediately apparent, however, when the senior rebels meet in secret conclave, and the self-interested, craven counsels of Belial and Mammon gain ascendency only to be rebutted by the manipulative policy of Beelzebub and the quick intervention of Satan to secure his own pre-eminence. Hell is a totalitarian society, grounded in the false individualism of mutual distrust and careerism, by which others are perceived in terms of what one can induce to happen in them. It is the image and obverse of the authentic participatory society of Heaven, which is grounded in and so confirms authentic personal individuation and self-effacement before the transcendent individuation of one's fellow-creatures and of God.

The closeness of individualism to the personalistic value, and of totalism to participation is crucial to our understanding of how 'Heav'n resembles Hell' in *Paradise Lost*. *The Acting Person* acknowledges this closeness when it describes 'conformism' as 'natural, in many respects positive and constructive or even creative' (345), but as being liable also to make the person servile, 'the subject of *what happens*' (346). The common good is 'that which conditions and somehow initiates . . . participation, and thereby develops and shapes . . . a subjective community of acting' (338), but 'nonauthentic attitudes' can develop in this area very easily. 'The touchstone . . . is the dynamic subordination to truth . . . reflected in the righteous conscience, which is the ultimate judge of the authenticity of human attitudes' (345). And this is surely distinction between the societies of Heaven and Hell in *Paradise Lost*. Satan's kingdom is a totalitarian monarchy of separate, self-preoccupied liars, God's a participatory providence of dynamic subordination to the Spirit of Truth in which a righteous conscience is the sign and consequence of the creature's free participation in the providential order.

But this in its turn describes the revolutionary society envisaged in Milton's writings on civil and religious liberty, and the principles professed by the *Szlachta* as democratised in nineteenth- and twentieth-century Polish literature. In other words, the vast structure of *Paradise Lost*, built so elaborately and yet so abstractly around the consciences and acts of its principal characters, and the Pope's no less elaborate and even more abstract analysis of the acting person, not only have a common source in the Aristotelian tradition of the will, but constitute a precisely apprehended political stance, a set of convictions about history which are at once deeply revolutionary and deeply conservative. The position of both writers may be summed up in the Pope's assertion that 'even when . . . acting is realized together with others' (334), its '*proper substantial subject*' is the human person. The fundamental political reality is thus a freedom of the human will sufficient to modify and even possibly transform the vast impersonality of what happens in history. Milton believes, and so does the Pope, that it belongs to the very nature of human society and human development that, in the strongest sense of each word, the possibility of persons acting together can never be discounted. Even in

Restoration England they can find courage to lay hold of an occasion. Because erasure — obliteration — can never be excluded from politics, solidarity is always an option.

14. But, the liberal sceptic might reply, has it ever happened? Has effective political activity ever been human activity? Has human activity ever been politically effective? It is of course possible that the true answer to all these questions is no. It is also possible that the very idea of human activity has never been entertained except as part of an ideological project, and that human beings have never acted freely. But then it belongs both to the nature of discourse and to the *actus humanus* that instances of freedom cannot be discursively vindicated. For the same reason, no account of free will can ever be given without its being possible and proper to read it in ideological terms. For the freedom with which we have been concerned in this essay can never be present; it operates only as an erasable trace. Alternatively we may say that it is present to us as an absence, as Milton is present to us in the heroic self-effacement of his final works. And to those *ad hominem* critics who deny this self-effacement, and assert that Milton is altogether too much with us, too ready to thrust himself on our attention, or too weak to prevent his unconscious from doing so, I can only suggest that their Milton, like the God of *Paradise Lost*, is a signifier only. The real Milton is concealed within the freedom which he offered to the English people, whether or not they heard and heeded him, and whether or not they ever will.

References and Quotations

JOHN MILTON

All quotations from Milton's poems are based on the text of *The Works of John Milton*, 20 vols, New York: Columbia University Press, 1931–40; however I have punctuated in accordance with *The Poems of John Milton* edited by John Carey and Alistair Fowler, London and Harlow: Longmans, Green and Co. Ltd, 1968.

All quotations from Milton's prose are from *Complete Prose Works of John Milton*, 8 vols, New Haven: Yale University Press, 1980; hereafter CPW. Milton's works in prose are referred to as follows:

Of Reformation Touching-Church Discipline: Of Reformation Touching Church-Discipline in England: And the causes that hitherto have hindered it. Two Bookes . . . written to a Friend (1641), CPW I

The Reason of Church-governement: The Reason of Church-governement Urg'd against Prelaty (1641), CPW I

The Doctrine and Discipline of Divorce: The Doctrine and Discipline of Divorce Restor'd to the good of both Sexes . . . (1643), CPW II

Of Education: Of Education to Master Samuel Hartlib (1644), CPW II

Areopagitica: Areopagitica; a Speech of Mr. John Milton For the Liberty of Unlicenc'd Printing. To the Parliament of England . . . (1644), CPW II

The Tenure of Kings and Magistrates: The Tenure of Kings and Magistrates: proving that it is Lawfull . . . to call to account a Tyrant . . . (1650), CPW III

Second Defence of the English People: Second Defence of the English People Against the Base Anonymous Libel . . . (Pro Populo Anglicano Defensio Secunda. Contra infamen libellum . . . (1654). Preface and Notes by Donald A. Roberts. Translation by Helen North, CPW IV

Christian Doctrine: Two Books of Investigation into Christian Doctrine (de Doctrina Christiana Libri Duo [*Posthumi*] 1825). Translation by John Carey; Notes by Maurice Kelley, CPW VI

Of Civil Power, A Treatise of Civil Power in Ecclesiastical Causes: shewing that it is not lawfull for any power on earth to compell in matters of Religion (1659), CPW VII

The Readie and Easie Way: The readie and easie way to establish a free Commonwealth; and the excellence thereof compar'd with the inconveniences and dangers of readmitting kingship in this Nation. The second edition revis'd and augmented (1660), CPW VII

The Art of Logic: A Fuller Course in the Art of Logic Conformed to the Method of Peter Ramus (Artis Logicae Plenior Institutio, ad Petri Rami Methodum concinnata, 1672). Edited and Translated by Walter Ong, S.J. and Charles J. Ermatinger, CPW VIII

A Declaration, or Letters Patent of the Election of this present King of Poland John the Third (Diploma Electionis S. R. M. Poloniae 1674), CPW VIII

HENRY JAMES

Quotations from *The Portrait of a Lady* (1881) are from the two-volume edition, London: Macmillan and Co., Limited, 1909.

OTHER WRITERS

Quotations from the Bible are from the Revised Authorised Version, 1884

Althusser L. (1970): 'Ideology and Ideological State Apparatuses (Notes towards in Investigation)' (1970) in *Lenin and Philosophy and Other Essays*. Translated from the French by Bill Brewster, London: 1977 edn

Bakhtin (1929): *Marxism and the Philosophy of Language (Marksizm i filosofija jazyka: osnovnye problemy sociologiceskogo metoda v nauke o jazyke*, 1929) by V.N. Volosinov. Translated by Ladislaw Matejka and I.R. Titunik, New York and London: Seminar Paper, 1973 (a work now generally attributed to Mikhail Bakhtin)

Barthes R. (1968): 'The Death of the Author' (*'La mort de l'auteur'*, 1968) in *Image Music Text*. Essays selected and translated by Stephen Heath, Glasgow: Fontana/Collins, 1977

—— (1971) 'From Work to Text' (*'De l'oeuvre au texte'*, 1971) in *Image Music Text*

Blake (1790–3): *The Marriage of Heaven and Hell* (1790–3), in Blake's *Complete Writings with Variant Readings*. Keynes G. (ed.), London: Oxford University Press, 1966 edn

Carey J. (1968) *Milton*. London: Evans Bros, 1969

Davidson, D. (1980) *Essays on Actions and Events*. Oxford: Clarendon Press

—— (1985): *Essays on Davidson. Actions and Events*. In Vermazen B. and Hintikka M.B. (eds), Oxford: Clarendon Press

Dennett D.C. (1984): *Elbow Room. The Varieties of Free Will Worth Wanting* Oxford: Clarendon Press

Derrida J. (1967(a)): *Of Grammatology (De la Grammatologie*, 1967). Translated by Gayatri Chakravorty Spivak. Baltimore and London: The Johns Hopkins University Press, 1976

—— (1967(b)): *Writing and Difference (L'écriture et la différance*, 1967). Translated, with an Introduction and Additional Notes, by Alan Bass, London: Routledge & Kegan Paul, 1978

—— (1979): 'The Supplement of Copula' in Harrari 1979

Eagleton T. (1976): *Criticism and Ideology. A Study in Marxist Literary Theory*. London: NLB

—— (1983): *Literary Theory: An Introduction*. Oxford: Basil Blackwell

Ferreira M.J. (1980): *Doubt and Religious Commitment. The Role of the Will in Newman's Thought*. Oxford: Clarendon Press

Foucault M. (1971): 'Nietzsche, Genealogy, History' (*'Nietzsche, la généalogie, l'histoire'*, in *Hommage à Jean Hyppolite*, 1971); *Language, Counter-memory, Practice, Selected Essays and Interviews*, edited with an introduction by Donald F. Bouchard and translated by Donald F. Bouchard and Sherry Simon, Oxford: Blackwell, 1977

—— (1975): *Discipline and Punish (*'Surveiller et punir'*, 1975). Translation

by Alan Sheridan, London: Allen Lane, 1977
——— (1979): 'What is an Author?' in Harrari 1979
Godwin W. (1798): *Enquiry concerning Political Justice and its influence on Morals and Happiness*. Photographic facsimile of the third edition (1798) corrected. Edited with variant readings of the first and second editions and with a critical introduction and notes by F.E.L. Priestley, 2 vols, Toronto: The University of Toronto Press, 1946
Hardy T. (1891): *Tess of the D'Urbervilles. A Pure Woman. Faithfully presented*, London: Macmillan, 1902
Harrari J.V. *Textual Strategies. Perspectives in Post-Structuralist Criticism*, London: Macmillan, 1980
Hill C. (1977): *Milton and the English Revolution*. London, Boston: Faber and Faber
Hume D. (1777): *An Enquiry concerning Human Understanding*, in *Enquiries concerning Human Understanding and concerning the Principles of Morals*. Reprinted from the posthumous edition of 1777 and edited by L.A. Selby-Bigge, M.A. Third edition with text revised and notes by P.H. Nidditch, Oxford: Clarendon Press, 1975
Husserl E. (1950): *Cartesian Meditations (Cartesianische Meditationen*, 1950), Translated by Dorion Cairns, The Hague: Martinus Nijhoff, 1977
Kant I. (1783): *Prolegomena to any Future Metaphysics that will be able to present itself as a Science (Prolegomena zu einer jeden kunftigen Metaphysic die als Wissenschaft wird auftret konnen*, 1783). A translation from the German based on the original editions with an Introduction and notes by Peter C. Lucas, Univesity of Manchester: University Press, Third Impression, 1962
——— (1787): *Critique of Pure Reason (Kritik der reinen Verunft*, 1787 ed.). Translated by J.M.D. Meiklejohn, London: J.M. Dent & Sons, 1934; reprinted 1969
Kenny A. (1975): *Will, Freedom and Power*, Oxford: Basil Blackwell
——— (1979): *The God of the Philosophers*, Oxford: Clarendon Press
Leavis, F.R. and Leavis Q.D. (1970): *Dickens the Novelist*, Harmondsworth: 1972 (Pelican Books)
Leitch V. (1983): *Deconstructive Criticism. An Advanced Introduction*, London: Hutchinson
Mackie J.L. (1982): *The Miracle of Theism. Arguments For and Against the Existence of God*. Oxford: Clarendon Press
Marx K. (1844): 'Critique of Hegel's Philosophy of Right' ('Kritik des Hegeleschen Staatsrechts', 1844), in *On Religion* Marx K. and Engels F., Moscow: Foreign Languages Publishing House, London: Lawrence and Wishart, second edition, n.d.
Milner J. (1981): *John Milton and the English Revolution. A Study in the Sociology of Literature*. London and Basingstoke: Macmillan
Miłosz C. (1969): *The History of Polish Literature*, London: Collier-Macmillan
Miner E. (1974): *The Restoration Mode from Milton to Dryden*. Princeton, New Jersey: Princeton University Press
Monod J. (1970): *Chance and Necessity. An Essay on the Natural Philosophy of Modern Biology (Le hasard et la nécéssité*, 1970). Translated from the French by Austryn Wainhouse, London: Collins, 1972

Newman J.H. (1835): 'On the Introduction of Rationalistic Principles into Revealed Religion', in *Essays Critical and Historical*, vol. 1, London: Basil Montagu Pickering, 1871
———— (1853): 'Papers of 1853 on the Certainty of Faith' in *The Theological Papers of John Henry Newman* on Faith and Certainty partly prepared for publication by Hugo M. de Achaval, S.J. selected and edited by J: Derek Holmes with a note of introduction by Charles Stephen Dessain, Oxford: Clarendon Press, 1976
———— (1870): *An Essay in aid of A Grammar of Assent*, with an introduction by Nicholas Lash, Notre Dame, London: University of Notre Dame Press, 1976
———— (1875): 'Letter to the Duke of Norfolk on Occasion of Mr Gladstone's Expostulation' in *Certain Difficulties Felt by Anglicans in Catholic Teaching*, vol II, London: Longmans and Green and Co, 1881
O'Connor D.J. (1967): *Aquinas and Natural Law*, London, Melbourne, Toronto: Macmillan
Parfit D. (1986): *Reasons and Persons*, Oxford, New York: Oxford University Press, reprinted with corrections
Pater W. (1873): *The Renaissance. Studies in Art and Poetry*. With an introduction and Notes by Kenneth Clark. London and Glasgow: Fontana/Collins, 1961
Plantinga A. (1974): *The Nature of Necessity*, Oxford: Clarendon Press
Polanyi M. (1962): *Personal Knowledge, Towards a Post-Critical Philosophy*, London: Routledge & Kegan Paul, Second Impression (with corrections)
Pope John Paul II: see Wojtyła 1969
Shelley (1820): Preface to *Prometheus Unbound*, in R. Ingpen and W.E. Beck (eds), *The Complete Works of Percy Bysshe Shelley*, London: Ernest Benn Limited; New York, Gordian Press 1965, vol II
———— (1840): 'A Defence of Poetry', ibid., vol. VII
Sheridan M. (1980): *Michel Foucault The Will Truth*, London and New York: Tavistock Publications
Sober E. (1984): *The Nature of Evolution. Evolutionary Theory in Philosophical Focus*, Cambridge, Massachusetts, London, England: MIT Press
Strawson, P.F. (1974): *Freedom and Resentment and other essays*, London: Macmillan
Swinburne R. (1977): *The Coherence of Theism*, Oxford, Clarendon Press
———— (1979): *The Existence of God*, Oxford: Clarendon Press
Wojtyła (1969): *The Acting Person (Osoba i czym*, 1969) by Cardinal Karol Wojtyła (Pope John Paul II). Translated from the Polish by Andrej Potocki. This definitive text of the work established in collaboration with the author by Anna-Teresa Tymieniecka for publication in the Reidel book series *Analecta Husserliana*, Dordrecht, Boston, London: D. Reidel Publishing Company, 1979

Index

There are separate entries for God, the Trinity, the Father, the Son, the Holy Spirit and Jesus Christ both in the main index and under the entries for those works of Milton which represent them as persons.